DATE DUE

Unless Recalled Earlier

APR 2 2 1994			
MAY 2 1 1994			
JUN 1 5 1994			
NOV 2 7 1994			

DEMCO 38-297

AFRICA'S
MEDIA IMAGE

AFRICA'S
MEDIA IMAGE

EDITED BY
Beverly G. Hawk

New York
Westport, Connecticut
London

Library of Congress Cataloging-in-Publication Data

Africa's media image / edited by Beverly G. Hawk.

      p.   cm.

    Includes bibliographical references and index.

    ISBN 0-275-93796-8 (alk. paper)

    1. Africa in mass media—United States.   I. Hawk, Beverly G.

P96.A372U535   1992

305.8′96—dc20   91-41633

British Library Cataloguing in Publication Data is available.

Library of Congress Catalog Card Number: 91-41633
ISBN: 0-275-93796-8

First published in 1992

Praeger Publishers, One Madison Avenue, New York, NY 10010
An imprint of Greenwood Publishing Group, Inc.

Printed in the United States of America

The paper used in this book complies with the
Permanent Paper Standard issued by the National
Information Standards Organization (Z39.48-1984).

10 9 8 7 6 5 4 3 2 1

Contents

Part III
The Southern African Story

Part IV
Changing African Coverage

Contents

I

The Media Debate

1

Introduction: Metaphors of African Coverage

Beverly G. Hawk

Interest in Africa waxes and wanes. Crises named Mau Mau, the Congo, Biafra, South Africa, and Ethiopia capture headlines. Many stories surge to the headlines and disappear quickly, leaving Americans with little understanding of the continent or the politics that drive it. From these points of information, the reader composes a constellation of understanding about Africa. Americans are left to believe that Africa is a confusing place with instability in government, society, and even country names. Most Americans have never visited Africa and will never visit Africa, yet there is an image of Africa in the American mind.

Americans' knowledge of Africa is formed by messages from many sources: school textbooks, the news media, church missionaries, and the entertainment industry. Among these sources, the media hold special importance, for it is to the media that individuals look to be informed. The media hold responsibility for the interpretation of the events they report, and their interpretations, in turn, define the understanding of events by readers and viewers. Some might argue that the media can just report the "facts," but there are no such things as facts without interpretation. As Edward Said puts it, "All knowledge that is about human society, and not about the natural world, is historical knowledge, and therefore rests upon judgement and interpretation. This is not to say that facts or data are nonexistent, but that facts get their importance from what is made of them upon interpretation."[1] The media give meaning to current events and identify for the reader those events that are important. Consumers of the resultant news programming and editorial opinion of the elite media consider themselves informed.

As one event after another occupies center stage, the American media present the story to readers and viewers, and Africa scholars, in their turn, assess this coverage. Common themes recur in each analysis of media coverage of Africa. An area specialist takes correspondents and editors to task for giving simplified and sometimes sensational views of the situation that the specialist understands in all its complexity. Given an opportunity to respond, editors and correspondents describe the constraints of finance, reader interest, and government censorship. This book brings the resulting debates among media researchers, Africa specialists, editors, and correspondents under one cover. Their analyses identify the language and metaphor used to communicate African stories in today's news. In this way, this book explores the implications of media coverage for the image of Africa in America.

THE AFRICAN STORY

The African story is different from other foreign relations stories. Americans attempting to understand the African story have a difficult time. Their social studies, history, and government schooling included only brief reference to African history and culture. Western education teaches that Europeans not Africans are the motive force in African history. To understand developments on the continent, Americans must recognize Africans as the major agents of change. Africa is special because there is little common understanding between Africans and Americans to provide context for interpretation. Further, unusual historical relations have shaped peculiar structures of knowledge regarding Africa. These repertories of knowledge, symbols, and a priori structurings of Africa are a Western creation. Where African news is concerned, then, American readers are in special need of contextual information with which to interpret the meaning of reported events.

Media presentation of needed contextual information about Africa is limited by commercial and financial considerations of editors, the personal opinions of editors and correspondents, and press restrictions of host governments. In Africa reporting, however, the limitations have an especially pronounced impact, given the peculiar cultural relations between the United States and Africa. Cultural receptors among readers are different for African news. Africa has been viewed as the "dark continent" by the West, an allusion not only to the skin color of its inhabitants but to their ignorance of European ways. Ever since Stanley was sent in search of Livingstone, Africa has been a wild adventure story and it continues to be perceived as such. The image of Africa in the American mind, then, is worse than incomplete, it is inaccurate. Interpretations of African events are based on media placement and description and their interaction with previous understanding of Africa. In the confusing environment of fascination with things African (as defined by outsiders), the media report the African story. Olav Stokke put the problem this way: "The factors at work when the mosaic of Africa, as transmitted by the international mass media, is created are probably more or less the same as those influencing international communication flow in general. However, specific structural and cultural traits may give this specific communication flow some qualities of its own."[2] From the massive array of conflicting political stimuli that strike an individual each day, an image is constructed that is coherent and corresponds to accepted beliefs, a comfortable and familiar image. Murray Edelman's words on the public's search for cues and comprehension are especially true in the African case:

Political events are largely creations of the language we use to describe them. For the mass of political spectators, developments occur in a remote arena where there can be no direct observation or feedback. The bewildering political universe needs to be ordered and given meaning. People who are anxious and confused are eager to be supplied with an organized political order—including simple explanations of the threats they fear—with reassurance that the threats are being countered.[3]

Although we might long for greater rationality among the American polity, reality is a construction of perception and misperception of ambiguous situations. The public's need for information about African political and economic change is met with the images and messages of media coverage.

African states sought, and many achieved, their independence prior to the Vietnam War and prior to the interest in the analysis of news coverage generated by that conflict. The impact of news coverage on public opinion toward that conflict demonstrated the power of the press in foreign policy. Conjecture concerning the comparative strength of the government and the media to shape the image of the conflict in the public's mind drove popular and scholarly discourse, creating a new appreciation for the press as an organizer and interpreter of international events for each of us. Todd Gitlin described this power clearly when he said,

They name the world's parts, they certify reality *as* reality—and when their certifications are doubted or opposed, as they surely are, it is those same certifications that limit the terms of effective opposition. To put it simply: the mass media have become the core systems for the distribution of ideology. That is to say, every day, directly or indirectly, by statement and omission, in pictures and in words, in entertainment and news and advertisements, the mass media produce fields of definition and association, symbol and rhetoric, through which ideology becomes manifest and concrete.[4]

One means by which the media shape an image is by the selection of news. After all, if a reporter has only a brief time or a small space in which to describe and explain a political event much, of necessity, must be left untold. For today's story of South Africans fighting for majority rule and its consequence, the end of apartheid, the media sifts from among African National Congress (ANC) demands those which will be published and those which will be ignored. In the shaping of Nelson Mandela into a Martin Luther King, Jr. figure, certain of his positions are not publicized while others are. To the journalist, they simply fit the story best. Yet, the selection is unavoidably ideological.

The public is saturated with news: newspapers, radio, television networks, and cable. The proliferation of news sources in recent years, however, has not created diversity of news content about Africa. They present a remarkably coherent picture of the African scene, because the homogeneous composition of news organizations assures the replication of familiar images. Most correspondents sent to cover South Africa are white and speak only English (not Afrikaans, Xhosa, Sotho, Tswana, or Zulu). As a result, reporters select as their sources government officials or white dissenters from government policy. There is very little of the beat reporting that fills local newspapers and news broadcasts. Indeed, this distance from African culture is often viewed as objectivity, an asset.

Africa is truly "covered" by the Western press in the sense that important stories go unreported. Hence, invisibility is a crucial issue to be addressed in the assessment of African coverage. Most African events are simply ignored by the media in its spotty coverage of the continent. Those aspects of African life covered by the foreign media are stories easily reported in brief dispatches and comfortably understood by the American audience. Such events are racial stories, coups and wars, and famine and disease. Stories communicating African history, culture, and values never reach the American public. Africa's history before the colonial period—for example, the peopling of South Africa—is not discussed. African rural economy is discussed only in conjecture concerning its potential for westernization. The confusing barrage that results has a common theme: Africa is a failure and needs our help. This pattern of coverage was set by the practices of Africa reporting during wars of independence on the continent.

Before the dawn of independence during the late 1950s, the international news agencies of the two major colonial powers—Reuters and Agence France-Presse (AFP)—had what amounted to almost a de facto monopoly of the mass-media communications to and from English-speaking and French-speaking Africa respectively. . . . Thus, before 1960 a large proportion of the news from Sub-Saharan Africa came via Paris or London.[5]

Prior to independence, the news agencies of the colonial metropole controlled news from Africa. Today's reporting of "tribal violence" quelled by the intervention of "security forces" has its origins in the reporting of colonial fears of majority rule.

By reporting those aspects of African life deemed to be important to the Western reader, the media select stories according to the Western values. As a result, African successes measured according to African values are never reported. Although a water pump in a rural area may transform a community and its economy, it hardly makes good copy. Coups and wars make better copy and can be succinctly communicated to a reader. Press coverage of Africa in the context of world events marginalizes things uniquely African.

AFRICA THE PRIMITIVE ARCHETYPE

As we look at the past, present, and future of Africa, it is constructed through metaphor. The metaphors selected for communication of the African story are not from Africa but from the news consumer's culture. The simplest way to communicate the African story in comprehensible form in limited space is by colonial metaphor familiar to the reader. To order events in Africa for readers and viewers, reporters resort to metaphors that communicate the complex African story to their American audience.

The enduring fascination with Africa and things African is revealed in the vocabulary of the metaphor. The vocabulary of the story reports "Africans" in "tribal" or "black-on-black" violence. Current violence in Soweto and Natal is reported in this frame of reference. Vocabulary defines the story as "African" and "tribal." The message for the reader or viewer is that African events require a different vocabulary than those in Northern Ireland or Yugoslavia. Implicit in this vocabulary is that African events do not follow any pattern recognizable to Western reason. It is "tribal" conflict. No one calls the violence in Northern Ireland white-on-

white violence, or tribal bloodshed. Current ethnic unrest in the former
Soviet Union and Eastern Europe is described as "ethnic," and scholars
even refer to it as the nationalities problem. There is, however, a special
language employed when describing African stories. To understand its
implications, it is necessary to examine its origins.

Africans did not historically refer to themselves by a single term;
African nations were referred to as "tribes" in the colonial vocabulary. The
act of naming "Africans" by one collective term may have been useful for
colonial goals, but it is not particularly useful for understanding culture.
At its "founding" Africans knew one another by their nations, and these
nations could be recognized by their linguistic boundaries and cultural
values. *African*, as it is used in the Western press, does not mean anyone
who lives on the African continent, but rather people who are black and
live on the African continent. It is a colonial label. North Africans and
descendants of European settlers are not included in the term. This narrow,
racial definition of Africa, structured by the language employed to tell the
African story, tells readers and viewers that the continent has a simple,
homogeneous culture.

The political boundaries left to Africa at independence do not correspond to its cultural boundaries, cultural boundaries which could have
properly been called *nations* in colonial times and could still be called
nations were it not for the western reification of the colonial boundaries.
The nations predating European rule on the continent and enduring despite
years of colonialism are called *tribes* by the media, their colonial designa-
tion. If South Africa is the nation, then we must use some other term for
pre-colonial African nations, and their sense of identity and pride in that
identity must be viewed as subversive. This reification of true nationhood
by the Western press is a political act, although the press itself is generally
unwilling to acknowledge its complicity at this time. Today's happenings
in South Africa are actually similar to the current political situation in the
former Soviet Union and Eastern Europe where nationalities reassert
themselves when the political climate will bear it. While newspapers have
taken space to explain the histories of Eastern European nations, they do
not provide histories of Southern African nationalities or explain the role
of apartheid in the reconstruction of those cultural identities. This may
correspond to the public perception of Africa, but it undermines respect
for the cultural complexity and historical depth of the continent. The many
cultures that comprise the African continent are diverse in their traditions.
Africans are not culturally monolithic, so it should come as no surprise
that there are political conflicts among Africans. We do not call political
disputes among white people white factionalism and when they turn

violent we do not refer to them as white-on-white violence. World War I or the more recent Cold War was never reported in these terms because diversity of nationhood is accepted for the white world.

The use of terms such as *black-on-black violence, black factionalism,* or *tribalism* serve the purpose of dehumanizing the conflict and casting it in racial terms. When television networks report "tribal warfare," their language casts political conflict in terms of a binary opposition between primitive and modern. Further, they do not report the more complicated forces shaping political change in the country. The Inkatha story is the story of the conflict between those people who have participated in the South African government for years and have a political patronage machine to show for it, on the one hand, and those people who have resisted the apartheid government and today threaten that patronage system. That more complicated story lacks the racial angle of a primitive modern dichotomy, so it is rarely reported. Reporting suggests that chaos might result from majority rule, but it is the chaos of ignorance within the mind of the reader or viewer, not chaotic and inexplicable political events in South Africa.

The existence of this view of primitive Africa is not new, nor is it limited to the press. Its origins can be found in colonial texts, justified by pseudo-scientific research. In colonial times, this view of Africa justified intervention and cultural surgery. In those earlier times, it was a moral judgment and the antidote was religious conversion. Today's story is more likely to be couched in terms of economic degradation, and the envisioned cure is described as economic intervention. Like anthropologists and explorers of the colonial era, journalists are empowered to paint an image of Africa by listing its deficiencies with respect to Western norms. Coverage of Africa which emphasizes poverty, disease, and famine corresponds to the existing view of Africans as have-nots. By comparing them to our economic and technological standards, we are able to create an image of Africa in the American mind that is a chronicle of its deficiencies to the Western standard. With moral evaluation soon replacing description, economic missionaries can justify intervention on the continent. Economic development is to the twentieth century what missionary evangelization was to the nineteenth century—a justification for intervention. This colonial legacy has left us the good African and the bad African, with the good Africans being those who are receptive to Western values.

Part I of this book sets out the current debate between Africanists and journalists; it offers us an appreciation for the complexity of the reporter's task. Bosah Ebo and Stanley Meisler state opposing viewpoints of media coverage. Ebo asserts that commercial demands and cultural arrogance, not a desire to inform the American electorate, determine foreign policy coverage.

The negative portrayal of Africa by American media is a deliberate and systematic process that is created and sustained by the bias in the way American media select foreign news stories. The process is manifested in the commercial, political, and sociocultural criteria that American media use to determine which nations and which foreign news events are newsworthy. These criteria treat American and Western cultural values as superior to Africa's and accordingly, news events from Africa are presented as abnormal or unnatural.

The resulting image, according to Ebo is, "a crocodile-infested dark continent where jungle life has perpetually eluded civilization." In defense of his trade, Meisler, a twenty-year veteran of foreign correspondence, insists his job is to report the story. In his view, those who criticize media coverage do not want Africa reported honestly, they simply want it reported positively. As Meisler puts it, "I am not Africa's public relations man. That's not the job of a foreign correspondent." Lest the reader imagine that the lines of the debate could be so clearly drawn, William Hachten explores the situation in the field when American correspondents meet African censorship. In this way, he provides a dose of realism to set the tone for this complex collection of essays.

This book is the first of its kind to include a wide geographic and historical breadth among its works. Articles that assess the coverage of Mau Mau, the War in Algiers, the Nigerian Civil War, the Cold War in Africa, and African famine lead Part II of the book. Some of these events preceded the Vietnam War and its impact on our understanding of the media. For this reason, they are especially important to reassess. The overview of coverage presented in Part II is completed by works on the African-American Press and *The New York Times*. These works, wide in their historic scope and divergent in their media of study, describe the coverage of various African events by America's newspaper of record, *The New York Times*, and this century's alternative media for the African case, the African-American press. The case studies presented in Part II provide specific examples to enliven the debate of media coverage.

Part III contains the work of prominent scholars and journalists who assess Southern African coverage and show the reporting of Southern African events to be reminiscent of earlier African reporting. Lisa Brock's work on the reporting of Inkatha shows that the paradigm of Africa the primitive, as described in Wunyabari Maloba's study of Mau Mau, remains a guideline for African reporting. Julie Frederikse also asserts that the South Africa story, like the Mau Mau story, has been racialized, and the shared history of struggle for majority rule has been oversimplified. From her history of ANC nonracialism, Frederikse demonstrates that important aspects of the South African story have been left unreported in the media's pursuit of a race war story angle. In his work on the Frontline states, Chris Paterson discusses another crucial story ignored by the press and seeks out the causes for its omission. News reporters stationed in Johannesburg could regularly report events in neighboring states but choose to exclude them from coverage. These articles are followed by a provocative piece of research by Elaine Windrich in which she demonstrates with relentless evidence the power of the South African government to manipulate the American press. Part III concludes with the views of a correspondent, David Zucchino. From his work, it is possible to get a peek inside the workday of a Western correspondent and see him attempt to communicate Southern African reality to readers who have never been there and to report the consequences of apartheid's racism without permitting its structure to frame his story. From these works, the consequences of media reporting practices on the construction of a South African reality in American minds are drawn in high relief.

Stories of Southern African decolonization and the march to majority rule have dominated recent coverage of Africa and promise to continue their prominence. The events in Southern Africa are given more space and time by the media than African events usually receive. Despite this increase in quantity, Americans turning to the news media for information find a story simplified into familiar symbol and metaphor. The South African story is a complicated, difficult one to tell in a short article or brief television report. To cope with the challenge, reporters resort to metaphor.

The present conflict in South Africa is a war of images. Nelson Mandela's release from prison was the first African news event carried live by the three networks. With his release, the coverage of South African politics as a replay of the U.S. Civil Rights movement, which had been rehearsed with Desmond Tutu, flourished at networks and newspapers. With the release of Mandela, the complex South African story began to be reported in terms of the man whose life has been a part of the struggle. The story shifted from the struggle itself, which lives in any person who shares its platform, to the leader of that struggle. Mandela's U.S. visit was a manufactured news event, as was his release. F. W. de Klerk's expert manipulation of the media has made it possible for him to have himself labeled as a moderate. The labels sketch a framework that is easy for any American reader to follow, and American voters are the market for this war of images. Mandela the peacemaker, de Klerk the moderate, the South African police as a security force, and the illusion of peaceful change are powerful visitors to the American home.

The presentation of the South African story as though it were a replay of the American Civil Rights movement is certainly the most striking feature of current reporting. For example, *The New York Times* covered the release with an article about the impact of the event in America. In an article entitled "Mandela Case Prompts Delight in the United States—South African's Release Recalls Push for Rights," the lead-in was: "From luncheonettes to classrooms to rallies and marches, American blacks are voicing a euphoria and pride in Nelson Mandela of a kind many said has not been seen since the height of the civil rights movement two decades ago."[6] During the live television coverage of Mandela's release, commentators made frequent reference to Martin Luther King, Jr. Indeed, the nonviolent movement for economic pressure, divestment, and sanctions used the rhetoric of the Civil Rights movement in its campaigns. This metaphor was chosen for its familiarity to the American readers and viewers, not for its appropriateness for the summary of South African events. This interpretation of the story was common to each network and newspaper that covered the release and Mandela's subsequent trip to the United States. *The New York Times* said that, in South Africa, "many whites and some blacks . . . had anticipated the kind of inspirational vision that distinguished the late Martin Luther King in the American Civil Rights Struggle of the 1960's."[7] Of course, it was not the South Africans who were looking for King at all, but the American journalists covering the event. American press coverage leads Americans to expect change in South Africa and underestimates the ramifications of that change. Those expectations leave readers unable to comprehend violence in terms other than racial bloodbath and primitive tribalism.

The American Civil Rights movement is an inappropriate metaphor for the present South African political situation because parallels between the two are few. The political environments of the two movements are not comparable. The American Civil Rights movement took place in a framework which guaranteed individual rights and press freedom at the federal level. The American Civil Rights movement benefited from the opinions of a friendly U.S. Supreme Court. The Supreme Court was one instrument through which the might of federal authority was imposed on the segregationist South. The American civil rights story was one of the federal government asserting control over state authority in the realm of voting rights and individual freedom. The American experience and the South African experience are incomparable. The present South African government does not need to respond to the demands of a mass movement it can crush with impunity. There is no right to freedom of assembly, the vote, or press freedom. When the minority government speaks of giving all South Africans the vote, they do not mean a vote for one parliament. In the language of South African politics, there can be a vote for a subservient lower house. Yet to an American reader, "the vote" is interpreted in the American civil rights context. There is good reason to believe that non-violence will fail today, as it failed at Sharpeville. The fundamental distinction between the two situations is that the South African turmoil is the result of a *majority* rights movement, it is not simply about inclusion, but a change in the power structure itself. The use of the American Civil Rights movement as metaphor for the present South African situation is inaccurate and incomplete.

Western beliefs about Africa have constructed an image of Africa as the repository of our greatest fears. The colonial image has become the media image. Image becomes fact. This image of Africa has important ramifications beyond American public opinion and foreign policy. Media set out the categories (primitive/modern) and define the concepts recognizable to readers and viewers. These metaphors frame the questions for American policymakers. The metaphors justify intervention, and they legitimate certain leaders and modes of change while delegitimating others. Taken together, the metaphors condemn armed resistance as dysfunctional and primitive. In this way, the metaphors used to communicate the story interpret that story for the reader and provide the value judgments that fuel subsequent political action. These paradigms were not chosen because they are an accurate summary of African reality and experience. They do not originate in Africa at all. They were chosen because they correspond to notions about Africa already existent in the minds of Westerners. The "news" is not new, nor challenging to colonial notions about Africa. The news is not a flow of information from the South to the North at all but a flow of information from the North to the North. Indeed, some would go so far as to claim that we do not really get any news from Africa. What is marketed to us as news from Africa is actually news created by Americans to the shape of an image Americans currently hold. The metaphor in which correspondents frame their stories and, indeed, the selection of the stories themselves tell us more about America than they do about Africa. The information we receive about Africa is the return of American ideas to the American market.

In the final section of the book, leading journalists and scholars assess directions in Africa coverage today. Tami Hultman, Thomas Winship,

Paul Hemp, and Danny Schechter bring diverse journalistic experiences and professional philosophies to the issues raised in this book. In their essays, they move beyond the analysis of coverage to suggest and predict changes for the future.

NOTES

The author wishes to thank Sally Baker, Pam Blake, Bob Edgar, Mary Glenn, Thoko Kadzamira, Virginia Morrison, and Grace Von Tobel for their assistance in the creation of this book.

1. Edward W. Said, *Covering Islam: How the Media and the Experts Determine How We See the Rest of the World* (New York: Pantheon, 1981), p. 154.

2. Olav Stokke, *Reporting Africa* (New York: Africana Publishing Company, 1971), p. 14.

3. Murray Edelman, *Politics as Symbolic Action* (New York: Academic Press, 1971), p. 65.

4. Todd Gitlin, *The Whole World Is Watching: Mass Media in the Making and Unmaking of the New Left* (Berkeley: University of California Press, 1980), p. 2.

5. Stokke, *Reporting Africa*, p. 12.

6. *The New York Times*, February 18, 1990, p. 28.

7. *The New York Times*, February 15, 1990, p. A21.

2

American Media and African Culture

Bosah Ebo

American news media have done less than an admirable job in their coverage of Africa. Much of what the American people know of Africa is derived from the negative and misguided images of Africa portrayed in American media. These images usually portray Africa as a crocodile-infested dark continent where jungle life has perpetually eluded civilization. Indeed, it is not surprising that American people usually associate Africa with the Hollywood images of Tarzan and the jungle, as these are regularly revived on American television. American news media have shaped the American image of Africa as a most unpleasant part of the world, where coups and earthquakes are staples of life. The underlying point is that Africa has no redeeming value to Americans or Western societies.

The increasing importance of mass news media as a source of information for Americans places great responsibility on them to give the American people an accurate, balanced, and realistic picture of the world. This responsibility becomes even more significant as the world becomes progressively interdependent. The ethnocentric attitude of American media, reflected in the portrayal of news events from Africa that do not accord with American expectations as abnormal or unnatural, precludes the fulfillment of this responsibility. Foreign news should not just reflect the expectations of American news consumers but must be presented in valid historical and cultural context.

The negative portrayal of Africa by American media is a deliberate and systematic process that is created and sustained by the bias in the way American media select foreign news stories. The process is manifested in the commercial, political, and sociocultural criteria that American media use to determine which nations and which foreign news events are newsworthy. These criteria treat American and Western cultural values as superior to Africa's and accordingly, news events from Africa are presented as abnormal or unnatural. This chapter examines the commercial, political, and sociocultural criteria that American media use in selecting foreign news and describes how these criteria undermine the cultural significance of news events from Africa by creating an appetite in the American media for the traditional coups and earthquake stories.

COMMERCIAL CRITERIA

The forces that shape global news substance and flow and the allocation of media resources can be better understood when analyzed in the larger context of the world capitalist system. Phil Harris points out, "The production and distribution of news stories in the present international arena is in fact the production and distribution of a commodity—information—within an international system whose base lies in a free trade concept of a market society and economy."[1] Even though American media present news as an objective and unbiased account of events in society, in reality news is a commodity, and like other commodities, is open to the impositions of commercial imperatives. Thus, profit maximization influences the determination of events as newsworthy by American media and also determines how they allocate their resources all over the world. Because the primary goal of American media is to make money, they select and present news stories in ways that make them commercially viable. In essence, the profit maximization motive prescribes a market concept of news, where the choice of news markets and media investments are calculated to maximize profits.

A major implication of the market concept of news is that American correspondents in Africa look for news stories that are easy and convenient to gather. As a result, these correspondents are readily attracted to exceptional and aberrational news stories. As one correspondent notes, "The Western taste for the sensational compounds ignorance."[2] Indeed, Western media practitioners generally acknowledge that the dominant formula of journalism in the world is a journalism of exception. Anthony Smith notes, "Foreign correspondents . . . are very often under great pressure to cover stories which emphasize the exceptional . . . [because] the foreign correspondent only really gets his or her chance to publish stories of major prominence in a paper when revolution or major change is taking place in the observed society."[3] The market concept of news partly explains why

American media prefer to emphasize coups and earthquake news stories and why the Tarzan and jungle image of Africa is so appealing to American media.

American media are not interested in meaningful development stories about Africa because they are mundane and commercially unattractive. An American correspondent observes that she has been to "many press conferences with African leaders where my Western colleagues' eyes have glazed over as the national newsmen deliver endless questions about school fees and rent control."[4] Ordinarily, these are not issues that Western media find interesting or commercially viable.

The geographic distribution of correspondents by American media reflects a de-emphasis of African news stories. A 1986 *Presstime* survey indicates that 31 percent of American newspaper correspondents are stationed in Europe, 23 percent in Latin America, 18 percent in Asia, 12 percent in the Middle East, 8 percent in Canada, and 8 percent in Africa.[5] The survey points out that Africa is underrepresented in global allocations of media resources because African news does not generate attractive revenues. The commercial criteria for foreign news have led to strong criticisms of American media by African leaders. They see Western journalists as "motivated only by the pursuit of the sensational—coups, corruption, chaotic economics, crocodile attacks, and quaint tribal rites."[6]

POLITICAL CRITERIA

It is well known in American journalism circles that the political significance of a country or a geographical region to America raises the newsworthiness of that country or region and provides political incentive for American media to allocate media resources and attention to that country or region. Roger Tatarian, former vice president of United Press International (UPI), acknowledges that the imbalance in news flow between America and the developing world reflects the military, economic, and political power distribution in the world.[7] The American media give superficial coverage to Africa because Africa is not considered an important player in global politics. Xan Smiley notes that, "Africa, vast as it is, no longer seems of great importance to the rest of the world. Journalists know . . . that the great power game will not be played out there."[8] Mary Ann Fitzgerald makes a similar observation, "Africa is no longer politically fashionable, instead the continent presents a repetitive litany of coups, corruption and famine."[9]

The only time Africa gets attention from American media is when major political events that threaten American political interest are taking place in Africa. American media gave lavish attention to Chad, Angola, Libya, and Liberia, when these ordinarily obscure and politically insignificant nations became crisis centers and American political interests were threatened. The American media covered Chad only because of Libyan involvement in the civil war and the perceived threat to American political interest. In fact, the war in Chad was acknowledged by the American media only when *The New York Times* added Chad to the itinerary for a roving African assignment, even though the war had been going on for years.[10] Chad was ignored because "editors had been used to discounting Chad as a place which was not important. But when the story was legitimized by the *Times*, it immediately became news, and other correspondents flew in to 'catch up.' "[11]

The war in Angola also received attention from American media because Cuban involvement in the war was considered detrimental to American interest. Even then, the war was usually reported by the American media as the result of Cuban and Soviet hegemony. The American media routinely blamed the Cuban forces for the atrocities on innocent civilians in Angola. Strong views that the war was really the result of the ideological conflict between America and Soviet Union being played out in Angola and that Jonas Savimbi's American-backed National Union for the Total Independence of Angola (UNITA) was responsible for much of the violence against civilians were rarely discussed by the American media. In fact, UNITA enjoyed strong support from the American right wing and received helpful spotlights in the American media.[12] The American media also gave attention to the Liberian civil war because American lives were at risk. Much of that attention, however, focused on the rescue mission to evacuate American citizens in Monrovia. Otherwise, general information on the war and the immense civilian casualty rate rarely made American news.

African countries ordinarily do not command high and sustained attention from American media. Usually, as soon as the temporary political significance of the crisis dies down, the country loses its limelight in the news. Smith points out, "There is an acknowledged tendency among Western media . . . to devote the greatest attention to the Third World in times of disaster, crisis and confrontations."[13] But then, the conflicts are usually reported as trivial tribal conflicts. The stories are not given historical context to avoid linking the West to the problem. After all, much of the political strife in Africa results from the collision of distinct cultural groups arbitrarily thrown into political entities by colonizers in their scramble for Africa.

In some cases, the sparse coverage Africa gets from the American media is slanted to support the political agenda of American and other Western governments. The American media coverage of black-on-black violence in South Africa is a good example. American television is filled with horrible images of South African blacks killing each other while at the same time they are agitating for a dominant role in the government. Underlying these images, of course, is a subtle message that these black people cannot run a country when they are having a difficult time running their lives. But the American media do not discuss the fact that much of the black-on-black violence in South Africa is encouraged by the South African government to give that very impression.

Andrew Breslau notes, "American media coverage of African affairs has been striking for its paucity and lack of sophistication. More alarming than this troubling state of affairs, however, is how that spare coverage has been shaped and used by various U.S. administrations to further specific political agendas."[14] American media coverage of South Africa during the Reagan administration is a good example of this point. Much of that coverage essentially reflected the position of that administration. Danny Schechter points out, "Just as the Reagan administration buys the South African line that the African National Congress (ANC) is a communist front, so much of the media uncritically parrots the same view."[15] The "ANC is invariably described as 'pro-Soviet' or Marxist. Yet, other groups are rarely called 'capitalist,' 'racist' or 'pro-American.' "[16] Indeed, the perspective of apartheid generally presented in the American media is usually slanted in ways that do not compromise American interest. The stories do not show how America and the Western economies benefit from the economic exploitation of blacks by the apartheid system. Instead, apartheid is presented as a system of racial discrimination and not economic domination.[17]

The South African government has had a well-orchestrated public relations campaign to get positive coverage from American media and clean its image in America. This propaganda machinery has successfully portrayed the ANC as a communist front and has been able to focus the apartheid debate in American media around that issue. An editorial in the *Nation* points out, "Rarely in recent years has the U.S. media so completely allowed a foreign power—in this case the Pretoria regime—to define the terms of debate."[18]

There have been cases where American media have presented news stories that have been detrimental to African countries because they supported U.S. government policy. An example is American media coverage of the events that led up to American bombing of Libya in 1986. American media did not seriously examine the government's evidence that

Libya was behind the West Berlin disco bombing on April 5, 1986, which precipitated American bomb attack on Libya on April 14. Breslau notes, "Strangely absent from the subsequent press account of the bombing was any serious inquiry into the nature of the 'evidence' used by the administration to justify its attack."[19] ABC News even had prior knowledge that the American government was planning the attack on Libya and chose not to publish the news.[20] Ironically, it was later revealed that the American government's contention that Libya was behind the disco bombing was part of a government disinformation campaign to justify the attack on Libya. In fact, the American government later planted other false stories in the press suggesting that it was planning another attack on Libya as a way of instigating a coup to destabilize Muammar Quadaffy.[21] While it is understandably difficult to sympathize with Quadaffy, it is still the duty of American media to seek out the truth.

Because American media see Africa as an insignificant player in global politics, African political groups and guerrilla movements are rarely given news coverage. African political groups are even delegitimized at times by American media if they have a different political orientation from the United States. The fact of the matter is that Africa does not have a high political priority for America or the West; consequently, American media do not see Africa as a newsworthy region. Fitzgerald points out, "For the most part, Africa is viewed as a vast black hole fringed by Libya and South Africa. With the exception of these two countries, both propelled by extreme convictions, it is not a player in the great global power game. In short, Africa is not deemed to be newsworthy."[22]

SOCIOCULTURAL CRITERIA

Another important reason for the negative and superficial portrayal of Africa in the American media is the tendency of foreign correspondents to analyze African news events from an American sociocultural mind-set. American correspondents are generally not sensitive to cultural nuances in African countries because they do not have the necessary training or background to explain the historical and cultural significance of African social events to American news consumers. The result is that American correspondents deculturalize news from Africa by stripping it of its social relevance and value. The traditional coups and earthquake stories are prime targets for foreign correspondents, because they can go in and write such stories and disappear, until another coup or earthquake takes place. More meaningful stories that need commitment to cultural knowledge about Africa, and the patience of explanation are shunned by the American media. Their correspondents do not have the cultural sensitivity or time to understand the social relevance of such stories.

American media coverage of the Ethiopian famine is a good example of how the American media deculturalize African news coverage. The American media did a fairly decent job in capturing the dramatic nature of the famine, but did little to put the story into a cultural context. As a result, American people became aware of the famine and its human toll, but did not know that the famine had effectively destroyed the cultural heritage and social traditions of the Ethiopian people. The lack of cultural sensitivity among foreign correspondents forces them to present foreign news from alien cultures in an American sociocultural mind-set. Foreign correspondents in Africa are mostly white and naturally respond to the impositions of culture, class, and color. These correspondents do not understand the problems and sufferings of the African people. For this reason, "foreign journalists are perceived by some African leaders mostly as racially imperious, ignorant of local cultures and social traditions."[23]

Another element in the sociocultural criterion for the selection of foreign news is the place of a country in the imaginary hierarchy of international social relationships. The Western media treat the cultures of the industrialized nations as superior and place them at the top of this imaginary hierarchy, while the cultures of the developing nations are placed at the bottom of the hierarchy.[24] Naturally, the wider apart two nations are in this hierarchy, the greater the tendency for imbalance to exist in the flow of news between the two nations, to the disadvantage of the nation in the lower level of the hierarchy. One study found, "The senders or initiators of communication tend to be found in the higher ranks and the receivers or imitators in the lower ranks."[25] America, in the higher ranks, is a provider of information while Africa, in the lower ranks, is a receiver of information. A study of the flow of news between the United States and South America supported this theory by showing that the United States is a "news giver" region while South America is a "news taker" region.[26] The imaginary hierarchy influences how correspondents and home editorial staff determine newsworthiness. News stories from countries on top of the hierarchy are treated with cultural respect by the American media while news stories from countries on the bottom are not treated as well.[27] For instance, the American media still see African cultural traditions as uncivilized, and even barbaric, and have not explained the relevance of these traditions to American news consumers.

DISCUSSION AND SUMMARY

Africa has endured a consistently superficial and negative image in the American media because the commercial, political, and sociocultural criteria that the American media use for selecting foreign news stories undermine the significance of African news events. Commercial criteria force correspondents to look for exceptional and aberrational news events. Meaningful stories about African cultural experiences are ignored because they are not commercially attractive to American media. This market concept news formula leads to distorted and superficial coverage of Africa and leaves the American news consumer with limited and incorrect knowledge of Africa. A good example is the persistent, derogatory image of Africa as uncivilized, attributable to the Tarzan and jungle image of Africa in the American media. This image, taken for granted by many Americans, influences the way Africans are perceived and treated by Americans. Many Americans still see Africans as half-clad savages roaming the jungles in pursuit of wildlife.

The American media shortchange the very people they purport to inform, American news consumers. The implication is even more alarming when we realize that many American elected officials and policymakers rely on the media for information. Smith points out an even more significant implication, "The struggle to escape from our bad image of the Third World is an essential stage in its struggle for independence. In this sense the journalism of the West is helping to arrest the historic process of development, and if there is any point at which the vicious circle of dependence can be broken, it is there, in the intractable issue of information."[28]

The superficial and negative coverage of Africa by American media has created animosity toward foreign correspondents on the part of African governments. John Edlin notes, "Foreign journalists are routinely denounced by African politicians as 'the enemy' agents of international imperialism, or mischief-makers bent on spotlighting domestic problems that don't exist."[29] African governments are particularly disappointed with American media coverage of South Africa, which they believe has been tilted toward the South African government's side of the story. The result was the Kadoma Declaration which was introduced by the information ministers of the Frontline states—the nations bordering South Africa—to ban foreign correspondents from reporting on them if they are based in South Africa.[30] Such a move, no doubt, hampers the free flow of information but one can hardly blame these countries for taking steps to protect themselves from unfair coverage by American media. African journalists are also disappointed with American media coverage of Africa and have even called for an international ombudsman to monitor the news coverage of international news agencies.[31]

Some African governments have found it necessary to use the services of American public relations firms to get positive coverage from American media. Togo, for instance, hired the public relations firm of David Apter and Associates, and has spent some $3 million on a public relations campaign to improve its image in America.[32] Part of the campaign was to bring Western journalists on an all-expense-paid trip to Togo, put them in luxury hotels and fete them with dinners during the twentieth anniversary of President Gnassingbe Eyadema's reign.[33] One wonders if Togo's approach is what it will take for African countries to attract the attention of American and Western media.

Any change in American media coverage of Africa must start with a reassessment of both the utility of foreign news and criteria for newsworthiness. The American media must not rely on commercial incentives as the primary criterion for selecting news stories, but must orient American news consumers to the value of African development news. As Herbert Schiller points out, "If the prevailing Western mode of treating news information as a commodity can be overcome, it will only be with an entirely different framework and purpose for information-gathering and dissemination."[34] As long as American news consumers' taste remains for the aberrational, African development news will never find a market in America. Fitzgerald observes, "Mass circulation newspapers (in America) are not interested in worthy development stories dealing with dam construction and rural health networks."[35]

The problem of inadequate coverage of Africa cannot be solved simply by increasing that coverage. More coverage will not necessarily mean better coverage. Part of the problem is that the symbols and criteria currently used by American media for selecting and presenting African news to American news consumers are not suited for telling the African story. American correspondents must be sensitized to the cultural and historical relevance of the African experience. For years now some journalism groups, such as American Society of Newspaper Editors (ASNE), Center for Foreign Journalists (CFJ), and World Press Freedom Development Committee, have developed programs to expose and sensitize Third World journalists to American news values and conventions. These organizations have yet to develop reciprocal programs to sensitize American and Western correspondents to African cultural experience. Academic institutions have not fared any better, either. Although schools have courses in international reporting, none has developed a cultural sensitivity course for foreign correspondents.

A handful of journalism groups are taking steps to improve American media coverage of the Third World. The Society of Professional Journalists has developed a program to teach reporters and editors the relevance of Third World stories. The National Association of Black Journalists (NABJ) sponsors occasional trips to Africa for minority journalists to help them get overseas posts and improve African coverage. Also, some news organizations have independently taken steps to improve Third World coverage. *CNN World Report*, for example, is a program designed to incorporate cultural relevance into news reports by using indigenous correspondents to report stories from their respective countries. The program's correspondents are usually well informed on their particular countries and know the cultural relevance of stories. These efforts indicate a willingness on the part of some news organizations to improve reporting of Africa.

In an increasingly shrinking world, where the media are an important part of the new global village, a news formula designed on a vertical international relationship model that arbitrarily treats some cultures as superior to others undermines the essence of intercultural compatibility. The media must develop and use a news model that looks at cultures horizontally by delineating the important contribution each culture can make to the new global village. The relevance of nations to the world community must not be measured in commercial benefits alone. Stories of the needs, aspirations, and endeavors of African people may not make viable commercial copy, but they may still tell an important story about humanity.

NOTES

1. Phil Harris, "Hierarchy and Concentration in International News Flow," *Politics* 9 (1974): 163.

2. Mary Ann Fitzgerald, "In Defense of the Fourth Estate," *Africa Report* (March–April 1987): 24.

3. Anthony Smith, *The Geopolitics of Information* (New York: Oxford University Press, 1980), p. 102.

4. Fitzgerald, "In Defense," p. 26.

5. *Presstime* (April 1986): 31.

6. John Edlin, "Perils of the Profession," *Africa Report* (March–April 1987): 29.

7. Roger Tatarian, "The Multinational News Pool," *Murrow Reports* (Medford, MA: Tufts University Press, 1978), p. 3.

8. Xan Smiley, "Misunderstanding Africa," *Atlantic Monthly* (September 1982): 70.

9. Fitzgerald, "In Defense," p. 24.

10. Mort Rosenblum, *Coups and Earthquakes* (New York: Harper and Row, 1981), p. 12.

11. Ibid.

12. Alana Lee and Andre Astrow, "In Search of Friends," *Africa Report* (March–April 1987).

13. Smith, *Geopolitics*, p. 90.

14. Andrew Breslau, "Demonizing Quaddafy," *Africa Report* (March–April 1987): 46.

15. Danny Schechter, "How We Cover Southern Africa," *Africa Report* (March–April 1987): 6.

16. Ibid.

17. Ibid.

18. Ibid., p. 7.

19. Breslau, "Demonizing," p. 46.

20. This information cam out during a February 1987 segment of ABC's "Nightline."

21. Breslau, "Demonizing," p. 46.

22. Fitzgerlad, "In Defense," p. 24.

23. Edlin, "Perils," p. 29.

24. Einer Ostgaard, "Factors Influencing the Flow of News," *Journal of Peace Research* 1 (1965).

25. Ibid., p. 47.

26. James Markham, *A Comparative Analysis of Foreign News in the Newspapers of the United States and South America* (State College: Penn State University Press, 1959).

27. Sophia Peterson, "Foreign News Gatekeepers and Criteria of Newsworthiness," *Journalism Quarterly* 56 (1979).

28. Smith, *Geopolitics*, p. 110.

29. Edlin, "Perils," p. 29.

30. Ibid.

31. Connie Roser and Lee Brown, "African Editors and the New World Information Order," *Journalism Quarterly* (Spring 1986). This study showed that 69 percent of African news editors were not pleased with international news agencies' treatment of Africa, and that 88 percent of the editors favored the idea of establishing an international right to remedy misrepresentations in international news.

32. Lee and Astrow, "In Search," p. 51.

33. Ibid.

34. Herbert Schiller, "Decolonization of Information: Efforts Toward a New Information Order," *Latin American Perspectives* (Winter 1978): 41.

35. Fitzgerald, "In Defense," p. 25.

3

Committed in Africa:
Reflections of a Correspondent

Stanley Meisler

I met Amos Zonke Khumalo, the plump and congenial foreign minister of Swaziland, on the eve of his new nation's independence on September 6, 1968. The fussy British government officials who still ran Swaziland had tried to keep me away from him, pleading the press of work on him at such a hectic moment in history. But the story of Swazi independence needed the spice of quotes from someone like Khumalo about his new country's dependence on neighboring South Africa, and I was determined to find him. I found him in his office in a dreary colonial building furrowing his brow over a yellowing form, a British government application for a passport. Swaziland had not yet printed new forms of its own.

There is little doubt that I was the first foreign journalist who had ever called on him. He grinned in pleasure but apologized that he could not talk about his new nation's foreign policy for a few moments. "I will be able to talk to you very soon," he said. "But first I must fill out this form for a passport. Perhaps you can help me."

Swaziland, the last British colony in Africa to receive independence, fit all the clichéd images of all the whites who called themselves old Africa hands. Swaziland was ruled by a sixty-nine-year-old chief of chiefs, King Sobhuza II, known throughout his little land as Ngwenyami, Swazi for Lion, a handsome, thick-bearded man with glinting eyes, a slight smile, a head of hair high and thick like a lion's mane, and at least eighty-five wives. Everyone expected independence to be a sham. Swaziland was dependent on white civil servants to get things done, on white farmers and tourists for income, and on the good will of the white South African government for transportation and trade. There were only 30 college graduates in its population of 400,000 and the foreign minister, like most of King Sobhuza's cronies, was not among them. All the old and smug Africa hands would chortle happily at the image of a foreign minister so ignorant of the world that he needed help filling out his passport application. I had stumbled on a very funny story.

But I could not bring myself to contribute to the ridicule of Africa. When I wrote my article on Swazi independence, I did not entirely suppress the story about the foreign minister and the passport. But I disguised Khumalo as "a very high-ranking and important Swazi official" and used the incident only to illustrate the pitiful lack of training among Swazi elites. My account did not sound funny at all.

I supposed some readers might feel like patting me on the back for my good will toward developing black Africa. But I have always felt a nagging little bit of shame and failure at the way I threw away that story. My good intentions had been founded on bad journalism. I had obviously acted as if I felt like some kind of guardian of Africa. I had trapped my professionalism in sentiment. I had acted like a public relations chief for Africa, trying to save Africa from ridicule or from itself. It was a foolish idea that did not last once I cornered it.

When *The Los Angeles Times* hired me in January of 1967 and sent me to Nairobi as its first foreign correspondent resident in Africa, I was neither an inexperienced reporter nor new to Africa, but I had never worked as a foreign correspondent before. I moved to the *Times* from the pompous-sounding position of deputy director of the Office of Evaluation and Research of the U.S. Peace Corps in Washington and knew Africa fairly well. I had spent most of 1962 travelling there on a Ford Foundation grant and dealt mostly with Africa in my two-and-a-half years with the Peace Corps. The Peace Corps, which seemed somehow above government in those heady days, attracted a good number of journalists, and I had joined its staff after almost a decade with the Associated Press in New Orleans and Washington. As rookie foreign correspondents go, I was rather old—all of thirty-five years—when the *Times* hired me.

The Los Angeles Times was then going through one of the great transformations in American journalism. It had long been looked on as a wealthy, conservative rag, more intent on promoting the likes of Richard Nixon than on informing its readers about the world.

In 1960, however, Otis Chandler took over the paper from his father as publisher. Otis was persuaded that the *Times* could not only remain rich but also become respected and influential if some of its earnings were used to create a newspaper in the same league as *The New York Times* and *The Washington Post*. The transformation of *The Los Angeles Times* began, and foreign coverage became the touchstone of that transformation. Editor Nick Williams and Foreign Editor Bob Gibson did not have the time to train a team of foreign correspondents but tried to assemble the best they could with the lure of salaries that were probably the highest in the business. The *Times* put together a staff that included *The New York Herald Tribune*'s imposing European correspondent Don Cook in Paris, China expert and novelist Bob Elegant in Hong Kong, Arabist Joe Alex Morris Jr. in Beirut, and *Newsweek*'s derring-do war correspondent Bill Tuohy in Saigon. Williams and Gibson were determined that each correspondent would be a specialist who would remain in his assignment for many years. There were not many Americans other than missionaries who qualified as Africa specialists in those days, and the *Times* had to be content with me.

Peace Corps officials, in their most philosophical moments, used to talk about commitment, and there is little doubt that I came on board the *Times* as a committed foreign correspondent, determined to look at Africa with a cold eye but explain it with sympathy. My readers, whether white or black, knew almost nothing about Africa, and I intended to instruct them even if I had to titillate them first to do so. I felt close to Africa and hoped to break down clichés about darkest Africa even though some readers might be surprised or even shocked as I did so. Proof that I was somehow succeeding came during my first year on the job when one irate though anonymous reader wrote me, "Anyone who spews out the kind of drivel that you do about Africa must be either (*a*) sexually obsessed with the African woman, (*b*) a member of the International Zionist Conspiracy, or (*c*) both of these."

For Africans, tribalism is a curse and a powerful security. It is the great reality of Africa, and any foreign correspondent who analyzes an election, a war, a coup, or a football match in Africa without analyzing its tribal machinations has failed at the job. The emotional loyalties to a tribe are still the only ties that almost all Africans feel beyond those to the family. People feel Ibo, not Nigerian, and, when they give their support by voting or by demonstrating and dancing in the streets or by plotting in bars, they do so for the political leaders of their tribes.

From time to time, I would receive a thoughtful letter from a reader protesting my constant use of the words *tribe* and *tribalism*. The protesters would insist on a phrase like *ethnic group* instead. I understood the problem. The word *tribalism* conjures up images of naked savages driving spears into the innards of other naked savages, images that reinforce all the hoary clichés about darkest Africa.

During my first months on the job, I tried to avoid the word *tribalism* but never could come up with anything better. More significantly, as the letters piled up, I began to realize that my critics were far less interested in the honesty of vocabulary than in the denial of a problem. Naked savages were not driving spears into the innards of other naked savages, but university-educated men in European suits were fuming with murderous hatred at other university-educated men in European suits even in the same government office. That was the depressing reality of Africa. Africans themselves knew that tribalism ruled their lives and had no hesitation using the term. I dropped my own hesitation soon enough. I could not have explained the Nigerian Civil War without analyzing the relentless force of tribalism.

For many years, there seemed no more frenetic, vibrant, jazz-colored town on earth than Lagos and no more self-confident country in Africa than Nigeria. Nigeria held the hope of Africa in its bouncing palm. Lagos bustled with migrants from the countryside, poor boys on the climb, hustlers on the make, fat cats corrupt with new and mind-boggling profits. The mammy-wagon buses carried defiant signs like "The Lord is my Shepherd; but Why?"

In 1962, Sam Jamiyatta Okudu, the administrative assistant to the principal of the University College of Ibadan, a handsome Ijaw with bloodshot eyes and a thick beard, was then thirty years old, a year younger than I. His moods changed often. He could be rash and then polite, nervous and then serene, angry and then silent, bitter and then resigned. "I am an angry young man," he said, smashing a fist into the palm of his hand, "but I do not know what to do." In those days, educated Nigerians of Sam's age liked to call themselves angry young men. Sam invited me, while I was at the University College of Ibadan as a Ford fellow, to spend a few days in Lagos visiting some of them, all old classmates and friends. Many worked for the civil service, and most were furious at their government. They complained constantly that thousands of pounds were pouring into the pockets of the corrupt ministers and that the northern-controlled government was filling some of the top civil service posts with dumb, incompetent Hausas from the North.

None of Sam's friends was more frenzied in his anger than poet and playwright John Pepper Clark. When we first met, J. P., an Ijaw like Sam, greeted me with a slapping handshake, swinging his hand in a wide arc, as if he wanted to spin me around. Short and dark with thick, bushy hair parted in the middle, thin, metal-framed eyeglasses, a heavy moustache, slight, tribal scars and the beginnings of a stringy beard, J. P. was loud, bitter, excitable, and very funny. J. P., features editor of *The Lagos Daily Express* in those days, felt like rebelling against all, smashing at the legacy of colonialism one moment, at tribal tradition the next.

We had tea one afternoon at the home of Sam Agbam, a high school and college classmate of J. P. and Sam Okudu. Tall, thin, and light-skinned, Agbam was not an Ijaw like the others but an Ibo. He worked on the European desk of the Ministry of Foreign Affairs and, though he wore a Western business suit every day to work, greeted us at his apartment in a long, Ibo skirt. He, his wife, and their infant boy had returned six months ago from London where Agbam had been a graduate student.

The conversation turned to newspapers, and Agbam complained about the sorry state of Nigerian newspapers, crowded with fluff and crime but short on world news and analysis. The complaint angered J. P. He jumped up, shouted, flapped his arms, and strode back and forth across the room. "You bloody fool," he shouted at Agbam, "would you pay five pence for a newspaper that had all those things you want? You would not. Newspapers are in business to make money, not to educate." The outburst provoked laughter from everyone including Agbam, and J. P. calmed down, shyly showing a little, mischievous smile.

These young men talked continually of the need for change. Sam spoke of the certainty of revolution, of even the need for a benevolent dictator. He and his friends speculated that the economy might collapse under the waste and weight of corruption, that the coming glut of university graduates on the market would lead to frustration and rebellion, that young army officers, as fed up as themselves, would seize power. "Nigeria," said J. P. after an evening of Highlife dancing at the Kakadoo night club, "is made up of a caste of corruption on the top and a caste of grumblers on the bottom." Sam intoned like a chorus, "The grumblers are angry." "No," J. P. insisted, "they are not angry yet. They still have too much."

We did not know then that we were scarcely five years away from the Nigerian civil war, the greatest scourge in Africa since the slave trade. The war, which I covered from both sides, would sear images in my mind of stick-boned, pot-bellied, flaky-skinned children sitting in their filth, so weak that the pressure of a finger tip could keel them over. After the war, the woeful wide eyes of the malnourished children would always symbolize Nigeria for me, pushing aside the memories of Lagos Highlife and the Kakadoo night club.

I returned to Nigeria in April 1967 on the eve of the war as the Africa correspondent of *The Los Angeles Times* and called on J. P., now a professor of English at the University of Lagos. He had lost the mischievous glint in his eyes by then. Much had happened in five years. J. P. had written an ill-tempered book about his stay in the United States, which had been shortened somewhat by Princeton's termination of his fellowship for refusing to attend classes.

We sat on the veranda of his home at the university and drank a beer or two. J. P. was warm but subdued, heavier now, married, well established as a writer. "I'm depressed," he said. "The market women are depressed. The dockworkers are depressed. Everyone is depressed. This is a very sad time for Nigeria."

Some of the Ibos in the old crowd like Sam Agbam had left Lagos for their tribal homeland in the East. "They were frightened men, and so they have run home," J. P. said. "I do not blame them. A man can live with his fear only so long. Yet their running home has hurt Nigeria, has intensified our divisions. Agbam did not know anything about his people at all. He is married to a northern girl, in fact. Then all this happened, and he had to run home, to people he did not really know. It is very sad."

Unlike the old days, he had no answers. "We need patience," he said, "a little time for self-examination. That's what we need most of all. Patience."

I met Sam Agbam again in Enugu a few weeks later, after patience had run out, after the Eastern Regional Government in Enugu had declared itself the Independent Republic of Biafra, an act that provoked civil war. After filing stories on the secession for two days from Lagos, I drove to the new and unrecognized republic to feel the mood of Biafra. On the night that we reached Enugu, Odumegwu Ojukwu received two British journalists and myself at State House, the old official residence of the regional governor.

Ojukwu, then 33, was a roughly bearded, well-educated young man with soft eyes and gentle tones and a showy contempt for his enemies in Lagos. Dressed in sports shirt, slacks, and sandals, sipping from a can of beer, Ojukwu, playing the grand man, seemed churlish and impatient, both with his aides and with questions that struck him as simplistic. He tinged his replies with bitterness and disdain. Did he believe Yakubu Gowon was bluffing with his threat to crush the secession by force? "No," Ojukwu replied with slow and mock thoughtfulness. "He is not bluffing. Bluffing supposes a very great deal of intelligence and thinking." Did he believe other governments would recognize Biafra? "The nigger in the woodpile in this," he said, pausing for his image to sink in, "is the outsider."

The corridors and lobbies of State House crowded with young Ibo civil servants dressed neatly in ties and suits. They kept chattering to visitors about the needs and wishes of "H.E." They quoted H.E. as if he spoke only in scripture. H.E. was an abbreviation for His Excellency, and almost every civil servant in Enugu used the initials when talking about Ojukwu. Sam Agbam was among them, a thin, light-skinned, well-dressed diplomat in the newly created Biafran ministry of foreign affairs. I cannot remember now exactly what he said. I only remember my disappointment then at hearing him mouth the same slogans, the same litanies as everyone else. Agbam had become faceless, boring, robot-like, and it was hard to fathom how he really felt.

A few weeks after the war began, Biafran troops, in a surprise strike outward, seized Benin and the Midwest Region of Nigeria. There has been a good deal of scholarly musing since that Biafra might have won the war then if its troops had taken full advantage of the surprise and rushed on to Lagos and Ibadan. But the troops consolidated, loitered, administered, and in a few months, gave way to counterattacking Nigerians and retreated back to Biafra. A furious Ojukwu needed traitors and saboteurs to blame for the loss of so great a prize so quickly.

Ojukwu arrested the army commander in Benin, two prominent Ibos, and an obscure diplomat named Sam Agbam. John de St. Jorre, the *London Observer* correspondent whose book on the war still dwarfs all others for clarity and evenhandedness, believes that, while the charges against the army commander were trumped up, the other three, including Agbam, had been trying to persuade prominent Biafrans, including military officers, that secession was hopeless and that Biafra therefore needed to work out some deal with Lagos. All four were sentenced to death and shot on September 24, 1967, four days after the fall of Benin to Nigeria. I heard the news by radio in Lagos a few days later.

When I returned to Ibadan during the early months of 1967, Sam Jamiyatta Okudu, now deputy registrar of what was now called the University of Ibadan, had once more tried to act as my guide. Warm, thoughtful, talkative, wide-eyed, he felt that I needed to encounter every shading of view on campus: Ibos ready to flee, Ibos prepared to stay, suspicious Northerners, proud and troubled Yorubas, minorities fervent for One Nigeria. It sometimes seemed that he had anointed me as the outsider who could best interpret Nigeria for the rest of the world and appointed himself as the Nigerian best able to lead me through the byways and morass. I felt closer to him than any other Nigerian. There was no doubt that Sam opposed Biafran secession, but he understood its roots, and he wanted me to understand them as well.

In late August, just three months after secession, two months after fighting began, I set down my views on the war for the Sunday Opinion section of the *Times*. Nigeria was a creation of British, French, and German diplomats drawing lines on a map in the late nineteenth century. Nigeria made no ethnic or geographic sense, and the British did not even attempt to rule the colony of Lagos, the northern protectorate, and the southern protectorate as a single British imperial administrative unit known as Nigeria until 1914. Even then, this unity worked better on bureaucratic paper than it did in the field. Putting the Islamic north and the Christian-pagan south together and calling it Nigeria was something like putting Ireland and Egypt together and calling it the United Irish Republic.

I realized that many African leaders feared that any successful secession of Biafra would trigger other secession movements throughout the continent and that many foreign specialists believed the economic development of Africa demanded large national units such as Nigeria. Yet these feelings justified no more than an attempt at a peaceful settlement that would bring a rather autonomous Biafra into a loose, largely economic Nigerian federation. The case for crushing Biafra by military force seemed outweighed by the tepid nature of Nigerian nationalism, the intense tribal feelings of the Ibos, the hatred of other tribes for them, and the poor chances of welding a real nation after the civil war. On balance, I wrote, it was hard to believe that a big Nigeria was worth all the bloodshed.

The piece did not attempt to hide a sympathy for the Biafrans. They were, after all, the aggrieved people, the Jews of Nigeria in anguish after terrifying pogroms. It was easy to fume with impatience at them. When I look back on the war now, I realize that the Ibos were brought down by their own arrogance and innocence, still believing the romantic, foolish maxims they had learned in imperial schools—God would save them, right would triumph, good Christians everywhere would never turn their backs on misery and injustice. They spurned all hands of compromise. They haughtily refused to accept anything less than their independence. In the end, they collapsed and salvaged nothing.

I was planning to visit Sam Okudu in Ibadan in October, but he had read a reprint of my article in *The International Herald Tribune*. Before I set out for Nigeria from Nairobi, I received a letter from him. The letter, a reply to my article, was hysterical, brimming with venom. "You are an enemy of Nigeria," he wrote, "and indeed of Africa! Could you have written the way you did to cater for certain American interests?" Where was my old friend who loved a good debate and clashing views? I was too depressed to ever call on him again.

The British had long looked on Uganda as a rare imperial jewel, a lush, tranquil, loyal protectorate in a dark and troublesome African empire. Winston Churchill came on it as a young newspaperman. "There is no region," he wrote in 1908, "which offers prospects to compare in hopefulness with those of the protectorate of Uganda." Yet no British journalist or politician praised Uganda during the last years that I covered it. General Idi Amin Dada ruled independent Uganda then with cruel and barbarous whim, a beefy, grinning man whose air of comical innocence could not obscure the delight he felt in his own murderous cunning. Africa has had few shames more sickening than Idi Amin.

Tribalism can explain the irony of so favorable a colony as Uganda falling into the clutches of Amin. Churchill had been excited not by Uganda but by the kingdom of Buganda on the shores of Lake Victoria. By the time of Ugandan independence in 1962, Buganda was one of the most modern and productive areas in Africa. But Buganda was not the same as Uganda. At independence, the people of Buganda, though granted some autonomy, found themselves in an independent country where other peoples—less modern and less educated—outnumbered them by more than five to one. Despite their numbers, the others, squabbling among themselves, felt threatened by the productivity and modernity of Buganda. Prime Minister Milton Obote, a northerner, was obsessed with the need to break the power of the kabaka or king, strip Buganda of all vestiges of autonomy, and render its people meek and impotent. To do the job, he created a monster, an enormous army of northerners led by a former hard-drinking sergeant who had won the heavyweight boxing championship of the Uganda Army. The commander was Amin, a poorly educated man with barracks English but quick humor, a northerner from another tribe than Obote. Amin routed the kabaka and broke the backs of the Buganda but then turned on his creator, ousting Obote in a coup in 1971.

But tribalism cannot wholly explain Amin. His dispiriting reign demonstrated how easy it was in Africa for a determined man, no matter how ignorant, to seize control of fragile institutions with a few thousand soldiers. Amin presided over a bloody and fierce instability until a few thousand soldiers from Tanzania finally drove him from Uganda in 1979. During these frightening times, Amin's soldiers murdered Nicholas Stroh, a stringer in Kampala for *The Washington Star*, and jailed Andrew Torchia of the Associated Press and a score of other correspondents for many days. Foreign correspondents in Nairobi felt fearful and hesitant about flying to Uganda to witness the terror.

In February 1973, General Amin gave us our opportunity. In a telephone conversation with an African journalist from Nairobi, he invited the Kenya newspapers to send reporters to Uganda to see what was going on for themselves. We seized on this. Agence France-Presse correspondent Bertrand Bellaigue phoned one of Amin's aides on behalf of the foreign correspondents of Nairobi and asked if the general would agree to see the "world press" as well. The phrase *world press* sometimes had a magical sound in Africa, opening doors that were closed to an ordinary foreign correspondent who represented no more than, say, *The Los Angeles Times* or *The New York Times* or *Time* magazine. The phrase conjured images of all the eyes of the planet turning slowly to focus on a little neglected patch of Africa. Once, during the Nigerian war, a Biafran escort officer grew furious with a soldier for stopping our car to check our papers. "You are delaying the world press," the escort officer shouted. In the face of this tirade, the soldier hurriedly pushed the papers back at us and waved us through the barricade. The world press was me.

General Amin agreed to meet the world press. Few of us would have taken the chance of going to Uganda alone, but we came as a group of fifteen foreign correspondents and felt reasonably sure that our numbers, invitation, and standing guaranteed us some safety from the hysteria of his soldiers.

General Amin welcomed us. "I think," he said, "Uganda is paradise country in Africa." An enormous man six foot three and weighing somewhere near 250 pounds, Amin seemed awkward in his civilian clothes, wearing a suit with red suspenders that failed to pull his trousers above his rotund middle. Like a country bumpkin out of place, he did not know where to put his limbs. He kept a huge hand out of the way by clutching his thigh. He spoke in an unschooled English learned in colonial days as an ordinary soldier in the King's African Rifles. Much like speakers of pidgin in West Africa, he dropped plural endings and used prepositions in an odd way. But his speech was free of malapropisms and easily understood. Talking about Tanzania, for example, he said, "But I have no time of quarreling with them. It is only Tanzania who is interfering with the internal affair of Uganda." If we had not known about the blood on his ham hands, we might have mistaken him for a peasant philosopher with a flair for comic, self-deprecating absurdity.

Amin told the journalists that he admired Prime Minister Edward Heath of Britain. "Mr. Heath is my best friend," said Amin. "Great Britain has one of the best prime minister. He is like Hitler. I like him very much. He is very strong." A German correspondent then asked him to talk a bit more about his admiration for Adolf Hitler. Amin, after all, had once sent a cable to United Nations Secretary General Kurt Waldheim praising Hitler for trying to exterminate the Jews. "Oh, no," Amin replied, "not Hitler. I meant Winston Churchill. Mr. Heath is like Winston Churchill. Please make that Churchill. I don't want to quarrel with my friends. I don't want to open a second-line front against me." Then he laughed heartily.

Amin said that Allah had told him in a dream to expel the Asians from

Uganda. The words of Allah had come at 5 A.M. on August 4. But that was not the only time that Allah had spoken to him in a dream. "I dreamed in 1952 that I would become commander of the armed forces, which is true, and president, and very popular, which is true," he said. "I was told how long I was going to live and when to die." Had there been any dreams since the Asian one? "I only dream when it is necessary," he replied. Could he reveal the date that Allah had fixed for his death? "That is confidential," he said.

Amin defended his army and denied the news reports about its massacres. "You must not talk bad word about the Uganda army," he said. "The Uganda army, including its air force, is really very good. And everyone can make mistake except God. The standard of my army and air force are purely international. The brain of the Uganda soldier is as good as the brain of any soldier in the world." Discussing his soldiers further, he said, "It seems that I am loved by them."

A correspondent asked Amin if he enjoyed the job of president. Amin replied that he did but added a philosophical note. "It is very hard," he said. "You must have a brain. You must work very hard. You must think before you act. It is very hard to be a president. And one thing I know as president, you must not be a coward." The manner and flavor of Amin's words were far more significant than their meaning, and I tried hard, in my reporting of the news conference, to lay the mood bare, in all its ugly comedy.

In 1973, I asked Foreign Editor Bob Gibson to transfer me from Africa. I had an ample case for a transfer: First-hand coverage was becoming difficult. African politicians and bureaucrats could not stomach the slightest hint of criticism, especially from someone who knew them well. I found myself barred from entry into South Africa, Zambia, Ethiopia, and Nigeria. Inefficient immigration police would probably have allowed me to enter Zaire, Upper Volta, Rwanda, and Burundi, but I would have risked expulsion, at the least, when other officials discovered I was there. I had a multiple-entry visa for Uganda but would have been foolish to use it.

I could also sense a certain staleness in my approach to the thirty-odd African countries that did let me in. I knew more about many of these countries than most American diplomats assigned there and found myself often briefing the diplomats instead of the other way around. That satisfied my ego at first but began to bore me later. On top of all this, the African story was depressing me. The plight of Africa was worsening. Its leaders were turning more tyrannical, tribalist, and greedy, refusing to look at the problems of Africa with any realism. Africa was sinking deeper into a morass, and nothing was being done about it.

In the fall of 1973, enroute to a new assignment in Mexico City, I was invited to speak at a seminar of the African Studies Center in the University of California at Los Angeles. Over the years, I had met and corresponded with several UCLA professors in African studies and felt we had a kind of kinship. In our different ways, we were both trying to explain Africa to a significant region of America. I expected to enjoy the exchange of ideas with the students at the seminar and felt pleased when I arrived to find the large room packed with more than a hundred students.

My pleasure did not last very long. It was still the era of political activism at American universities, and the students had come armed with a furious litany of complaints against me. For more than two hours, the angry students, disguising their diatribes as questions, accused me of racism, neoimperialism, distortion, and omission.

Some of the accusations were directed less at me than the American press in general. "Why do you keep calling General Amin 'Big Daddy,' " asked one frowning youth, "when you know that is not his name?" Although no one in Uganda ever called him that, some sensationalist journalists, especially those of the British press, had coined the nickname, which seemed so apt, by twisting it out of his full name Idi Amin Dada. But I had refused to fall into the practice of ridiculing him with a phony nickname. If they examined my stories carefully, I explained, they would see that I had never once called him Big Daddy. "Well, if you didn't call him Big Daddy," the student said with contempt, "*Newsweek* did." One student complained about the lack of depth in my coverage of the Sudanese civil war. Since the *Times* had recently published a series of my articles on the war, I asked him what in the series had troubled him. "I did not bother to read it," he said with a good deal of haughtiness.

The students insisted that I had failed to appreciate the greatness of Kwame Nkrumah, had devoted too much space to the capitalist system of Kenya, had neglected significant developmental problems, and had treated Africans with condescension. One thread ran through all the complaints: I had somehow let down the side in Africa. "The kind of things that you write about General Amin," said one smug young lady, "hurt the cause of the black movement in the United States." I protested. "I am not Africa's public relations man," I said. "That's not the job of a foreign correspondent. Your quarrel isn't with me. It's with General Amin."

4

African Censorship and American Correspondents

William Hachten

The Nigerian press spokesman smiled at the room full of reporters, paused dramatically, and said, "Gentlemen, I've got some good news for you today. We are lifting press censorship." In the commotion that followed, one reporter was heard to shout: "Can we report that?" "Unfortunately not," replied the spokesman. "You see, we never really said publicly that we were imposing press censorship. Therefore, we can hardly announce today that we are lifting it."[1]

This Catch-22 incident occurred at the end of the Nigerian civil war and was not uncommon; wars and civil unrest have long been difficult to report in Africa yet direct wartime censorship is only one of the many faces of censorship in Africa. Censorship is a central concern for journalists and writers reporting on Africa. African journalists themselves are less free and must work under more government restraints than their colleagues in other regions of the world. These same conditions make it difficult as well for foreign journalists and broadcasters who come in to report about Africa. Clearly, Africa's image in the global community has been affected by the restraints and pressures on the men and women who have tried to report, write about, and explain Africa to the world. Assessing the effects of censorship is difficult to measure but unquestionably there is some distortion from various efforts to repress and manipulate the flow of news.

This is not to say that news does not get out. It does. Few major stories stay buried for long, if there is the will and effort to get the information out. The day-to-day news out of Africa often seems like a trickle but a great deal of information is available about Africa, and ironically, the best places to obtain it often are in Western capitals such as London, Paris, or Washington, D.C., not African cities.

Let us begin by trying to define what we mean by censorship. Narrowly defined, *censorship* means direct government restraints on what is printed or broadcast. *Direct censorship* is a bureaucratic process wherein reporters must submit their material to a government official for approval before it can be printed or broadcast. Africa has had comparatively little direct restraint, except for time of war, because African governments have not been that efficiently bureaucratic or totalitarian. So here we use a broader definition—*indirect censorship*—that is, any action, whether by government or not, that inhibits or represses expression or the reporting of news. As we see, this includes a wide variety of restraints on the free flow of news and information, including self-censorship—a special problem for Africa.

Africa's image has been distorted, for example, by other indirect factors such as the sparsity of foreign correspondents outside of South Africa, inadequate telecommunications and transportation systems (foreign reporters in Africa must fly much farther and to many more nations to cover stories than correspondents anywhere on earth) and the lack of interest about, and understanding of, Africa in the outside world.

Primary factors inhibiting news flow relate to the inadequacies of the African news media themselves. During the 1960s, government ownership and/or control of most instruments of mass communication became the norm in independent Africa—an inevitable outcome of one-party governance or of military regimes which often took over after the frequent coups. Most post-colonial governments either acquired or established major newspapers, monopoly radio and television broadcasting services, a national news agency, and an extensive government information service—all under official control and directly accountable to those in power. This control required the media's unquestioning support of the nation's leaders and policies and persistent exhortations to the public to do likewise. Thus, most newspapers and broadcasters practiced self-censorship, avoiding both investigative reporting and criticism of government and leaving any dissent or growing discontent among the people without even meager outlets. Under such circumstances, direct government censorship of the media was hardly necessary.

Journalist David Lamb explained what had happened to the African press: "In almost every country of Africa, the prime role of the media is to serve the government, not to inform the people. This is a propaganda vehicle, used to manipulate and organize and control; any questioning voice is a potential threat and only the government is wise enough to know what the people need to know. . . . News was censored and managed to the point that what got into print was little more than government news releases."[2] The frustrations of African journalists were well expressed by a leading Kenyan journalist, Hilary Ng'weno: "In respect to the all pervading power of government, nothing has really changed from the bad old days of colonialism. Only the actors have changed; the play remains the same. Instead of a colonial governor, you have a president or a field marshal. . . . Newspapers were taken over and those which were totally opposed to being incorporated into the government propaganda machinery were closed down."[3]

Africa's kept media, then, have been an extremely inadequate source for news about Africa. And the rights and effectiveness of foreign reporters are directly related to how free and competent the local media are. In most countries, foreign journalists rely on the local media for much of their basic news and enjoy about the same amount of freedom or restraint as their local colleagues. (One important difference is that a local reporter may be jailed, or worse, while a foreigner is more likely to be deported.)

Local and foreign reporters often help each other as well as compete for news. In South Africa, for instance, local reporters sometimes gave to foreign newsmen a story they knew they could not publish. Then, after the story appeared abroad, South African papers could pick it up from the news services.

World news agencies such as Associated Press (AP), Reuters, United Press International (UPI), or Agence France-Presse (AFP) rely on the local media to cover the basic news; when the local media are inadequate, the agencies' task is much more difficult. When Reuters closed its bureau in Accra, Ghana, it made an agreement with the Ghana News Agency (GNA) to exchange news reports so that Reuters could continue to cover Ghana for both its worldwide and African services. The only problem was the GNA was an official government mouthpiece and hence lacking in credibility about any story that might reflect badly on the Ghanaian leadership or its policies.

Sudan, where civil war has raged off and on for more than twenty years, offers a special kind of challenge, or example, to the Associated Press. AP has no clients there, largely because the Sudan News Agency, which distributes news to local media, lacks the hard currency to buy the satellite-beamed AP world service report. Local media are not credible as news sources because they are subject to official controls and the AP cannot justify maintaining a full-time correspondent in Khartoum. Therefore, AP covers Sudan by using a local stringer, who may work for the government; periodically AP may send a staff correspondent to Sudan to do background or roundup stories. Hence, the largest nation in Africa, an important one, goes mainly unreported in the world's major news agency.

Despite the widespread availability of communication satellites, computers and high-speed telecommunications, collecting news in Africa is an erratic and imperfect process. "What is commonly referred to as the world flow of news," AP correspondent Mort Rosenblum wrote, "is more a series of trickles and spurts. News is moved across borders by a surprisingly thin network of correspondents. . . . The smaller countries are squeezed into rapid trips during lulls between major stories in the larger countries."[4] Some significant events are either not reported or reported well after the fact. Much of Africa rarely gets into the world's daily news flow. Datelines from such capitals as Niamey, Bamako, Khartoum, Ouagadougou, Lome, Freetown, Conakry, Bangui, Yaounde, Nouakchott, or Brazzaville seldom appear in Western newspapers unless the stories concern natural disasters, violent conflict, or a coup d'etat.

In Africa, profound disagreements exist between professional journalists and government officials over the nature of news. To the journalist, news is the first report of a happening that editors think will be of interest to their readers or viewers. To most government officials, news is positive information that reflects well on their nation (and hence their leaders) and thus serves their country's general interests and goals. Yet those same leaders want the unvarnished facts about what is happening outside their borders. News is what a government official wants to read about somewhere else; propaganda is what the official wants the world to read about him and his country.

African governments treat the foreign press in a variety of ways. Some, at times, just keep out all foreign reporters, as Guinea did for many years and Nigeria did for several years while under military rule in the 1970s. Or reporters may be permitted in but access to news sources or officials is severely limited. On a visit to Tanzania, Henry Kamm of *The New York Times*, was told by a government official that he should have submitted his precise program in writing long before arrival so that a special government committee could rule on his requests. Because he had not done so, Kamm was told he could see no government official and must not leave the capital at risk of arrest. The only official help he received for a story on Tanzanian development was a collection of speeches by President Julius Nyerere, the most recent of which was three years old.

David Lamb of *The Los Angeles Times* believes that doors have been closing for the Western press. "Across the continent," he wrote, "news management is becoming tighter, restrictions on journalists more severe and access to countries more limited. More than a quarter of Black Africa's

44 governments ban foreign correspondents or admit them infrequently and under such controlled conditions that news, in effect, is managed or blacked out. Others admit journalists only for self-serving group tours, then send them on their way."[5]

African leaders feel strongly they have a sovereign right to control information crossing their borders and, in Africa, censorship may be achieved in a variety of ways. For example, a foreign journalist arriving at a national airport to investigate a rumored coup, may be denied a visa to enter the country and thus miss the story. Or a foreign reporter may be denied the use of transmitting facilities; in many African nations, there may be only one government office with telex or telephone facilities. (Some reporters believe inability to transmit a story out of Africa is a greater problem than direct censorship.)

Or, foreign journalists may be subjected to harassment in a variety of forms. In the Central African Empire in the 1970s, AP reporter Michael Goldsmith was brought handcuffed into the presence of Emperor Jean-Bedel Bokassa I. The ruler suddenly clubbed him to the ground, stepped on his glasses and began kicking him mercilessly. The rest of the party joined in and Goldsmith quickly lost consciousness. He awoke in a tiny detention cell where he spent the next month. Through diplomatic intercession, Goldsmith was finally released. He later said that what happened to him could happen to any correspondent in countries where the ruler is unstable and regards objective reporting as hostile.

The drawn-out invasion of Uganda by Tanzanian forces was reported mainly from neighboring Kenya because of hostility to foreign journalists from both sides. In the later stages of the conflict that finally drove Idi Amin from power, two West Germans, Hans Bollinger and Wolfgang Stiens, and two Swedes, Arne Lemberg and Earl Bergman, who were entering Uganda to report on the war, were murdered by soldiers loyal to Amin.

Such political instability exacerbates the reporters' work. During the first twenty-five years of independence, more than 70 leaders in 29 nations were deposed by assassinations, coups, and purges. The 44 new nations were rocked by 20 major wars and 40 successful coups between 1957 and 1981. Such conditions force many reporters to cover individual countries by proxy by monitoring radio or interviewing diplomats or refugees leaving the country. Ghana, Guinea, Guinea Bissau, Benin, Equatorial Guinea, and Angola have at various times been covered from afar because access was denied to Western correspondents. When an attempted coup occurred in Cameroon in 1984, the story was covered by monitoring the Cameroonian radio service in Abidjan, Ivory Coast, because there were no foreign reporters in Cameroon at the time. In some places, such as Morocco, government officials often do not talk to any reporters and the foreign press is sometimes reduced to getting information from foreign embassies or from intelligence sources.

Efforts of some African governments to inhibit coverage of Africa's disastrous famines of recent years have cost lives. The drought and famine in Ethiopia that made world headlines in 1985 and again in 1988 and 1990, brought in a good deal of Western relief aid, but the famine itself had been unreported for at least two years in that country. One observer noted, "Actual starvation began to ravage the country as early as 1983. Relief agencies knew it. Many Ethiopian officials knew it, but the government banned any reporting of the oncoming catastrophe in its own media until late 1984. Even when the ban was lifted, coverage had to focus on government 'relief and rehabilitation' efforts, not on the famine itself."[6] In neighboring Sudan, Mike Kilongson, a Sudanese journalist, was forced to flee to Kenya in 1986 after he had been imprisoned and tortured by the authorities following his reports for the BBC about the famine in the Sudan. On the other hand, widespread starvation has rarely occurred in a country with a free and active press, because in such places, famine conditions are more likely to be reported, and hence, the government and the international aid community are more likely to act to avert starvation.

By trying to cover the news that African authorities do not want reported, reporters face the threat of expulsion. Over the years, a good number of Western journalists have been forced out of Africa and refused visas when they sought re-entry. Colin Legum, a leading British journalist, was barred from South Africa for many years because of his incisive reports on apartheid. Peter Webb, who once covered Africa for *Newsweek*, said,

One has to weigh one's words carefully to think of the possible repercussions before committing them to print. As a result, I think most foreign correspondents on this continent exercise a form of self-censorship which may, in some way, be no bad thing. To paraphrase Sam Johnson, the thought of having to pack up one's whole household within 24 hours concentrates the mind wonderfully. Should he or should he not file a certain story, knowing that it may get him into trouble? Every correspondent has to overcome the problem in his own way. My own rule of thumb is that if the story is sufficiently important then publish and be damned, but if it is essentially trivial and will be forgotten by tomorrow then perhaps it is better to pass it by. Reporting Africa is like walking through a minefield; you have to be careful where you put your feet.[7]

A British journalist, Xan Smiley, believes that heavy self-censorship has become a standard feature of Western reporting about Africa. A sense of guilt and the hope of returning to report again cause many reporters to pull their punches and not report to the full extent how badly things have gone in Africa. "Above all," Smiley wrote, "if he is to survive in respectable journalistic circles, he must paint over rank incompetence, cruelty, and corruption of the new elites—be they right wing or left wing—and ignore the amorality and inertia among the common people."[8] Critics have charged that the American television networks—ABC, CBS, and NBC—have softened their coverage of South Africa and avoided stories critical of the ruling Afrikaners during the turbulent mid-1980s to maintain their bureaus in Johannesburg.

Those African journalists and publications which were courageous enough to speak out against their governments, often became the targets of repressive actions. Idi Amin shut down virtually the entire Uganda press, harassed and killed several journalists, and banned all foreign reporters. In 1986, one of Nigeria's leading investigative journalists, Dele Giwa, editor of *Newswatch*, was assassinated by a car bomb—a few days after being interrogated by the state security service. Critical journalists have had a hard time in Ghana and their papers are often closed down. "It is very unfortunate," said Elizabeth Ohene, the first woman editor of a Ghanaian newspaper, "that so many governments in Africa believe that journalists should be part of the political process. . . . This is dangerous both for government and the press, because the people need to know that, in the last resort, they can turn to the press to defend them against official abuses."[9]

SPECIAL CASE OF SOUTH AFRICA

In many ways, the Republic of South Africa, the last bastion of white supremacy on the African continent, is a special case. As it is Africa's most industrialized nation, all white people and some urban black people have enjoyed a high standard of living. (Rural black South Africans live at a poverty level comparable to other nations throughout the continent.) The republic is an unusual mixture of the First and Third Worlds; this may explain why the world is so fascinated with it.

Since the Soweto uprising of 1976, South Africa has received a great deal of foreign media attention, while most of black Africa has been largely ignored. In recent years, the number of accredited foreign journalists has been about 170 to 200, mostly based in Johannesburg. This was more than were based in all of Africa. Despite repression and censorship of both the domestic and foreign press, the story of apartheid has gotten out. Americans and other Westerners know little of black Africa but quite a bit about the apartheid struggle in South Africa. Nonetheless, the foreign press in South Africa has long been criticized by both whites and blacks.

The National Party leaders who have ruled South Africa since 1948 have long been troubled and annoyed about the resident foreign correspondents. Many Nationalists believe the overseas media, especially in Britain and the United States, present a warped and biased picture of the republic. As the apartheid laws began appearing after 1948, so did legislation restricting the press, so that today there are more than one hundred laws that circumscribe press coverage. There has been little direct censorship, most laws restrict access to such apartheid-sensitive areas as news of police and jails, military and security matters, prisons, riots and protests, communist activities, and terrorism. All journalists, domestic and foreign, face sanctions if they contravene these myriad laws; journalists rely heavily on lawyers to avoid contravening the statutes. The government enjoys broad legal powers to close down newspapers (as happened to several leading African papers), to ban and jail journalists, or worse, detain them without charge for long periods. Foreign correspondents are subject to the same draconian laws and during the turbulent mid-1980s about a dozen were expelled from the country. Critical reporters are often barred from re-entering South Africa.

During the extended period of violence from late 1984 until 1986, the Botha government gradually tightened the clamps on the foreign press. After months of protest and violence throughout South Africa claimed more than a thousand lives, and all of it fully reported by Western media, the government imposed sweeping restraints on foreign press coverage. New regulations required that all reporters in print and broadcasting could cover scenes of unrest and protest only under police supervision. Most tellingly, television and still pictures and sound recordings of unrest in those areas were prohibited. If the purpose of the ban was to remove images of violence from foreign television screens, then it worked. Subsequently on June 16, 1986, on the tenth anniversary of the Soweto uprising, the government imposed a state of emergency and banned the use of communication satellites for live television coverage of *any* news coming out of South Africa. So while violent confrontation between blacks and whites continued unabated (more than four thousand were killed by 1989), the vivid images of that violence disappeared from television screens.

Despite an earlier tradition of press freedom (mostly for whites), the press of South Africa today enjoys little real freedom and can basically only report what the government will permit it to report.

South Africa has been unusual in Africa for the extent to which it has used propaganda and public relations to improve its tarnished image abroad. A number of tools have been used to counter what South African authorities consider to be hostile, misleading, and erroneous criticisms, especially from foreign journalists. Domestically, the South African Broadcasting Corporation (SABC), a government monopoly in television and radio, has been a major propaganda tool of the Nationalists to give all South Africans their version of reality, to counter their critics abroad and in their own English-language press, and to control the political process. In addition, their propaganda has been reinforced by part of the press, *The Citizen,* and most Afrikaans language newspapers, although less today than earlier due to the independence of *Beeld* and new critical papers such as *Vrywe Weekblad.*

To persuade the influentials overseas, the government spent generously in its lobbying efforts. The Muldergate scandal of 1977–79 provided a marvelous picture of extensive illegal and covert efforts to influence public opinion overseas, especially in the United States and Western Europe.[10] During the 1970s, about $100 million was surreptitiously spent on some two hundred projects to improve the image of South Africa. Among the projects revealed that relate to media were $14 million of government funds to secretly fund a new English-language daily, *The Citizen,* which was ostensibly a private newspaper; $17 million to secretly subsidize *To The Point,* an international news magazine supporting South Africa; over $10 million given to Michigan publisher John McGoff, who tried to buy *The Washington Star*; unregistered funds given to oppose successfully the reelections of Senators John Tunney of California and Dick Clark of Iowa, both of whom were outspoken critics of South Africa in the U.S. Congress; efforts to buy major European publications such as *L'Express* and *Paris Match* in France; and trips funded for U.S. congressmen and journalists to visit South Africa. Revelations, mainly published in the *Rand Daily Mail* and *Sunday Express*, brought down the government and ended the political careers of Prime Minister John Vorster and Information Minister Connie Mulder. But the National Party itself survived the scandal and has continued to rule South Africa.

Since Muldergate, South Africa has relied on more conventional efforts to polish its image. For its sophisticated efforts in international broadcasting, Radio South Africa sends out strong short wave signals, broadcasting about 223 hours weekly, aimed mainly at black Africa but also the United States and Western Europe. Subtle propaganda messages are wrapped in hard news reports. In addition, the South African government spends about

$1 million annually in the United States on lobbying and legal represen-
tation with most of it spent in Washington, D.C.

Since the current government of Prime Minister F. W. de Klerk has
freed Nelson Mandela and some other political prisoners during 1990 and
called for negotiations with the African National Congress, the media
situation has become relatively open and unimpaired. Both the foreign and
local media have been outspoken and critical in reporting current developments. Investigative stories highly embarrassing to the government
have been published without repressive action by government officials.
How long this comparative freedom of expression will last will depend on
political developments, for the laws and habits of controlling the press and
manipulating public information are still very much in place and controls
could return with full force at any time.

GETTING AROUND CENSORSHIP

Africa's image suffers because, outside of South Africa, there is comparatively little news about Africa in U.S. news media. In fact, U.S. press
coverage of Africa is the most inadequate and sparse of any region in the
world. Further, there is less coverage of Africa today in U.S. media than
in the heady, optimistic days after political independence in the early
1960s. Africa has slipped down the list on the Western world's news
agenda, well below Europe, the former Soviet Union, and the Pacific Rim.
And in my opinion, this lack of news about Africa is a more serious
problem than is the nature of African news. Africa is being seriously
ignored, much more than it is being misreported.

Added to this are the efforts of African governments to censor or repress
news, and I believe these efforts ultimately fail because important news
does get reported. Because their own media are often so controlled and
inadequate, educated Africans have long relied on overseas media for news
about themselves and Africa in general. Publications like *Le Monde,
International Herald Tribune, Time, Newsweek, Financial Times, Daily
Telegraph,* and the *Economist* and others are widely read in Africa.
International short wave broadcasters such as BBC World Service, Voice
of America, Radio France Internationale, Deutsche Welle, and others have
large audiences in Africa, particularly during times of crisis when local
media either shut down or fail to report the news. The BBC is especially
impressive in reporting a political crisis by calling on its stringers and other
experts on the scene. With the demise of the Cold War, international
broadcasters are putting more stress on news and less on propaganda.

Diversity of information is available in another way because London and Paris have become publishing centers for numerous magazines, newsletters, and weeklies specifically edited for African audiences. Many expatriate African journalists, forced out of journalism at home by politics, have helped produce such influential publications as *West Africa*, *Jeune Afrique*, *Drum*, *Africa Events*, *Talking Drums*, and others, plus the influential newsletters, *Africa Confidential*, and *African Research Bulletin*. These publications contain a good deal of hard information and, being based in Paris or London, they are free from censorship and political pressures.

Some foreign correspondents get around censorship by sending out free-lance articles under pseudonyms to publications other than their own. Others write long interpretive articles or books after their tour in Africa has ended. A good example is Joseph Lelyveld of *The New York Times*, whose book on South Africa, *Move Your Shadow*, won the Pulitzer Prize.

In sum, then, censorship as an inhibitor of the news flow from Africa is only part of the problem of Africa's media image. But censorship certainly is related to and contributes to other aspects such as cultural differences between Africans and Westerners and the lack of understanding and indifference among many Americans toward Africa and the Africans. Perhaps, as African nations move toward multiparty democracy, censorship—direct or indirect—will become less of a factor in distorting Africa's media image.

NOTES

1. Sean Kelly, *Access Denied: The Politics of Press Censorship* (Beverly Hills, CA: Sage Publications, 1978), p. 10.

2. David Lamb, *The Africans* (New York: Random House, 1982), pp. 244–45.

3. Hilary Ng'weno, "The Third World Dilemma: Can a State Press Be Free?" *The Weekly Review* (Nairobi), June 2, 1979.

4. Rosemary Righter, *Whose News? Politics, the Press and the Third World* (New York: Times Books, 1978), p. 70.

5. William Hachten, *World News Prism*, 2d ed. (Ames: Iowa State University Press, 1987), p. 119.

6. Roberta Cohen, "Censorship Costs Lives," *Index on Censorship*, 5/1987, p. 15.

7. William Hachten, *Muffled Drums: The News Media in Africa* (Ames: Iowa State University Press, 1971), p. 78.

8. Xan Smiley, "Misunderstanding Africa," *Atlantic Monthly* (September 1982): 70.

9. Colin Legum, "Africa's Journalists Battle Uphill to Get and Keep Press Freedom," *Christian Science Monitor* (November 24, 1986).

10. William Hachten and Anthony Giffard, *The Press and Apartheid* (Madison: University of Wisconsin Press, 1984), pp. 229–61.

II

Patterns in African Coverage

5

The Media and Mau Mau: Kenyan Nationalism and Colonial Propaganda

Wunyabari Maloba

Kenya, Algeria, Zimbabwe, and South Africa formed what came to be known as settler colonies in Africa. In these colonies, a considerable number of resident white settlers appropriated land from Africans and controlled the political structure of the territories. Usually the society formed was racist. South Africa today offers the vivid and most prominent example of this color bar ridden society under its policy of apartheid.

In Kenya, the Mau Mau revolt must essentially be seen as an uprising of peasants (principally from Central Province) against the colonial state, its policies, and agents in 1952. One of the most important aspects of this revolt was its portrayal in the local and especially Western international press. This portrayal, which was negative, set the tone and structure of Western media coverage of African nationalist struggles. Subsequent Western media coverage of African nationalism and political problems became riddled with the adjectives, descriptions, and generally negative portrayal that had been first employed with particular effectiveness against the Mau Mau revolt. A study of Western media coverage of the Mau Mau movement is therefore a study in propaganda and also an effort to trace some of the origin of the negative portrayal which Africa, and especially African nationalism, continues to suffer in the West.

THE ORIGINS OF AFRICAN RESISTANCE

The history of settler occupation in Kenya from 1900 is indissolubly linked to the railway, then called the Uganda railway. The railway was built using British government funds estimated at about £5 million. This represented the most expensive British expenditure in the newly acquired territory. It also demonstrated the British government's commitment to securing a firm foothold not only in Uganda but also in British East Africa, a territory that came to be known as Kenya after 1920. Once the railway had been constructed, it had to be put to profitable use. Because Kenya and Uganda lacked an abundant supply of minerals, the railway could only be profitable if it stimulated agricultural production in the interior.

In the early years when Kenya was a protectorate, several schemes were encouraged by the Foreign Office in London to stimulate agricultural production in the territory. On the one hand, the Foreign Office considered making Kenya the "Americas of the Hindus" by encouraging Indian colonization. Others in the Foreign Office favored Jewish colonization of the territory. In the end, European colonization of Kenya was settled on as the most viable alternative. This outcome that favored the white settlers' occupation of Kenya was achieved largely through the efforts of Sir Charles Eliot, appointed high commissioner in 1901. Together with the few newly arrived settlers congregated around Nairobi, Eliot took the view that the newly acquired territory would have to be developed as "a whiteman's country." He proceeded to bar Indians from occupying the "white highlands," allowing only a few to occupy the low lying areas.

At no time in these discussions was any serious thought entertained of using indigenous Africans as the agents of commercial agricultural production in Kenya. It was postulated that Africans were so primitive, so disorganized that it would be centuries before they would be able to assume the gigantic task of being commercial farmers. Sir Charles Eliot thought that although "the African is greedy and covetous enough . . . he is too indolent in his ways, and too disconnected in his ideas, to make any attempt to better himself, or to undertake any labour which does not produce a speedy visible result. His mind is far nearer the animal world than is that of the European or Asiatic, and exhibits something of the animal's placidity and want of desire to rise beyond the stage he has reached."[1] In the mind of Sir Charles Eliot and subsequent governors of Kenya, the development of the territory could not be left in the hands of such a race that inhabited "a section of the world which has hitherto been a prey to barbarism."

Eliot initially turned to South Africa, and it was from there that a majority of settlers in Kenya, up to 1912, came. This initial South African majority had several implications for Kenya. M. P. K. Sorrenson asserts that "the European settlement in Kenya highlands was in a very real sense (though not legally) a South African colony."[2] These settlers saw their position as being similar to that of earlier settlers in other British dominions such as Canada, New Zealand, Australia, and of course, South Africa. They were in Kenya to found a "whiteman's country" modeled on South Africa. Africans would have to be disciplined and controlled, and they would also have to provide labor to give settlers the prosperity needed to lead a comfortable, secure life. In the years up to 1923 and beyond, the settlers agitated for self-rule in one form or another and especially for severe legislation in dealing with Africans, or "Kaffirs."

The most important step taken by the colonial state to demonstrate its commitment to European settlement in Kenya, was the alienation of African land. In 1896, "the Land Acquisition Act allowed the administration to acquire land compulsorily for the railway."[3] This was followed by the Land Ordinance of 1902 which enabled settlers to acquire land, allocated by the commissioner for 99-year lease. The 1915 Land Ordinance increased the lease years from 99 to 999 years. The governor could "grant lease or otherwise alienate, in His Majesty's behalf, any Crown Lands for any purpose and on any terms as he may think fit."[4] What all these ordinances meant to the economic future of Africans in Kenya is that their access to land, their principal means of production and livelihood, was severely limited especially in Central Province—home of the Kikuyu. This, together with the labor needs of settler capitalism mediated through the colonial state, drastically reduced and eventually destroyed the economic independence of the African population.

In Central Province, population increase coupled with lack of room for expansion, led to serious agrarian problems. Some Kikuyu migrated to the Rift Valley to work as squatters on European farms, while others migrated to urban centers. In either case, the migrants led a precarious existence. As early as 1937 the settlers urged the government to repatriate undesirable squatters back to the reserves. The urban centers, especially in Nairobi, had massive unemployment after 1945. Industrial development in Kenya at this time was minimal even with the boost from wartime production. The colonial government had some information about overpopulation, congestion on the land, soil erosion, unemployment, and falling living standards in Kikuyuland from 1934 up to the outbreak of the state of emergency in 1952. What is however sadly apparent is that the colonial government was not at all convinced that these problems required a radical and urgent solution to the question of land ownership. A consistent view of the government was that white settlers' occupation of the highlands had to be protected at all costs. Therefore, the solution to the African agrarian problems had to be found in the African reserves.

It is not surprising that land was the emotional issue around which a lot of African protests revolved. Land alienation on behalf of settlers and labor needs greatly alarmed Africans. From as early as 1920, Africans started to demand compensation of alienated land and later a complete return of stolen lands. A combination of these economic and political grievances gave rise to the formation of protest movements, organized by literate Africans, initially in Central Province (especially among the Kikuyu) and in Nyanza Province (among the Luo and Abaluyia).

The Kikuyu Association (KA) formed in 1919, was the first movement organized by Africans during the colonial period to articulate their grievances and present them to the colonial authorities for redress. Kikuyu Association would later be followed by Harry ThuKu's East African Association (EAA), and then the more radical Kikuyu Central Association (KCA) formed in 1924. In each of these associations, the demands remained similar: return of "stolen lands," increased educational opportunities, improved labor conditions, and decreased unemployment.

The colonial government nonetheless remained unmoved by African political protests. After the establishment of Local Native Councils (LNC) in 1925 under official control, the government viewed them as the only appropriate channels for the expression of African complaints. In its view, African political parties were therefore redundant. It persistently obstructed the establishment and expansion of such parties, considering them as agents of disruption. It is significant that no major shift of official policy especially over land in the highlands was adopted as a result of African petitions.

The formation of the Kenya African Union (KAU) in 1944 marked the first attempt to organize an African political party with territorial ambitions—the first attempt at territorial nationalism. As expected, it was formed by the mainly Nairobi-based African elite, many of whom were employees of the government. It afforded the opportunity to continue the politics of moderate petitions to the government, a strategy that had yielded almost no results since 1919. It was also correctly seen as a party of the educated; as a result, very few ordinary peasants showed any marked enthusiasm for it. Still, on a national level, KAU was recognized as the legitimate outlet of African political demands. These expectations were heightened in 1947 when Jomo Kenyatta assumed the party's presidency.

Returning to Kenya from England in 1946, Kenyatta was a towering figure in African politics. Although he had acquired immense political sophistication, he did not encourage unchecked radicalism or confrontational politics. He believed that many of the problems facing the Kikuyu would be solved through meaningful cooperation between the colonial state and his people and also through individual initiative and hard work.

Such sentiments were out of tune with the times. Many landless peasants, squatters, and unemployed workers were not keen to listen to speeches or to be admonished about their laziness and insincerity in business. The colonial state also saw no need to cooperate. It granted no reforms. From 1946 to 1950 KAU failed to register any victory. It also failed to expand its influence beyond Nairobi and Central Province.

Constitutional nationalism as advocated by KAU under Kenyatta entailed gradualism. This gradual approach to African nationalism was doomed to failure because of the intolerable economic conditions of the African masses. KAU's constituency was restive and demanded immediate solutions. This restiveness and the deeply felt need to forge a radical alternative gave rise to the oath as an instrument of mass politicization. Inaugurated at Ex-Senior Chief Koinange wa Mbiyu's home in Kiambu in 1950, the oath drive was under the control of Parliament.[5] Parliament wanted the oath taking campaign to proceed slowly with caution and to convince even the educated elite to join the underground movement to achieve complete unity of all the Kikuyu people. Armed rebellion was not entertained by Parliament nor did it ever abandon politics of petition.

The Nairobi radicals (many affiliated to trade unions) who had participated in Parliament proceedings became convinced by 1951 that oath taking had to be expanded even further and that an armed uprising against the government might become inevitable. To this end, these radicals led by Fred Kubai and Bildad Kaggia among others, organized a super-secret committee known as Muhimu to direct and coordinate oath taking in Nairobi and in the northern districts of Nyeri and Muranga.

By July 1952, the Batuni or platoon oath was introduced for warriors. This was administered to those young men and women of exceptional courage who would take up arms and fight the British from Mt. Kenya and the Aberdares. Accumulation of arms was undertaken and a few guerrilla units were dispatched to the mountains. The underground movement still faced a lot of problems pertaining to the coordination of its various facets, recruitment of would-be warriors, and planning of strategy. By October 1952, when the state of emergency was declared, the Mau Mau movement was not yet ready to declare war on the British.

In spite of these difficulties, the guerrillas, many of them ordinary peasants, entered the forests to fight with minimal weaponry but with tremendous courage and ingenuity. For more than three years they fought the government security forces with unflinching determination unaided by any external source, indeed shut off from the rest of the world. The revolt functioned entirely without external friends or influence, nor did it receive any arms from outside Kenya. No correspondence existed between any external body or government with the guerrillas; they were never recognized as a legitimate liberation movement by any government or international organization. Theirs was a lonely struggle fought in the Reserves and mountains. At the start of the state of emergency, the government thought that it would crush them in a short time. The tenacity of the guerrillas made this impossible. Compared to the various units of government forces, the guerrillas were outgunned throughout the duration of the revolt. *Pangas* and *simis* (long, sharp, double-edged knives) and occasional pistols, were no match for Bren guns and automatic rifles. This mismatch in weaponry ultimately broke their effectiveness. The presence of government loyalists (Home Guards) also shut off local support making it impossible for the guerrillas to survive in the mountains.

Nonetheless, their ability to harass and intimidate government forces and Home Guards must surely be seen as remarkable. They attacked small Home Guard posts continually and generally established a sort of aura of ruthless courage around themselves. When Dedan Kimathi, one of their key leaders, was shot and captured in 1956, the revolt had essentially come to an end. The guerrillas had been militarily defeated and untold misery had been inflicted on the people of Central Province. The need for reforms had, however, been urgently pointed out by the revolt. British financial expenditure and military commitment to the revolt led to a rethinking of the whole colonial situation in Africa. The intensity of the revolt persuaded even "influential conservative political figures in Britain to bow to the winds of change in Africa."[6]

THE MEDIA AND THE MAU MAU MOVEMENT

The major aim of government's propaganda offensive against the Mau Mau locally and internationally was to discredit African nationalism as being basically a criminal endeavor. The government also sought to show a direct linkage between Kenyatta, the most prominent nationalist leader, and the Mau Mau. In the famous Kapenguria trial of 1952–53 Kenyatta was accused of managing an unlawful secret and criminal society. Kenyatta had also visited the Soviet Union between November 1932 and September 1933, and was automatically suspected by the colonial government, and especially by the local white settlers, of being a communist. The settlers saw in the Mau Mau movement a communist plot to take over the country using violence and intimidation. Occurring against the background of Cold War between East and West, it was easy and expected for the settlers and their supporters to see communist plots behind every form of nationalist agitation.

The defense lawyers retained by KAU made sure the Kapenguria trial was given immediate and significant international publicity. Led by D. N. Pritt, these lawyers argued that their clients had no criminal case to answer but rather they stood accused as nationalists and, therefore, this was a political case with African nationalism on trial. The government denied this contention. The judge sentenced Kenyatta and his associates to seven years of imprisonment with hard labor; he came back to the point of drawing a distinction between a political and criminal case. He ruled that although the accused had "engaged in politics over a number of years," this did not "make the trial a political trial." Rather, it was "an ordinary criminal trial on ordinary criminal charges."[7]

On the whole, however, the limited positive publicity that African nationalism as organized under KAU enjoyed during the Kapenguria trial, did not extend to the Mau Mau. Kenyatta and his associates and their defense team all dissociated themselves from the Mau Mau movement. Even those external friends of African nationalism found it necessary to make a scrupulous distinction between the Mau Mau movement and nationalism. Why was it necessary to make this distinction? The reasons lay in most part in what the government through its spies and missionaries and the press reported about Mau Mau oaths, said to be central to the revolt's political and military offensive. "It cannot be denied," Fenner Brockway wrote, "that many of the practices of Mau Mau represent a reversion to primitive barbaric mentality" and added that "this has shocked, perhaps most deeply, those of us who have cooperated in the political advance of Kenya Africans."[8]

Official propaganda was given considerable boost by the British Parliamentary Delegation to Kenya in January 1954; later it published a white paper on its visit. In the report, the delegation characterized the Mau Mau movement as "a conspiracy designed to dominate first the Kikuyu tribe and then all Africans and finally to exterminate or drive out all other races and seize power in Kenya."[9] Mau Mau oaths were singled out for special consideration. The delegation found details about these oaths to be so nauseating and objectionable as to be "unfit for general publication." Leaving the details unpublished was just as effective as publishing them for the public (local and foreign) was left to indulge in extravagant imagination as to how foul these oaths really were and also to believe any stories and rumors that sounded incredible.

In London, the colonial secretary stuck to his opinion that Mau Mau was a secret society, not "the child of economic conditions." According to him it was essentially "an anti-European, anti-Asian and anti-Christian" movement that committed the worst crimes "you can imagine."[10] If the revolt was not "the child of economic conditions," then the white settlers and the government were to be seen not as heartless villains whose policies had triggered the revolt but rather as victims of unprovoked barbarous assault by Africans under the spell of magic and foul oaths.

The portrayal of Mau Mau in foreign press, especially in Western countries, tended on the whole to emphasize the alleged "atavistic nature" of the movement. In its issue of November 10, 1952, *Time* magazine devoted two pages of pictures to Mau Mau. On one page was the picture of a dead cat "left hanging from a bent sapling in a forest clearing" which bore a threat "written in blood that any person who works for whites will be destroyed by the power of this Oath."[11] The magazine also suggested without proof that Mau Mau were in the general habit of "nailing headless cats to their victims' doors."[12] This was seen as evidence of callousness and cruelty of the rebels who also employed magic.

Life magazine informed its readers that in Kenya, "natives use violence and voodooism to terrorize the British" and that although the "Mau Mau embrace modern concepts of national independence, they go back to a primitive voodooism to gain their ends."[13] *The New York Times*, while discounting the influence of communism, nonetheless reported that the Mau Mau revolt stemmed from "the frustrations of a savage people neither mentally nor economically able to adjust itself to the swift pace of civilization."[14] The foreign press characteristically concentrated on how the Mau Mau were rebelling not on why they were rebelling. Without discussing in detail the reasons behind the revolt and exposing the ruthless British response, the Mau Mau movement appeared to the world as a revolt without cause, except for the desire of Africans to kill, maim, and terrorize. The world, therefore, woke up one morning confronted with a murderous movement guided by voodooism and without cause or aim, "except to kill and disembowel as many whites, chiefs, headmen and non–Mau Mau Kikuyu as possible."[15] Portrayed thus, it was difficult for the Mau Mau to be liked or tolerated.

The foreign press did not stop at merely showing that the revolt was senseless. Most of the coverage consistently described in emotive and graphic imagery the killings attributed to the Mau Mau. As far as possible, the stories never failed to mention that the victims had been "hacked to pieces." This tendency toward an emotive and graphic imagery was particularly employed if the victims were white.

Throughout the state of emergency only thirty-two settlers were killed by Mau Mau, although the general impression created by the press and government propaganda machinery seemed to suggest that the "highlands were strewn with eviscerated bodies of white settlers."[16] In those cases

where settlers' murders were reported, emphasis was placed on the particularly cruel ways in which these had been carried out, "usually with the
help of trusted servants." Settlers were depicted as betrayed benevolent
employers. The Mau Mau were seen as not only "striking from their jungle
hideouts" but also from the kitchen. "There is no way to be sure," Robert
Ruark wrote, "that a servant is not a member of the secret terrorist society.
The news may come some dark night when he opens the door to his fellow
Mau Mau, who will chop you into small bits."[17] To be sure, there were
servants who turned on their employers or facilitated the entry of Mau
Mau into homes of their employers. But this was a relatively small number
and many Kikuyu house servants continued to work for settlers and other
Europeans at the height of the state of emergency with no dramatic
incidents. It would therefore appear that the general fear which "affected
the European community, was largely psychological."[18]

British and African soldiers together with Home Guards were not
exempt from official propaganda. Soldiers, it has been said, do not define
the enemy; they leave this task to the politicians.[19] It is the politicians who
isolate particular groups of people and communities and instruct their
military forces to attack and destroy. Sam Keen correctly argues that, "as
a rule, human beings do not kill other human beings," and therefore,
"before we enter into warfare or genocide we first dehumanize those we
mean to eliminate."[20] In war situations, propaganda takes on the responsibility of dehumanizing "those we mean to eliminate" so that they may
be killed without the soldiers or their civilian bosses feeling guilty. In the
war against the Mau Mau, all soldiers and especially British soldiers were
given information about the guerrillas' use of "foul oaths." Many of the
soldiers had arrived in Kenya with very little information about the Mau
Mau. Frank Kitson for example, who later played a crucial role in
counterinsurgency operations recalled that while in Britain he had seen
the picture of Kenyatta as "the leader of the revolt." "Unfortunately, he
had appeared in an animal skin and a spear," so Kitson had "a distorted
idea of the rebellion from the start."[21] After his arrival and subsequent
briefing by his superiors, the Mau Mau became associated in his mind,
"with all that was foul and terrible in primitive savagery."[22]

Official propaganda aided by media coverage succeeded in dehumanizing the guerrillas and ensuring that the soldiers saw them not as people,
but agents of evil. In killing them, the soldiers were killing an evil idea;
thought had been paralyzed. As the troops fought in the forests they looked
at their operations as a "big game hunt, the Kikuyu as a particularly clever
species."[23]

CONCLUSION

The propaganda campaign against the Mau Mau must rank as one of the most concerted and excessive assaults against a nationalist movement in post–World War II Africa. It is the killings attributed to the Mau Mau that graced newspapers, official reports, and sermons. In the end, the Mau Mau forces were equated with the devil. After restating that "The Mau Mau oath is the most bestial, filthy and nauseating incantation which perverted minds can ever have brewed," Oliver Lyttelton, the colonial secretary, concluded that he could not recall any instance when he had felt the forces of evil to be so near and so strong as in Mau Mau. "As I wrote memoranda or instructions," Oliver Lyttelton recalled years later, "I would suddenly see a shadow fall across the page—the Horned shadow of the Devil himself."[24] It can hardly be denied that the major objective of this negative portrayal was to deny the revolt any legitimacy or respectability. Consistently, the Mau Mau movement was portrayed as a criminal, ruthless, secret society that committed the "worst crimes you can imagine."

The Mau Mau leaders did not have any comparable form of propaganda machinery to challenge the distortions actively being spread about it or to explain its practices. In this propaganda war, the colonial government (aided by the media) was quick to claim its first major victory over Mau Mau fighters. The image created by the media of the revolt being a ruthless, barbaric, and purposeless form of violence has haunted the Mau Mau movement for a long time.

The insistence by the Western media to portray the African continent as a land of violent savages living in jungles alongside lions and other wildlife, has had the effect of reinforcing the old myths. These myths fashioned to justify slave trade and other forms of exploitation have over the years been used with devastating effect not only against Africans on the continent but also in the diaspora. The media in the West looks at Africa as an area of peripheral interest and only reports those stories that are dramatic and graphic; for example, violent demonstrations or hunger and starvation. Such coverage reinforces the myth of Africa being a land of violence and brutality and Africans being helpless beings who cannot look after themselves. There are also terms that are reserved for Africa alone, such as *tribe* and *tribalism*. Any time there is political upheaval or demonstration in Africa, it is attributed to tribalism. This is not the case when similar incidents are reported in the United States, Europe, or even the former Soviet Union. The net effect is to reinforce the myth that Africans are irrational and their political struggles are not guided by nationalism, ideological strife, class struggles, but by blind forces rooted in tribalism. Such a portrayal clearly makes it impossible for the West to understand the complexity of African nationalism, its ideological content, and the lingering legacy of colonialism.

NOTES

1. Sir Charles Eliot, *The East Africa Protectorate* (New York: Barnes & Noble, 1966), p. 92.

2. M. P. K. Sorrenson, *Origins of European Settlement in Kenya* (Nairobi: Oxford University Press, 1968), p. 1.

3. E. S. Atieno-Odhiambo, "The Colonial Government, the Settlers, and the Trust Principle in Kenya, 1939," *Trans-African Journal of History* 2, no. 2 (1972): 97.

4. The Crown Lands Ordinance (Ordinance No. 30) in *Kenya Select Historical Documents 1884–1923*, G. H. Mungeam, ed. (Nairobi: East African Publishing House, 1978), p. 346.

5. Carl G. Rosberg and John Nottingham, *The Myth of Mau Mau* (New York: Hover-Praeger, 1966), p. 259.

6. Lord Michael Carver, *War Since 1945* (New York: G. P. Putnam's Sons, 1981), p. 263.

7. Rosberg and Nottingham, *The Myth*, p. 283.

8. Fenner Brockway, *African Journeys* (London: Victor Gollanz Ltd., 1955), p. 169.

9. *Report of the Parliamentary Delegation to Kenya* (HMSO, 1954), p. 4.

10. *The Times* (London), November 7, 1952.

11. *Time* (November 10, 1952): 30–31.

12. *Time* (November 3, 1952): 36.

13. Ibid., p. 34.

14. *The New York Times*, October 20, 1952.

15. *Time* (March 30, 1953): 31.

16. Elizabeth Hopkins, "Racial Minorities in British East Africa," *The Transformation of East Africa*, Stanley Diamond and Fred G. Burke, eds. (New York: Basic Books, 1966), p. 114.

17. *Life* (February 16, 1953): 120.

18. Mss. Brit. Emp. S. 486 Papers of Sir Arthur Young (Rhodes House Library, Oxford, Box 5, file. 1): 11.

19. Sam Keen, *Faces of the Enemy* (San Francisco: Harper & Row Publishers, 1986), p. 12.

20. Ibid., p. 25.

21. Frank Kitson, *Gangs and Counter Gangs* (London: Barrie and Rockliff, 1960), p. 2.

22. Ibid., p. 2.

23. Hopkins, "Racial Minorities," p. 116.

24. Oliver Lyttelton, *The Memoirs of Lord Chandos* (New York: New American Library, 1963), p. 380.

6

Dateline Algeria: U.S. Press Coverage of the Algerian War of Independence 1954–1962

Robert J. Bookmiller and
Kirsten Nakjavani Bookmiller

In the eyes of most Americans, Algeria used to be a far-off desert where Foreign Legion types defended Beau Geste forts against howling Arabs on camels. Then there was the Casbah . . . dark ladies, exotic music. . . . Last week, however, Americans were beginning to realize that Algeria could easily become another Korea.

—*Newsweek*, November 1960

The Algerian War of Independence, like other anticolonial struggles of the same period, presented American foreign policymakers with a serious quandary. While greatly sympathetic to the Algerians' desire for independence from France, the United States had other significant considerations. Chief among these were its NATO relationship with France as well as the American fear that communism was advancing into Africa.

American press coverage of the Algerian War was not immune to the clash between anticolonial ideals and communist dread. This tension shaped and molded press portrayals of the major parties to the conflict. As a result, foreign correspondents stationed in France and North Africa provided American readers with a dizzying jumble of images. Paris was at once pragmatic and foolhardy for prolonging the war. Algerian nationalists first portrayed as mere bandits were later recognized as legitimate representatives of their people. And reporters depicted native Algerians one day as impoverished victims of colonial oppression and the next as Muslim fanatics.

This chapter surveys the complex coverage of the Algerian War on four levels: the indigenous Algerians; their nationalist movement, the Front de Liberation Nationale (FLN); North African regional politics; and media treatment of the Algerian conflict in the larger Cold War context. *Time* and *Newsweek* as well as two elite newspapers, *The New York Times* and *The Washington Post* are used in this content analysis.[1] The study focuses on the period between November 1, 1954, the outbreak of the war, and July 5, 1962, the day of independence.

The objective of surveying U.S. press coverage of the Algerian War is to reveal how the inherent tension of American ideals permeated reporting of this particular anticolonial struggle. Moreover it is to provide a foundation on which to critique and understand American reporting of similar conflicts in Africa and elsewhere.

BACKGROUND TO THE ALGERIAN WAR
OF INDEPENDENCE

France's 132 years of colonial domination of Algeria began in July 1830. The French government of Charles X, in a bid to boost its popularity and provide military service for thousands of soldiers left over from the Napoleonic wars, invaded this North African country. Numerous attempts at indigenous resistance occurred throughout the nineteenth century, but they were quelled by the French occupiers. Before long Algeria became more than a colony. Paris considered the territory to be an integral province of metropolitan France. As one prominent Frenchman noted years later, "the Mediterranean crosses France the way the Seine crosses Paris."

French power waned following defeats suffered during both world wars, and Algerian nationalists took up arms again in 1945. Although the French brutally crushed the uprising at Setif, it provided the rallying point for the anticolonial revolt in 1954. France's humiliating defeat at Dienbienphu, Indochina, by non-Europeans that same year further encouraged Algerians to vie for independence.

The Algerian conflict caused the collapse of France's Fourth Republic and brought Charles de Gaulle back to power in 1958. Many conflicting interests hampered de Gaulle's attempts to achieve a negotiated peace to this costly and bloody war. He sought to balance the needs of one million Europeans in Algeria with the legitimate aspirations of nine million Arabs. In addition, France wanted to keep Algeria's fertile coast, oil, and Saharan atomic test sites.

The war also had larger Cold War implications, particularly for the United States, which tended to view the world in polar terms. Washington was caught between its support of France, its wish to keep Paris in NATO, its fears of communist inroads in Africa and its anticolonial position and support for self-determination. Consequently, the Eisenhower administration did not publicly address the issue of Algerian self-determination until de Gaulle did so. The Soviet Union, for much of the war, refrained from openly backing the FLN. Instead Premier Nikita Krushchev hoped his tacit support of France could be used to split Paris from its NATO allies. When China provided nominal support to the rebels, however, it prompted Moscow (which feared China would gain too much influence) to rally to the Algerian side in 1960.

France finally relented to Algerian independence in 1962. The eight-year war was marked by brutality on both sides, especially between 1961 and 1962 with the advent of the rightist French Secret Army Organization (OAS). By its end, close to one million people had been killed, almost two million Algerians were relocated by the French to concentration camps and most of the one million Europeans had fled.

THE MEDIA PORTRAYAL OF
INDIGENOUS ALGERIANS

Categorizing European perceptions of the Islamic world during the eleventh century, Maxime Rodinson wrote that to the Europeans Islam "was first and foremost a hostile political and ideological system but, it was also an utterly different civilization and a remote and foreign economic sphere."[2] A similar description could characterize mid-twentieth-century press representation of indigenous Algerians. Primarily referred to by their Islamic faith to distinguish them from European colonists in Algeria, reporters called them "Muslims," "Algerian Muslims," "Muslim natives" and the "Muslim masses." In utilizing this type of identification, rather than their ethnic categorization as Arabs, the press could play on and reinforce commonly held American notions of the Islamic world.

While the media did not regularly cover the societal or religious background of Algerians in depth, over the duration of the war it did provide a composite picture which was strongly negative. For example, in December 1954, *The New York Times* presented a sympathetic piece on the European colonists who were described as "always fearful of Arab xenophobia and Moslem fanaticism."[3] An extensive 1956 *Newsweek* article on Islam provided maps with labels such as "Danger: Islamic World," and warned its readers: "To the devout [Muslim], a jihad (holy war) will never cease until the entire world has been converted."[4] *Time* in 1959 identified one Algerian Muslim sect as a group "whose 40,000 members are not quite ready to be yanked out of the Middle Ages."[5]

Time and *Newsweek* were particularly fascinated with the treatment of Algerian Muslim women. Both newsmagazines were intrigued by the young marriage age of Muslim brides, the fact that a man could divorce by stating, "I divorce you," three times, the practice of polygamy, and the nature of traditional female dress.[6] In 1962, *Time* not only hailed the independence of Algerians but also the new freedom for Algerian women: "In the forced draft of revolution . . . Moslem society has changed more than in centuries. In many traditional pious families, the daughter of the house has changed from a haik and face veil to blue jeans, and from the harem to the underground."[7]

The French arrival in Algeria, therefore, was a much needed dose of civilization. The American press portrayed Algeria's colonization as a positive watershed in its history. *Time* referred to France as bringing "Western civilization into the desert," and also to the "great French civilizing mission."[8] *Newsweek* commented that the "French have made Algeria bloom" and explained that "over the past century, the French have transformed Algeria . . . from its primitive past into an advanced community."[9] *The New York Times* even compared the initial French colonization to early U.S. history: "Like the Americans in the West, the early Europeans in Algeria farmed with the rifle near at hand. The breaking of the Moslem power was difficult but in time Algeria was more or less at peace."[10]

What exactly did the French do for Algeria? The media seemed impressed with the level of modernization and industrialization Paris had introduced. The French brought wine vineyards (although as Muslims, Algerians did not drink). Paris built roads, railways, and later airports. Cities were turned into modern urban centers with sparkling apartment houses and buildings. Mechanized farming was introduced along with a new educational system. In addition, the French ushered in tremendous advancements in health care, eradicating many regional diseases such as cholera and malaria as well as greatly reducing the infant mortality rate. As *The New York Times* sarcastically commented, "Many of the dissident Moslems would never have been on hand at all" if France had not cut the infant mortality rate.[11]

Although awed by the rapidity of Algerian modernization, the press unanimously recognized that "the very achievements of French rule have served to increase the misery of the Moslem masses."[12] *Time* and *Newsweek* in particular allowed that indigenous Algerians were the last to reap the benefits of French "civilization." They noted the slums which were adjacent to the modern urban centers, the high unemployment among Algerians and the general bleak picture for non-Europeans. *Time* explained: "For any Algerian Moslem who sought to rise in the world, the odds were staggering. In 1954 only one out of five Moslem boys and one out of 16 girls went to school. The lucky ones read French textbooks speaking of 'our ancestors, the Gauls,' but in French army messes, Moslem noncoms drew only two-thirds of the food allowance of Frenchmen of equal rank."[13] The press occasionally coupled this understanding of the Algerian's plight with an anticolonial stance against France, reversing its reverence for the French presence in North Africa. *The New York Times* wrote: "The native populations were not consulted about the dominion placed over them."[14] *Time* reprimanded Paris by stating, "Morally [the French] had an obligation to keep their unkept promises to the Algerians," and that "France gave North Africa roads, hospitals and the works of Voltaire, but not the political liberty it demanded."[15]

Although the press did recognize that Algerians had legitimate grievances, it was terrified by their display of anticolonial anger and the possibility of unity with other Muslim Arabs. *Newsweek* warned that "leaders of the Pan-Arabic crusade in the Middle East were inciting Algerians to 'holy war' against 'French imperialism.' "[16] It later carried a special report on Muslim unity entitled: "Moslems on the March: 350 Million Strong—Is It Zero Hour for Holy War?"[17] The article discussed the "seething" new Islamic nationalism, and warned that the United States was a special target because of its association with the European colonial powers.

The implication of this type of reporting was that Algerian nationalism was solely Islamic. While religion had a part to play, the Algerian war and the larger pan-Arab movement were predominantly secular in orientation. Even when the press highlighted the Arab nature of the conflict, it tended to depict nationalism in similarly negative terms. *Time* repeatedly referred to Algerian discontent as "fanatical Arab hatred."[18] *The New York Times* wrote about "nationalist flames," the "politico-religious fervor" and warned that the "poverty-stricken Arabs have been fired by the flames of nationalism that burned throughout Asia and Africa in the post-war era."[19]

THE PRESS IMAGE OF THE ALGERIAN NATIONALIST MOVEMENT

What was the Algerian conflict? An outbreak of blind terrorism? An anticolonial struggle? A civil war? This was one of the many challenges American reporters faced in describing the Algerian nationalist movement and the violence which it committed during the eight-year conflict. The confusion resulted in varying media portrayals of the FLN and its tactics.

The press continually reinvented the Algerian nationalist leaders. Yesterday's "extremists" became today's "moderates." For example, at the outbreak of the insurrection, the press like all observers, scrambled to identify those who had launched the initial attacks. Immediate blame was placed on Messali Hadj for instigating the revolt. Messali was routinely described as the leader of an "extremist nationalist party."[20] When it became apparent that Messali had relatively little to do with the outbreak and indeed was in conflict with the FLN, he rapidly became the "moderate" and others were deemed "extremists."

FLN leaders Ferhat Abbas, Ben Youssef Ben Khedda, and Ahmed Ben Bella also metamorphosized in all four publications. Their media labels were not only shaped by their political views but also by their relationships with France, other North African leaders, and the superpowers. Abbas underwent two transformations. He was a "moderate" before joining the FLN in early 1956. Contributing to this label was his occupation as a pharmacist, the fact that he spoke better French than Arabic, had a French wife and that he once wrote disparaging passages about Algerian nationalism. After Abbas joined the FLN and was appointed premier of the Provisional Government (GPRA) two years later, he became an "ex-moderate" or the "formerly moderate Abbas." However, *The New York Times* went to great lengths to distinguish between actions done on behalf of the GPRA and his personal beliefs.[21] For example Abbas' 1960 trips to China and the USSR were reportedly undertaken against his wishes.[22] When Ben Khedda, an "anti-West leftist" replaced him as premier, Abbas returned to a "respectable" and a "moderate" position once more.[23]

With Ben Khedda's assumption to power, *Time* reported that control of the FLN "shifted to a clutch of hard-eyed terrorists who had survived street battles and mountain skirmishes" with the French.[24] Ben Khedda, while not a communist, was noted for his contacts and visits to China and Cuba, as well as for his approval of "such communist techniques as the nationalization of industry and the political instruction of the Algerian masses."[25] His selection, the press reported, opened the possibility of increased communist penetration of North Africa. The press dubbed Ben Khedda the "moderate" following his change of heart on agrarian reform and the conclusion of a cease-fire agreement with France in March 1962.[26]

The new "extremist" became FLN leader Ahmed Ben Bella who fought with Ben Khedda over the direction of the revolution. Known for his close association with Egyptian President Gamal Abd al-Nasser, Ben Bella was identified as a "revolutionary extremist" and "Marxist-minded." He may not be a communist, *Time* noted (echoing the same sentiments it used to describe Ben Khedda earlier), "but he spouts the Marxist line and would work with the communists if he thought that this could get him to power."[27] Later, beneath his picture on a *Time* cover, was a caption which read: "Algeria's Ben Bella, Another Castro?"[28] The *Post* also utilized an emotive analogy and likened Ben Bella to Hitler. It claimed the Arabic word *zaim*, which his followers called him, "might be translated Fuehrer."[29] The correct translation is simply "leader."

As a political movement, the FLN was also recast by the press during the war. At the beginning, the FLN consisted of "bandits" and "outlaws" whose only support among the population came from those who were coerced to join.[30] Even as late as 1956, when the FLN was a recognized organization, some publications refused to legitimize it. Algeria, unlike Tunisia and Morocco, was said to still be without a representative body.[31] By 1962, in the euphoria of independence, *Time* reported that no group in history was better prepared to assume power than the FLN and *The New York Times* referred to the Algerian leadership "as a group of relatively young men [who] looked at the ferment in the colonial areas of the world after World War II and decided that history was with them."[32]

The FLN or any indigenous Algerians who engaged in violence were described variously as "rebels," "guerrillas," "nationalists," "terrorists," or a combination thereof, such as "rebel terrorists" or "nationalist guerrillas."[33] *The New York Times*, for instance, noted in November 1954, "Algeria contracted the terrorist disease that has plagued" Tunisia and Morocco.[34] The "terrorist" label ebbed somewhat as the struggle endured, but the press continued to use this term for indigenous Algerians until the end of the conflict. At the other end of the political scale, the charge of terrorism was reserved only for violence which was committed by the ultra-rightist OAS which carried out brutal acts of violence both in Algeria and in France. Violence (or torture) perpetrated by French authorities or individual European colonists was not called "terrorism," but seen as legitimate governmental action or self-defense. In the vicious cycle of "reprisals," "terrorism and counterterrorism," or "violence and counter-violence," the press generally treated it as Algerians beginning the round of violence and the Europeans responding. Thus readers were left with the impression that the Europeans simply were operating out of defensive positions and not initiating the violence itself.

Reporters often placed the Algerian conflict into a comparative perspective with other anticolonial clashes. Factional infighting between Algerian nationalists and the cycle of violence between the FLN, the French and the OAS were frequently compared to the fighting in the Congo. As *Time* pejoratively noted after the particularly bloody month of January 1962: "These bloodlettings take place not in the primitive backcountry of the Congo but in highly developed cities; the killing is not done by savages but by men who, in one way or another, purport to be part of French civilization."[35] Algerian "terrorism" against the French was also equated with Kenyan "terrorism" against the British, but the media concluded that the FLN soon surpassed the Mau Mau in the type and frequency of violence. *Time*, for instance, stated in 1955, "They are nationalists-turned-terrorists," and their revolt "has long since dwarfed the Mau Mau War in Kenya; it now threatens France with another Indo-china, this time in Europe's backyard."[36]

This latter reference to Indochina was one of many found in the coverage of Algeria. The French experience in Indochina was tailor-made for media accounts of the Algerian War. Many of the same reporters who had covered Indochina were now reporting from Algeria. *New York Times* correspondent Tilman Durdin explained in 1957, "The Algerian rebellion has many aspects in common with the former war in Indochina, particularly its early years, when the communist-led Vietminh depended mainly on sabotage, guerrilla raids, and terrorism. The barbed wire, the body search of persons who entered public places, the sandbagged police posts, the atmosphere of unease in Algiers is Saigon all over again."[37] However, he did stipulate that presently the Algerians lacked the "subtlety and sophistication" which the Vietnamese possessed and which ultimately led to French defeat. While all four sources utilized Indochina analogies, *Newsweek* seemed particularly taken with the comparison. "Algeria, Shades of Dienbienphu" was the title of one story in 1956, while in 1960, *Newsweek* entitled another, quoting de Gaulle, "Never a Dienbienphu."[38]

THE "BAD" VERSUS THE "GOOD" NORTH AFRICAN: NASSER AND BOURGUIBA

Media and U.S. foreign policy perceptions of the predominant North African leaders also colored coverage of the Algerian nationalist movement. Nasser, Tunisia's Habib Bourguiba and King Mohammed V (and later his son, King Hassan II) of Morocco had prominent roles to play in the shaping of the Algerian War's press image. Correspondents portrayed Algerians as caught between two opposite poles—that of the "extremist" Nasser and that of the "pro-Western" Bourguiba and Mohammed. While journalists and policymakers lavished praise on the latter two leaders, they came to view Nasser as the very embodiment of evil.[39] To understand how

Algeria fit into this spectrum, the media portrayal of these North African leaders must first be illuminated.

Nasser's efforts to promote pan-Arabism and his support of anticolonial movements in Africa clashed with the perceived interests of the United States, France, and Britain in the region. Between 1952 and 1955, the Western powers sought to temper Nasser's ambitions by working with him. This policy changed in mid-1955 with Nasser's recognition of China, the receipt of Soviet aid for Egypt's Aswan Dam, and acceptance of Czechoslovakian arms ("Nasser Defies West on Arms," as the *Post* headlined).[40]

These events coupled with his stands on the Suez Canal and Israel only increased Western enmity. *Time* called him the "dictator of the Nile." He was "pro-Red" to *The Washington Post* and *Newsweek*. Even though the press acknowledged that Nasser was not a communist, his friendly gestures toward Moscow and his advocacy of nonalignment, certainly placed him outside the "Western camp."[41] At the very least, the press declared, Nasser was "the instrument Russia has used to expand her influence in the Middle East."[42]

Nasser's support of the Algerian resistance also put him at odds with the West. This support manifested itself in a number of ways: (1) he allowed Cairo to be a base of operations for the FLN; (2) the powerful force of Egypt's radio, "The Voice of the Arabs," beamed programs and propaganda to Algeria; and (3) Nasser placed his own considerable prestige behind the nationalist cause. Indeed, from the outbreak of the war through 1956, France claimed the war was being directed from Cairo and, thus, was not an indigenous expression of discontent with French colonialism. Successive French governments held the view that the Algerian revolt would collapse if Nasser were somehow removed from the scene. This "outside agitator" theory was given credibility by the American media. *The New York Times*, for example, ran stories with headlines such as "Cairo Broadcasts Irk London, Paris," "Inflammatory Talks to Africa Incite Natives to Revolt Against Imperialists," and "Fate of Algeria Linked to Nasser."[43] Its "News of the Week in Review" section frequently stated that North Africa has "been swept by the winds of nationalism emanating from Cairo."[44]

If Nasser exemplified the pro-Soviet, extremist, "bad" North African leader, then Mohammed, Hassan, and Bourguiba were his polar opposites. They were constantly referred to as "moderate," "pro-Western," or "pro-French" in the media. Their actions and statements were viewed as a voice of reason in revolutionary Africa.[45] Mohammed and Bourguiba were frequently described as "disturbed" by Nasser's "excesses" and FLN acceptance of "Red" support.[46]

Perhaps the most laudatory press treatment is that given to Bourguiba. This *Time* account is typical: "[France] is dealing with the most moderate and responsible of Arab nationalist leaders. He has a French wife and an admiration for the products of French culture. He conspicuously resists the anti-Western line of Egypt's Nasser and disdains Nasser's brand of opportunist neutralism."[47] Bourguiba's French wife and French education were frequently mentioned in all four media sources. Often the press referred to him as "one of the best friends France has in the Arab world."[48]

Bourguiba's attitudes toward the West were presented in stark contrast to those of Nasser. While Bourguiba's autocratic rule was overlooked or downplayed, the same attributes in Nasser were condemned. The Tunisian's advocacy of independence but interdependence with France was held by the West and the media as an example for other nationalist movements to follow. As *Time* intoned, "Dapper, quick-witted Habib Bourguiba may be just the man" to smooth over the differences between France and the FLN.[49]

The Algerian nationalists were portrayed as caught between these two North African forces: that of "Nasser's propaganda-saturated Cairo" and the "relatively French-friendly atmosphere of Tunis [and Rabat]."[50] Statements from FLN political headquarters in Cairo or from Algerian nationalists such as Ben Bella were delegitimized as part of the Nasserite or even communist campaign against Western influence in Africa. Meanwhile FLN "moderates" such as Abbas, were generally more acceptable to the media as a result of their association with Bourguiba.

When the FLN established its military base in Tunisia, this was a good sign to the media that Bourguiba would have a moderating influence on the organization. A similar assumption could be found in press coverage of Tunis and Rabat's recognition of the provisional government. Journalists perceived this as a means of keeping the FLN wholly out of Nasser's camp. As the FLN and Paris moved closer to accommodation in 1961, the press presented Nasser as attempting to sabotage the accord, which "moderate" Bourguiba had helped forge.

By the end of the conflict, Morocco and Tunisia were considered advocates of "pure African nationalism," which was synonymous of course with pro-Western attitudes.[51] Nasser was seen as being directed by his "communist masters" and in turn dictating policy to those Algerians, like Ben Bella, under his control. Consequently, Ben Bella and his cadres were often portrayed as not operating for purely Algerian interests and their statements and actions were skeptically viewed.

ALGERIA AND THE INTERNATIONAL SETTING

As the conflict coincided with the height of the Cold War, Algeria assumed a particular significance far beyond that of a localized conflict with France. Reporters used powerful symbolism to impress on their readers that Algeria was the next domino ready to fall to communism and that the future of the West was at stake.

The peril that the war posed for the West had a number of different angles. Paris transferred some of its NATO troops to help suppress the nationalist outbreak, leaving the alliance understaffed in Europe.[52] There was concern that France itself would simply flounder due to the constant physical and fiscal drain caused by the unending war.[53] Lastly, the Western Alliance was troubled by the potential "loss" of Algeria from its sphere of influence, an area which was a "huge, rich, strategic keystone of the western Mediterranean."[54]

Moreover, the Western Alliance—in particular the United States— begrudgingly acknowledged that the Soviet and Chinese communists were successful in associating themselves with nationalist movements like the one in Algeria. In addition, Moscow and Peking successfully portrayed the United States as both "imperialist" and a colonial power because of its association with France.[55] For example, *Newsweek* explained the particular appeal of Chinese communism to the Algerian nationalists:

To millions of Afro-Asians, the Chinese revolution does not mean revolt against capitalism so much as a two-front revolt against backwardness and against the white man. Prosperous Moscow may still be the official capital of Communism, but many officials there and in East Europe look to China for guidance. And it is Mao who preaches the worldwide revolt . . . Mao himself recently told an FLN delegation: "Europeans and Americans despise us and they despise you. We have that bond."[56]

As the GPRA courted both East and West to win independence, reporters forewarned that the entire fate of the West was to be determined by the political orientation of the Algerian nationalists.[57] In a story headlined "Peking Presses Algerian Rebels," *The New York Times* wrote that the nationalists had to choose between two alternatives—communism or the "free world."[58] In a later article entitled "Algerians Now Play East Against West," the *Times* stated that "most North Africans still hope the West will ride to the rescue before it is too late."[59]

In the end, it was not simply the fate of Algeria that was threatening to the West. It was fears that Algeria could be used as a springboard for communist advancement south to the rest of Africa and east to the Arab heartland.[60] As the *Post* explained: "If this process is allowed to continue, a decade or two from now, all Asia and all Africa will be a solid Communist bloc, anti-Europe, anti-West and anti-America."[61]

CONCLUSION

Media labels such as *extremist, moderate, terrorist*, and *pro-West* obscured many of the real issues associated with the Algerian War. For example, the use of *Islamic nationalism* by the press veiled the reality that individual Arab states had very different conditions, problems, and aspirations from other Arab states. The juxtaposition of "extremist" Nasser with "moderate" Bourguiba also concealed the fact that they utilized similar governing styles domestically.

American press overage in the 1950s is understandable given as Edward Said notes, "Most of what the West knew about the non-Western world it knew in the framework of colonialism."[62] In addition, correspondents were reporting on unfamiliar cultures and religions at the height of the Cold War when fears of communism were very real. These factors affected American reporting and obscured U.S. support for the self-determination of other nations. They also shaped Algeria's media image for Americans and more specifically, the next generation of U.S. correspondents.

Similar themes can be found in U.S. coverage of Algeria today. "Militant Muslims Grow Stronger as Algeria's Economy Weakens," warned one *New York Times* article, subheaded: "For West's Leaders, a Grave Quandary."[63] A *Washington Post* story entitled "Victorious Islamic Party Sets Demands" commented that "shock waves [are] still reverberating around the Arab and European shores of the Mediterranean."[64] These reports followed Algeria's first free election in which Muslim party candidates trounced the FLN at the polls.

Algeria past and present is not the only place where American press coverage reflects and reinforces misperceptions and fears about non-Western peoples. In the past decade, the Iranian revolution revived old apprehensions that Islam was again on the march. Within North Africa, Libya's Muammar Quadaffy became the new media menace as he challenged the Western order, and particularly the United States. By association, all Libyans became terrorists. Meanwhile Tunisia and Morocco, still "pro-West," remained two constant moderate friends in the region.

These labels frame issues in purely Western terms. If we are to understand Algeria and North Africa on its own terms, this vicious cycle of categorizations must end. Only when Americans learn how these labels influence their perceptions of other cultures will they finally get the real story in North Africa and elsewhere. Borrowing from Maxime Rodinson once again:

How other peoples of different persuasions have reacted to Islam, to Muslims, to their virtues and to their crimes is exceedingly instructive. It provides a model by which foreign peoples and ideas can be understood, misunderstood, loved and hated. An awareness of the laws and principles that have made this model work in the past and present is an important tool for coping with the many ordeals from which future events, in all likelihood will not spare us.[65]

NOTES

1. After combining with *The Washington Times-Herald* in March 1954, *The Washington Post* became the capital's dominant paper. It joined *The New York Times* as a large-circulation daily read by policymakers and citizens alike. While *Life* and *Look* had larger circulations than *Time* and *Newsweek*, the latter were chosen for their predominant news focus.

2. Maxime Rodinson, *Europe and the Mystique of Islam*, trans. Roger Veinus (Seattle: University of Washington Press, 1987), p. 8.

3. *New York Times*, December 19, 1954, p. A4.

4. *Newsweek* (March 19, 1956): 53–55.

5. *Time* (February 23, 1956): 26.

6. Ibid. See also *Newsweek* (October 12, 1959): 54.

7. *Time* (March 16, 1962): 26.

8. Ibid., p. 24. *Time* (March 23, 1962): 23.

9. *Newsweek* (February 20, 1956): 42. *Newsweek* (February 8, 1960): 26.

10. *New York Times*, January 25, 1960, p. A3.

11. *New York Times*, May 19, 1958, p. A4.

12. *Time* (October 13, 1958): 26.

13. Ibid.

14. *New York Times*, August 28, 1955, p. E5.

15. *Time* (August 29, 1955): 22; *Time* (October 10, 1955): 32.

16. *Newsweek* (July 11, 1955): 36.

17. *Newsweek* (March 19, 1956): 41, 53.

18. See *Time* (August 29, 1955): 23; *Time* (April 8, 1957): 28.

19. *New York Times*, November 7, 1954, p. E9; *New York Times*, August 28, 1955, p. E5; *New York Times*, October 19, 1955, p. E1.

20. See *New York Times*, November 7, 1954, p. A9, for example.

21. Another semantic difference concerned reporting about the provisional government. *The New York Times* and Associated Press wire service, which the *Post* carried, generally reported on the government and ministers without placing these words in quotes. *Time*, *Newsweek*, and the other wire services usually referred to the "provisional government" or "premier" with quotes, thus questioning their underlying legitimacy.

22. *New York Times*, October 24, 1960, p. A1. On September 20, 1958, when reporting on the formation of the provisional government, the *Times*'s headline read: "Moderate Rebel, Ferhat Abbas" (p. A4), while the *Post*'s read: "Algeria Picks Ex-Moderate as Premier" (p. A4).

23. *New York Times*, August 30, 1961, p. A2.

24. *Time* (September 8, 1961): 33.

25. Ibid.

26. See *Time* (February 19, 1961): 43–48.

27. *Time* (July 13, 1962): 34.

28. *Time* (August 13, 1962).

29. *Washington Post*, April 29, 1962, p. E1.

30. *New York Times*, November 7, 1954, p. 19.

31. See for example, *Newsweek* (February 20, 1956): 40–42.

32. *Time* (March 16, 1962): 23; *New York Times*, July 2, 1962, p. 10.

33. One of the strangest labels was "the rebel party of Allah." *New York Times*, July 1, 1956, p. A1.

34. *New York Times*, November 4, 1954, p. A9.

35. *Time* (February 9, 1962): 20. See also (August 13, 1962): 16.

36. *Time* (November 26, 1955): 23.

37. *New York Times*, February 3, 1957, p. E5.

38. *Newsweek* (May 7, 1956): 40–41; *Newsweek* (March 14, 1960): 51.

39. A particularly interesting comparison of Nasser and Bourguiba was made by *Newsweek* on October 27, 1958, pp. 42–43.

40. *Washington Post*, May 20, 1956, p. A4. Washington turned down Nasser's request for Aswan funding and Western arms before he turned to Moscow for aid.

41. See *New York Times*, May 24, 1956, p. A1.

42. *New York Times*, May 18, 1958, p. E2. *Time* also utilized this theme, see for example, May 13, 1957, p. 30.

43. *New York Times*, March 1, 1956, p. A2; and July 17, 1958, p. A14. Nasser was presented in menacing terms. Following the Iraqi Revolution, the *Times* started a front-page story with, "The shadow of Nasserism fell full across the Arab Middle East today. Washington awoke to it and did not like it." (July 15, 1958).

44. *New York Times*, March 11, 1956, p. E1; and May 13, 1956, p. E1.

45. See *Time* (November 5, 1956): 40.

46. *Newsweek* (November 5, 1956): 57. Bourguiba's statements on communism were given considerable press. *The New York Times* headlined: "Tunisia Warns West on Algeria, Bourguiba Says While U.S. Waits, North Africa May Slide to Communism" (February 7, 1958, p. A1); see also *New York Times*, October 16, 1960, p. A9.

47. *Time* (April 23, 1956): 39.

48. See *Washington Post*, April 8, 1956, p. A13.

49. *Time* (February 17, 1961): 25.

50. *Time* (July 29, 1957): 17; see also *New York Times*, October 24, 1955, p. A9.

51. See *New York Times*, March 3, 1961, p. A5.

52. *New York Times*, November 12, 1954, p. A1.

53. *New York Times*, November 22, 1960, p. A11.

54. *Newsweek* (November 14, 1960): 38; and (November 25, 1960): 32.

55. See for example *New York Times*, October 30, 1960, p. E8; and March 5, 1961, p. E1.

56. *Newsweek* (June 27, 1960): 29.

57. See for example *Washington Post*, June 27, 1960, p. A1.

58. *New York Times*, June 19, 1960, p. A30.

59. *New York Times*, October 30, 1960, p. E8.

60. See for example *Newsweek* (November 28, 1960): 32.

61. *Washington Post*, June 27, 1960, p. A10.
62. Edward Said, *Covering Islam* (New York: Pantheon Books, 1981), p. 155.
63. *New York Times*, June 25, 1990, p. A1; see also July 30, 1990, p. A6.
64. *Washington Post*, June 14, 1990, p. A31.
65. Rodinson, *Europe*, p. xv.

7

Tribes and Prejudice:
Coverage of the Nigerian Civil War

Minabere Ibelema

When Nigeria plunged into a civil war less than seven years after independence, it occasioned further reflection on African tendencies. The war, which lasted from July 1967 to January 1970, has been described "as black Africa's first large-scale war fought with modern weapons in which the armies were manned, trained, led and sustained by Africans."[1] Credible estimates of casualties vary from half a million to one million.[2] The Biafran war, as it is more commonly known, attracted considerable international press coverage not just because of its scope but also because of its elements of melodrama. It involved the diverse peoples of Africa's most populous country as they grappled with the post-independence challenges of establishing national cohesion. It pitted—at least in the conception of some observers—the westernized and industrious Christian Ibos against the Muslim culturally conservative Hausa-Fulanis. It involved a classic clash between the principles of self-determination and territorial integrity. There were charges of genocide. Starvation was widespread. And the outcome of the conflict was hardly predictable. The war therefore presented a wide range of angles for coverage. The angles pursued and the images presented are instructive on the patterns of portrayal of black Africa.

Studies of Euro-American media coverage of the Third World and African countries in particular have identified at least three dominant themes.[3] The first is what has been called "the tribal fixation."[4] This is the tendency to analyze African conflicts as primitive rivalries and behavior

rather than as contemporary sociopolitical situations with inherent complexities. The second is what may be called the Cold War fixation: the
coverage of Third World issues in the light of capitalist-communist
ideological rivalry.[5] The third is cultural affinity, or the extent people or
events are judged to conform to Euro-American norms.[6] This chapter
ascertains whether, and if so how, these themes were manifested in the
coverage of the Nigerian civil war.

In a brief assessment of U.S. media coverage of the war, Mort
Rosenblum, himself an American journalist, writes that:

Neither side was right or wrong. Biafran leaders wanted to secede, and the federal
government wanted to keep the country intact. There were mixed feelings among
both. On a few fronts, Nigerian and Biafran soldiers played football together and
assumed their battle positions only when officers came for inspection. On others,
there was savage fighting. As in all wars, there was a complex mixture of
atrocities, brotherliness, corruption, blame and suffering. But it did not come
across that way.[7]

This chapter explains why. The emphasis is on rhetorical-analytical evidence, supplemented with quantitative data. Underlying much of the
analysis is the tenet that the rhetoric of reporting can be more consequential
and revealing than the facts reported.[8] The primary medium of analysis is
Time magazine. Coverage by *The New York Times* and a medium-sized
Midwestern American daily were also systematically examined for comparative purposes.[9]

Nothing in this chapter suggests that people who crusaded for humanitarian assistance, expressed concern, or took either side of the conflict
were necessarily misguided. It is the belief of this writer that the world's
conscience is a moderating element in global conduct, and it should be
brought to bear as necessary. However, the expression of this conscience
can be unwittingly prejudiced, as we demonstrate. Media coverage and
public perception of the war derived from the interplay of the harsh
realities of the war, the political exploitation of those realities, and prejudicial racial views. Logistical difficulties in covering the war and the
absence of reliable sources of data were also factors in the coverage.[10]
However, editorial selection played a crucial role in distorting the coverage. We first review events of the civil war and American public image of
the war, then examine how the image came about, and suggest some
implications.

BACKGROUND TO BIAFRA

Events leading to the war may be traced at least back to 1914 when the British protectorates of northern and southern Nigeria were amalgamated.[11] Years before the protectorates were created, the area of West Africa that now constitutes Nigeria was made up of disparate clans, city-states, kingdoms, and empires. From the onset of British colonial rule in the mid-1800s, these entities were systematically brought under one political umbrella for administrative convenience and to facilitate British colonial goals.[12] After more than half a century under British rule, Nigeria attained independence in 1960 and adopted the British parliamentary system of democracy, with a prime minister as the head of government.

At that time, Nigeria had three political divisions: the Northern Region, the Eastern Region, and the Western Region, the latter two being the South. Each region had a dominant ethnic group: the predominantly Muslim Hausa-Fulanis in the North, the Christian and animist Ibos in the East, and the roughly half Christian and half Muslim Yorubas in the West. The rest of Nigeria's diverse peoples were dispersed among the regions, including the Midwestern Region, which was excised from the West in 1963. Formation of national political parties followed regional lines. When national elections were held, the party that was based in the most populous region, the North, won the parliamentary plurality and chose the prime minister. For about five years, Nigeria was considered the "showcase of stable African democracy."[13] But the appellation was short-lived. As Henry L. Bretton predicted, the political tension inherent in regional/ethnic-based politics was to intensify as the country's diverse peoples jousted for political advantage amidst mutual fear of dominance.[14]

In 1965, the tension reached a breaking point in the West following an electoral crisis. The party in power in that region faced considerable popular opposition, and a regional parliamentary election was expected to resolve the situation. But the election was widely believed to have been flagrantly rigged by the ruling regional party, with the assistance or connivance of the national ruling party. Over objections from the opposition, the prime minister declared his Western regional ally a winner. Major riots broke out in the region, seriously threatening the country's fragile democracy. The ensuing tension and related political problems were precariously hanging over the country when the army intervened in January 1966 in Nigeria's first military coup.

The coup, led for the most part by Ibo officers, was bloody. Several political and military leaders of Northern origin were killed, including the prime minister, Sir Abubakar Tafawa Balewa, and the premier of the Northern Region, Sir Ahmadu Bello, who was also the spiritual leader of the Hausa-Fulanis. Some Yoruba leaders were also killed, including the controversial Western Regional premier, Chief Samuel L. Akintola. No Ibo military or civilian leader was killed, except for Lieutenant Colonel Arthur Unegbe, a Midwestern Ibo who refused to join the coup.[15] The coup stalled, however, and leadership of the country was handed over to the general officer commanding the Nigerian army, Major General Aguiyi Ironsi, an Ibo.

Although the forced change of government was very popular in the South, it initially received mixed reactions in the North. As the political implications sank in, the Northern reaction quickly metamorphosed into anger and resentment. The reaction was further intensified when General Ironsi decreed a unitary government that would abolish the once powerful regions. The decree which seemed logical to counter the divisive effects of regionalism, only fueled Northern fears of domination.[16] Anti-South (especially anti-Ibo) sentiments soon reached a crescendo in the North. Riots broke out in various Northern cities, resulting in the killing of several Southerners, especially Ibos. In July 1966, the Northern officers mutinied, killing General Ironsi, Lieutenant Colonel Francis A. Fajuyi (the military governor of Western Nigeria) and several other Southern officers and men. Lieutenant Colonel Yakubu Gowon, a member of a Northern minority group, assumed leadership of the country. About a month later, a report by a neighboring foreign radio that some Northerners had been killed in the East sparked what became the worst outbreak of massacres of Ibos in the North. Mobs in several Northern cities, with the apparent support of some military units, murdered thousands of Ibos in search-and-kill operations.[17] Such was the tension and insecurity so generated that most Nigerians living elsewhere in the country were forced to flee to their regions.

Lieutenant Colonel Odumegwu Ojukwu, the governor of the East, refused to recognize Gowon as the national leader and called for a confederal system by which each region would be largely autonomous with separate armies. Gowon insisted on continued federation and chose instead to break up the regions into twelve states, partly to diminish their power and partly to meet the aspirations of various minority people in the country who had long sought such a division. Ojukwu rejected the division and on May 30, 1967, declared the Eastern Region the sovereign state of Biafra. The civil war began about five weeks later on July 6.

PUBLIC IMAGE AND MEDIA COVERAGE OF THE WAR

The Nigerian civil war gained considerable international attention. Polls show that in 1968 it was the most salient foreign relations issue in Europe and second only to Vietnam in the United States.[18] The dominant view was that the war was being fought to subjugate a progressive segment of the Nigerian nation, and many people believed that the ultimate goal was to annihilate the Ibos.

By mid-1968, activist groups sympathetic to Biafra's cause or Biafrans' plight had emerged throughout the United States, including college campuses. Activities in support of the Biafran cause easily meshed with efforts to alleviate human suffering, making the distinction hardly discernible. Advertisements sponsored by the American Committee to Keep Biafra Alive, Inc., appeared in newspapers bearing the caption: "President Nixon, do you want one Nigeria over the bodies of 10 million people?"[19] At the University of Dayton (Ohio), a group called Brothers of Biafra erected a "thermometer" to indicate the rising death rate in Biafra. By February 26, 1969, the thermometer was indicating 2.5 million.[20] A letter in *Time* magazine compared the fate of the Ibos with that of the Jews in Nazi Germany. The quest for one Nigeria, would "ultimately result in the death of 8,000,000 Ibos if nothing is done," the letter states. If that happened, the letter continues, it "may turn out to be one of the worst examples of genocide and savagery in history."[21] Another letter contends that Ibos should never have been a part of Nigeria to begin with, and noting that it was too late, adds: "There won't be any of them left when the federalists get through with them. God help the Ibos. It seems no one else has the courage to do so."[22]

The expectation that Ibos would be annihilated persisted to the end, even after teams of international observers repeatedly reported to the contrary. When the war ended, the Euro-American community expected the worst. The wire services carried reports of activities "to rally help for Biafran refugees against possible massacres."[23] The French government instructed its Cameroonian ally to open its borders for Ibo refugees, who would be fleeing from the expected massacre. Examination of media coverage of the war provides some evidence that while there were reasons to be concerned about the welfare of Ibos, perception of inherent African savagery may have contributed to the widespread conviction that genocide was imminent.

Among the reasons for concern were the massacres in the North, war atrocities, and the indiscriminate bombing of Biafra. As noted early, up to eight thousand Ibos and other Easterners were killed in riots and mutinies. However, massive as the killings were and "while the violence may have been politically inspired, it was more like anarchy than genocide."[24] Regarding war atrocities, John de St. Jorre, one of the European journalists who covered the war, writes that it "was, in short, a war not different from any other and it is disturbing that Westerners should have been . . . so patronizing and so remarkably devious in our interpretation of its worst manifestations."[25]

Biafran propaganda also played a crucial role in creating the expectation of genocide, but as Karen Rothmyer has demonstrated, the U.S. press was an unquestioning transmitter.[26] Other studies and appraisals of media coverage of the war also suggest that it had the overall effect of reinforcing Biafra's propaganda. Rosenblum notes that "federal atrocities were recounted in grim detail, relieved by colorful portraits of Odumegwu Ojukwu. . . . The picture that emerged was one of an oppressed people fighting nobly for their ideals against imperialistic tyrants who forced their children to starve."[27] Euro-American media coverage emphasized Biafran suffering and relied considerably on visual images.[28]

Time magazine's coverage mirrors these findings. However, *Time* did not rely so much on visual images as it did on rhetorical devices. Of the thirty-four photographs (not including maps) it published on the war between July 1967 and December 1969, only ten were of war casualties (dead or living). An additional eight were of war scenes, such as soldiers in trenches. The rest were of personalities involved in the war, with Gowon and Ojukwu appearing about as many times as mercenaries and missionaries.[29] *Time*'s coverage of the crisis was relatively low-keyed and dispassionate through the early months of the war, even while it laid the foundation for the slanting that was to follow. For the first coup, it noted the role of ethnic differences, rivalry, and mutual suspicion. For the second coup and the related killings, *Time* cited these factors, as well as "pent up anger" over the killing of "the nation's two most prominent Northerners" and the "trimming away of their regional authority."[30] When Ojukwu threatened secession, *Time* emphasized the political differences between him and Gowon, especially over the creation of states, while also noting Ojukwu's professed intent to protect the Ibos. *Time* continued the relatively dispassionate coverage, through the first story on the outbreak of war, in which it noted that federal forces were under orders to "fight a clean fight" and avoid atrocities.[31]

Late in 1967, after Biafra was back on the defensive following its short-lived occupation of the Midwest, *Time*'s reportorial tone became increasingly skewed in favor of Biafra. The complex issues and chain reactions that led to secession and war were reduced to the "persecution" and "hatred" of Ibos. One reason for Ojukwu's quest for autonomy, which earlier was his fear of "a repeat of recent massacres," was upgraded to his utter conviction "that the Ibos faced annihilation in a united Nigeria."[32] Another reason, the creation of states, which earlier made "sense enough" later became the "gerrymandering of Ibos."[33] By 1968, *Time*'s coverage had intensified and become decidedly pro-Biafran. That year it carried fourteen stories for a total of 485 column inches. (In contrast, it carried ten stories in each of the years before and after 1968, for a total of 185 column inches in 1966, 155 in 1967 and 298 in 1969.) The most concentrated coverage was in August 1968, when it carried one major story in each of the five issues, for a total of 280 column inches (including 210 for its only cover story).[34] Also, the only letters to the editor on the conflict were published at this time, and all six were pointedly pro-Biafra.[35] In October 1968, *Time* began to use Biafra in its datelines for the first time.

Time's increased coverage corresponded with its greater use of graphic detail on Biafran casualties, juxtaposed with evidence of Biafran resolve. An account of a federal air raid, for instance, is placed in the context of the serene setting in which two teenage school girls prepared evening meals as Red Cross volunteers. Federal bombers strike and kill them both, the correspondent narrates before providing a wider view: "Under tall shade trees outside an already filled mortuary lay a score of corpses, including pregnant women and months-old babies, charred, disfigured and mangled. Amid the tearful cries of keening women, workers carried into the morgue mashed human fragments piled on stretchers, and limbs and torsos balanced on shovels."[36] In a similar story, a correspondent describes the death of an eleven-year-old girl who was hit while returning from school. As nursing nuns prayed beside the girl at her request, she whispered: "I really tried to hide from the plane. I went behind a tree, but it found me all the same. I'm sorry."[37] And so saying, she died. This narrative evidently suggests that federal pilots went the extra length to seek out and hit individual children.

Time also used statistics to supplement its evocative reportage in much the same fashion as Rothmyer notes with regard to general coverage of the war.[38] In its July 12, 1968, issue, *Time* cities international relief agencies' reports that three thousand Biafrans were dying daily and that two million may be dead by the end of August. It notes that "those figures may be exaggerated," but then a little over a month later it makes the ultimate claim that "slowly and surely, eight million Biafrans are starving to death."[39] Still later, *Time* reports that: "When the conflict began, the Ibo tribesmen of Biafra were a nation of 15 million people. They are now, by their government's estimate, reduced to 7,000,000 in an island of 9,000 square miles."[40] There is nothing in the report to indicate whether the reduction was through death or absorption into federal-held territory. Since *Time* consistently reported that Biafrans either retreated en masse or were massacred by "mop up"federal soldiers, the impression that eight million Ibos had died could hardly be avoided.

From the outset, coverage of the conflict underscored the difference between Nigeria's dominant ethnic groups. The overriding theme was that the Ibos were cast in the Euro-American mold and the rest of Nigerians were not. Citing a British missionary, a *New York Times* correspondent writes that Ibos may not have been negroid in origin, but may have migrated from the Nile Valley. The evidence cited was that some Ibos are light-skinned and "the faces on their masks and carvings are not negroid, but Eastern."[41]

Time magazine underscored this supposed difference in virtually every article on the conflict. Its descriptions of the major ethnic groups left no doubt as to who were the heroes and the villains. In a story early in the conflict, *Time* describes the Ibos as "ambitious," the Yorubas as "ebullient" and the Hausa-Fulanis as "feudal."[42] Later in the story, *Time* goes into detail to describe the Ibos as "Christian, democratic, enterprising;" the Yorubas as "farmers and small traders whose passions are Highlife music and politics, often accompanied by endless draughts of pungent palm wine;" and the Northerners as "rigid Moslems, suspicious of outsiders, wary of progress, ruled by reactionary emirs whose palaces are made of mud and whose law is adamantine." About midway through the war, it describes the Ibos as "ambitious and clever," the Yorubas as "a tribe known for its profusion of gods . . . and joie de vivre," and the Hausa-Fulanis as "haughty, devout Moslem peoples governed locally by feudal emirs."[43] And, having reported that the Ibos were "among the most primitive people" the British encountered in Nigeria and having attributed their advancement to their receptivity to "Western values and education," *Time* describes them as "quite possibly Africa's most capable people and, by force of energy and intellect, the dominant tribe of newly independent Nigeria." It goes further to report that Ibos "won for themselves the nickname 'Jews of Africa,' and they were, in a sense, a chosen people."[44] A letter in *Time* points to several other perceived Europhilic attributes: "The Ibos are regarded as the Irish of Africa—ready-witted, strong-willed, carefree and gay, with a burning sense of patriotism for their own."[45] Both the tribal fixation and Euro-cultural affinity themes are evident here.

By extension, Ojukwu was similarly adulated. As noted earlier, coverage of the war was "relieved by colorful portraits of Odumegwu Ojukwu, the saintlike Oxford-accented secessionist leader."[46] Indeed, the use of the phrase Oxford-educated in the general coverage seemed compulsive, and Ojukwu's endowment was directly or by implication credited to his European enlightenment. *Time* writes, for instance: "With an Oxford education, a rare gift for rhetoric and a deep sense of the tragedy encompassing the war, he is endowed with the best that the white man has given Africa and beset by the worst of Africa's many ills."[47] This statement perhaps best sums up the theme that Africa's problems are rooted in African nature and its successes are of European origin.

The theme is manifested in various other aspects of the coverage. In its report on the January 1966 military coup, *Time* notes that it was brilliantly planned and executed and goes on to quote an English resident in Nigeria: "Sandhurst training certainly leaves its marks."[48] But when Sandhurst-trained or otherwise European-educated Nigerians participated in actions judged unbecoming, *Time* turned to African nature for explanation. In explaining the essence of the conflict, for instance, *Time* writes: "The absence of neighborly compassion among the tribes is a fact of African life." And earlier in the same article: "To the African mind, a political group is either for the government or against it, and if the latter, it has no business existing." On Biafran leaders' refusal to accept relief through federal-controlled territories because it might be poisoned, *Time* writes that the claim "is not so ridiculous as it seems to Western mind: the traditional way of doing in an enemy in Africa is to poison him." And on heavy artillery shelling by federal forces before infantry advance, *Time* claims that "such tactics, or at least the attitude behind them, are not confined to Nigeria's federal troops; they are commonplace with most African armies."[49] Polemical response to these claims may note the thinking behind U.S. bombing of Hiroshima and Nagasaki; Euro-American development of chemical weapons; and political strife in Italy, Northern Ireland, Rumania, and some former Soviet republics. But that is beside the point. What is of interest here is how the European-African dichotomy is reflected in the slanting of *Time*'s coverage.

EUROPEAN-AFRICAN DICHOTOMY
AND MALCOVERAGE

In Ulf Himmelstrand's assessment of Euro-American commentary on Africa, he notes the particular problem arising from the general "tendency to perceive conflicts as ranging between good and evil forces."[50] Himmelstrand further notes that an even more natural tendency is to support the good. *Time*'s coverage of the civil war manifests these tendencies not just in the slanting of what is covered but also by its omission or downplaying of facts and developments that were necessary for a comprehensive understanding.

The most manifest element of the slanting is that brutality and incompetence were exclusively ascribed to the federals, who were cast as true Africans, and bravery and competence were the exclusive attributes of the Ibos, the perceived embodiments of European ideals. Unlike *The New York Times*, which strove to be even-handed,[51] *Time* reported no atrocities by secessionist forces.[52] Instead, it recounted Biafran successes in laudatory and heroic terms and derided federal forces as using modern equipment "like dilettantes."[53] When Biafran forces invaded the West, for instance, they were "clobbering [Gowon's] best troops."[54] In contrast, "Nigerian mortar bombs and small-arms . . . splash about aimlessly, killing here, falling sterile there."[55] So strong was *Time*'s perception of federal incapability that in July 1969, when Biafra held only one major city, *Time* reported that federal outright victory "may be impossible."[56]

Time attributed practically every federal success in the war to its numerical superiority, arms supply, and outright brutality. No credit was given to thought or strategic planning. When the war reached a stalemate, *Time* would deride another "final offensive." In contrast, Biafra's successful repulsions of federal assaults were credited to ingenuity, resolve, or white mercenaries. Biafra certainly demonstrated considerable ingenuity, technological creativity, and resolve, but as Chinweizu, an Ibo intellectual, has noted, Biafran resourcefulness could have been replicated by the other side if it were in a similar circumstance.[57]

Besides, while the military challenge facing Biafra was formidable, insights that have since been offered by some of Biafra's top leaders show that Ojukwu's much glorified leadership may have been a liability for Biafra. *Time* reports that "he runs Biafra as a wartime democracy, frequently seeking the advice of his consultative assembly of Ibo elders."[58] But few of Biafra's principal players support this view. Among others, Alexander A. Madiebo, who was the general officer commanding the Biafran army during much of the war, and N. U. Akpan, who headed the civil service, both assert that Ojukwu distrusted all but a handful of Biafra's top leadership, both military and civilian.[59] So distrustful was he, according to Alexander Madiebo, that he never took his army commanders into confidence about Biafra's arms stock and supply. The distrust converted into general lack of confidence in Biafra's senior officers, most of whom were branded saboteurs in the course of the war. Madiebo believes that, besides foreign support of federal Nigeria, this "crisis of confidence" was "the most important reason . . . we lost the war."[60]

On a related matter, *Time* surmises that Ojukwu declared secession only after yielding to public pressures and that he received undivided support thereafter. But while public opinion in the East was at a boiling point over the massacres of Eastern people, it may never be known how many people were in favor of secession and how many merely yearned for revenge. St. Jorre writes, "The facts of the massacres alone probably would not have been enough to produce the kind of sustained popular support that the government needed to carry the East out of the Federation. It was only when their horrific detail had been hammered home in a pervasive and gifted propaganda campaign . . . that the East was ready both to pull out and to fight for its newly acquired independence."[61] Similarly, Akpan asserts that "the majority of people in former Eastern Nigeria, including the Ibos, did not initially support secession, and would have rejected the whole idea if they had been freely and fairly consulted."[62] Indeed, while the Ibo populace and some other Easterners embraced Biafra following the intense propaganda, hushed but potent opposition continued after secession, culminating in the execution in September 1967 of four top Biafran officers, including Major Emmanuel Ifeajuna, one of the leaders of the January 1966 coup.[63] *Time* reported the execution in one sentence, without noting its significance. Also, by December 1968, when *Time* reported Biafran resolve, Madiebo notes that the Biafran situation was such that "it appeared as if the majority of the people simply wished for nothing but to see an end to the war at all costs."[64]

In explaining how the fragile coalition that constituted federal Nigeria was able to wage a war successfully, *Time* is content to point to arms and numerical superiority and to claim that Nigeria's "15 major tribes . . . [found] common ground against the Ibos," the common ground being envy and hatred.[65] But only the North was committed to the war before Biafran occupation of the Midwest. And several authorities have pointed to the minority factor, the preference of smaller ethnic groups in all the regions for a federal structure that would mitigate the dominance of their more populous neighbors.[66] *Time*'s coverage ignored this factor. However, in an indirect reference, *Time* reports that the declaration of secession was precipitated by "a plan for twelve Nigerian states that would have cut the Ibos off from their oil and their coastline."[67] (*Time* must have known that the Ijaws, Ibibios, and other smaller ethnic groups are natives of the Niger delta and southeastern coastlines, where much of Nigeria's crude oil is located.)

Not only did *Time* ignore aspects of the conflict that would have enhanced its readers' understanding of the war's complexity, it also overlooked or downplayed those aspects that contradicted the theme of

African savagery and hatefulness. At the beginning of the war, Gowon issued a code of conduct that demanded in specific terms that federal forces fight fairly and humanely.[68] The code, which St. Jorre describes as "a revealing and unique document," also required officers to acquaint themselves with the Geneva Convention.[69] *Time* covered it in one phrase at the beginning of the war and referred to it about two more times, not to note its significance, but to point out its violations.

During the war itself, Ibo property in the North and most other parts of Nigeria was safeguarded and, after the war, returned to the owners, in some cases with accumulated revenue.[70] And there was fraternization across some war fronts. Madiebo narrates that federal troops threw drinks and cigarettes to Biafran soldiers, who after initial suspicion began to retrieve and consume the scarce items. The gesture led to exchange of visits, and "before long Biafran soldiers in many fronts began to cross into enemy lines to attend frequent food and drinks parties."[71] In at least one front, the commanders signed a local peace accord and fired only to mislead their superiors.

Such developments in the war were virtually ignored in the coverage. Reports that refuted the imminence of genocide were so qualified or isolated that they were no match for those in support. Such were the cases of *Time*'s report of a federal commander's summary execution of one of his officers for the unprovoked shooting of a Biafran captive,[72] and in another front, that "there has been little genocide in the ground advance, if only because almost no civilians remain behind."[73] (The phrase "there has been little genocide" has to be one of *Time*'s most curious. The Webster's New Collegiate Dictionary definition of *genocide* seems to preclude the qualification "little," even in the negative.) Himmelstrand writes that such accounts may have been downplayed because Euro-Americans probably doubted that "primitive Africans [can] possibly be as civilized as these reports seem to indicate, when even civilized Americans during the Second World War seriously maltreated American citizens of Japanese descent!"[74]

One could have attributed *Time*'s lapses to the limitations of coverage noted earlier. However, as Himmelstrand suggests, its end-of-war coverage was so much more judicious that it is reasonable to conclude that the malcoverage was at least partly intentional. Contrary to the thrust of its wartime coverage, *Time* notes that many Ibos had "deserted through gaps in the battleline to take their chances with the Nigerians;" that by the end of the war "more Ibos [were] living outside Biafra [-held territory] than inside" and "many of them went to work for the central government;" that "Gowon's . . . tactics for three years have been designed to limit casualties;" and that "minorities under Ojukwu's rule seemed so unhappy."[75] That it did not report these highly relevant facts during the war makes the ultimate point of this chapter. And *Time* was not alone in this respect. A study of three television networks' coverage of the war also concludes that "it appears they chose not to report contextual information necessary for reasoned assessment of the situation. . . . [T]heir selective perception in this task totally depends on what they expected to see and select or leave out."[76]

CONCLUSION

Time's coverage clearly fits the themes of tribal fixation and Eurocultural affinity identified earlier in this chapter. The third theme identified—the Cold War fixation—is however hardly present. That is not surprising given that ideology was not an issue in the war.

It may be useful to reiterate that the goal of this analysis is not to indict *Time* magazine (and other news media) for pro-Biafran coverage, per se, or to vilify support for Biafra. *Time* has traditionally taken an editorial position in its news coverage, and its support of Biafra violates no journalistic standards or ethics.[77] But *Time* seems to have gone beyond an editorial stand to doctoring its coverage and promoting stereotypical racial themes. Of course, we cannot know whether a less prejudicial coverage would have produced a different public attitude. Still, it is clear that *Time* did not give its readers the broadest possible perspective from which to assess the situation and choose the best course of action in furtherance of that assessment. It is entirely possible, for instance, that public and media fixation on the imminence of genocide may have complicated or detracted from the search for a political solution and efforts to ease human suffering. The reaction of the Nigerian government with respect to end-of-war relief assistance certainly points in that direction.[78]

As the issues of the Nigerian civil war become increasingly clarified, the war may well be remembered for what could be its most significant irony: That while in both its reality and distorted portrayal, it represented some of Africa's most horrific hours, in its fraternal ending, it embodies Africa's humanism. For, as Stremlau notes, "Despite the high degree of international interest and involvement during the conflict, Nigerian reunification was finally achieved without external assistance, foreign mediation, international peace-keeping or security guarantees."[79] And as St. Jorre observes, "In the history of warfare there can rarely have been such a bloodless end and such a merciful aftermath. . . . The internal reaction was not vindictiveness, as many people had expected, but mercy and magnanimity."[80] Perhaps a measure of the growth of humanism in Euro-America could be an improvement in its ability to see and interpret African reality without resort to racial stereotypes.

NOTES

1. John de St. Jorre, *The Brothers' War: Biafra and Nigeria* (Boston: Houghton Mifflin, 1972), p. 273.

2. Ibid., p. 412.

3. Since the term *West*, its derivatives, and related terms are used extensively in reference to Nigerian political structure, the word *Euro-America* is substituted for *West* as a global geopolitical reference.

4. William Artis, Jr., "The Tribal Fixation," *Columbia Journalism Review* (Fall 1970): 48–49.

5. See, for instance, Edward S. Herman, "Diversity of News: 'Marginalizing' the Opposition," *Journal of Communication* 35 (Summer 1985): 135–46.

6. See, Herbert J. Gans, *Deciding What's News: A Study of CBS Evening News, NBC Nightly News, Newsweek and Time* (New York: Vintage Books, 1979), pp. 32–33; and Umar Mohammed, "Nigerian News in Four United States 'Elite Dailies': An Analysis of the Coverage of Civilian and Military Governments (1960–1966; 1966–1979)" (Ph.D. diss., Florida State University, 1981), p. 98.

7. Mort Rosenblum, *Coups and Earthquakes: Reporting the World for America* (New York: Harper & Row, 1979), pp. 174–75.

8. Richard Weaver, "Language Is Sermonic," in James L. Golden, Goodwin F. Berquist, and William E. Coleman, eds., *The Rhetoric of Western Thought* 2d ed. (Dubuque, Iowa: Kendall/Hunt, 1978), pp. 202–11. See also, Percy H. Tannenbaum and Mervin D. Lynch, "Sensationalism: The Concept and Its Measurement," *Journalism Quarterly* 37 (Summer 1960): 381–92.

9. With a global circulation and reach of 6.05 million and 32 million, respectively, *Time* is easily one of the most influential news media in the world. See *The 1987 Media Guide* (New York: Harper & Row, 1987).

10. Paul Harrison and Robin Palmer, *News Out of Africa: Biafra to Band Aid* (London: Hilary Shipman, 1986).

11. Michael Crowder, *A Short History of Nigeria* (New York: Frederick A. Praeger, 1962).

12. Ibid., pp. 155–224.

13. *Time* (January 28, 1966): 21.

14. Henry L. Bretton, *Power and Stability in Nigeria: The Politics of Decolonization* (New York: Frederick A. Praeger, 1962). See also A. H. M. Kirk-Greene, *The Genesis of the Nigerian Civil War and the Theory of Fear* (*Research Report No. 27*) (Uppsalla: The Scandinavian Institute of African Studies, 1975).

15. Possible reasons for the differential execution of the coup are summarized and evaluated by B. J. Dudley, who concludes that "the coup was motivated by partisan considerations." Dudley, *Instability and Political Order: Politics and Crisis in Nigeria* (Ibadan, Nigeria: Ibadan University Press, 1973), pp. 106–9.

16. Major-General Joseph N. Garba, *"Revolution" in Nigeria: Another View* (London: Africa Books Limited, 1982).

17. St. Jorre puts reliable estimates of the death toll at 6,000 to 8,000; however, during

the war Biafran officials revised the figures from 10,000 to 30,000 to 50,000. See St. Jorre, *Brothers' War*, p. 86.

18. John J. Stremlau, *The International Politics of the Nigerian Civil War 1967–1970* (Princeton, N.J.: Princeton University Press, 1977), p. xii.

19. See, for instance, *New York Times* (January 21, 1969), p. C3.

20. *Journal Herald* (Dayton, Ohio: February 26, 1969), p. 21.

21. *Time* (August 30, 1968): 8.

22. *Time* (September 6, 1968): 7.

23. *Dayton (Ohio) Daily News* (January 11, 1970), p. 5A.

24. Stremlau, *International Politics*, p. 38.

25. St. Jorre, *Brothers' War*, p. 287.

26. Biafra's successful propaganda is very well summarized in Karen Rothmyer, "What Really Happened in Biafra?" *Columbia Journalism Review* (Fall 1970): 43–47.

27. Rosenblum, *Coups*, p. 174.

28. John A. Sambe, "Network Coverage of the Civil War in Nigeria," *Journal of Broadcasting* 24 (Winter 1980): 66. Ikechukwu Enoch Nwosu, "Crisis Reporting: A Comparative Analysis of Four Black African Cases (1967–1979)," Vols. I & II (Ph.D. thesis, University of Minnesota, 1981), p. 464.

29. Sorting and categorization of the photos were done by the writer.

30. *Time* (October 10, 1966): 45.

31. *Time* (July 14, 1967): 17.

32. *Time* (April 7, 1967): 32; and (August 23, 1968): 20. Since there were no further massacres between the April 1967 report and the declaration of secession in May 1967, one has to conclude that the change in interpretation was occasioned by editorial rather than factual considerations.

33. *Time* (October 9, 1966): 43; and (June 9, 1967): 45.

34. *Time* had another cover story at the end of the war which content is compared with its wartime coverage.

35. Publication of letters at this point is significant, however the selection of letters is interpreted. Some studies suggest that published letters are a measure of public opinion (see, J. S. Foster and C. J. Frederich, "Letters to the Editor as a Means of Measuring the Effectiveness of Propaganda," *American Political Science Review* 31, no. 1 (1937): 71–79; David B. Hill, "Letter Opinion on ERA: A Test of the Newspaper Bias Hypothesis," *Public Opinion Quarterly* 45 (Fall 1981): 384–92; while others conclude that letters are more indicative of editors' selection. See David L. Grey and Trevor R. Brown, "Letters to the Editor: Hazy Reflections of Public Opinion," *Journalism Quarterly* 47 (Autumn 1970): 450–56. If the latter finding is correct, that would be further indication of *Time*'s increasing pro-Biafran crusade. If the former is applicable, it may be said that *Time*'s crusade has at last galvanized its readers. Similarly, that *The New York Times* published both pro-Biafra and pro-federal letters may be indicative of the effect of its more balanced coverage or a continuation of such coverage.

36. *Time* (May 10, 1968): 45.

37. *Time* (July 4, 1969): 30.

38. Rothmyer, "What Happened?"

39. *Time* (July 12, 1968): 20; and (August 23, 1968): 20.

40. *Time* (July 4, 1969): 32.

41. *The New York Times Magazine* (June 11, 1967): 30. In reality, the Fulanis are the native Nigerians of non-negroid origin. See, Crowder, *Short History*, p. 21. For additional comment on the *Times*'s claim, see Artis, "Tribal Fixation."

42. *Time* (October 7, 1966): 45.

43. *Time* (August 23, 1968): 21.

44. Ibid. *The New York Times* similarly adulated the Ibos, but in comparison with *Time*, it was also generous in noting the capability and achievement of Nigeria's other dominant ethnic groups.

45. *Time* (September 6, 1968): 7.

46. Rosenblum, *Coups*, p. 174.

47. *Time* (August 23, 1968): 20. *Time* was also complimentary of Nigeria's non-Ibo leaders Balewa and Gowon, but equivocally so. Balewa was "shrewd and prudent" and Gowon was Spartan in lifestyle and skilled in managing the federal coalition. But Gowon lacked Ojukwu's intellect and both he and Balewa were mere fronts for the "backward" Hausas. See, *Time* (August 12, 1966): 27; and (August 23, 1968): 20.

48. *Time* (January 28, 1966): 21.

49. *Time* (August 23, 1968):20–24, 27–28. Ojukwu lent credence to this racial analysis by expressing "anger with those who made devastating weapons available to primitive men." *Time* (May 10, 1968): 46.

50. Ulf Himmelstrand, "The Problem of Cultural Translation in the Reporting of African Social Realities," in Olav Stokke, ed., *Reporting Africa* (New York: Africana Publishing, 1971), p. 122.

51. A plausible explanation of *The New York Times*'s evenhandedness, in contrast with *Time* magazine, is that its perception of Ibo Euro-affinity is counterbalanced by its preference for a united Nigeria, as expressed in its editorials.

52. The closest *Time* came to mentioning Biafran atrocity was in its coverage of the killing of eleven mostly Italian oilmen by Biafran commandos. *Time* (June 13, 1969): 44.

53. *Time* (April 4, 1969): 36.

54. *Time* (September 1, 1967): 21.

55. *Time* (April 4, 1969): 36.

56. Ibid., p. 32. The perception of African incapability is not limited to *Time* or other news media. A report by Britain's International Institute of Strategic Studies in 1968 contended, in effect, that Nigeria's federal army could not overrun Biafra because "few such armies have developed a sufficient number of leaders in the field to stand up to casualties without a breakdown of the command system." Quoted in Stremlau, *International Politics*, p. 149.

57. Chinweizu, *The West and the Rest of Us: White Predators, Black Slavers and the African Elite* (New York: Vintage Books, 1975), p. 327.

58. *Time* (August 23, 1968): 27.

59. Alexander A. Madiebo, *The Nigerian Revolution and the Biafran War* (Enugu, Nigeria: Fourth Dimension, 1980). Ntieyong U. Akpan, *The Struggle for Secession, 1966–1977: A Personal Account of the Nigerian Civil War* (London: Frank Cass, 1971).

60. Ibid., p. 379.

61. St. Jorre, *Brothers' War*, p. 114. For an analytical overview of the crusade for and opposition to secession, see pp. 98–122.

62. Akpan, *The Struggle*, p. 180. Akpan is presumably being hypothetical. A plebiscite was hardly feasible in the circumstance.

63. Adewale Ademoyega, *Why We Struck: The Story of the First Nigerian Coup* (Ibadan, Nigeria: Evans Brothers, 1981), pp. 152–73 passim.

64. Madiebo, *Nigerian Revolution*, p. 290.

65. *Time* (July 4, 1969): 32.

66. See, Kirk Greene, *Genesis of the Nigerian Civil War*; Stremlau, *International Politics*, p. 55.

67. *Time* (August 23, 1968): 24. In its end-of-war coverage, *Time* more correctly rephrased this claim to read "deprived the Ibos of control over." *Time* (January 26, 1970): 21.

68. The code is reprinted in A. H. M. Kirk-Greene, *Crisis and Conflict in Nigeria: A Documentary Sourcebook, Vol. I, January 1966–July 1967* (London: Oxford University Press, 1971), pp. 455–57.

69. St. Jorre, *Brothers' War*, p. 282.

70. Garba, *Revolution*, p. 120.

71. Madiebo, *Nigerian Revolution*, p. 327.

72. *Time* (September 13, 1968): 30.

73. *Time* (October 4, 1968): 36.

74. Himmelstrand, *The Problem*, p. 126.

75. *Time* (January 26, 1970): 18–24.

76. Sambe, *Network*, pp. 66–67.

77. Gans, *Deciding*, pp. 5, 103.

78. At least partly in an attempt to ensure that foreigners did not take credit for the magnanimous ending of the war, the Nigerian government barred direct relief assistance by international agencies to the war-affected area, precipitating the final outcry about imminent mass starvation.

79. Stremlau, *International Politics*, p. 357.

80. St. Jorre, *Brothers' War*, pp. 404, 406.

8

Reporting African Violence: Can America's Media Forget the Cold War?

Rodger M. Govea

African nation-states have for years criticized the United States for its obsession with the superpower conflict.[1] In fact, during the early Reagan years, several African nations—particularly Nigeria—raised objections with a congressional delegation that the United States was excessively concerned with communism and inadequately concerned about the issues of apartheid and democracy in South Africa.[2] Most students of African politics have a similar concern. They argue that unrestrained anticommunism is blind to the reality of Africa's serious problems, and may even limit U.S. influence on the continent.[3] Meanwhile, America's media have had problems covering Africa, due in part to the ignorance of the public and even of government officials. A vivid example of government ignorance came when Deputy Secretary of State William P. Clark admitted at his 1981 confirmation hearing that he could not identify the prime ministers of Zimbabwe and South Africa.[4]

Some believe that this ignorance has led newscasters and commentators to communicate by using Cold War themes or superficial analogies such as "the shadow of Vietnam."[5] Reliance on the East-West theme appears to have had a paradoxical effect. On one hand, it has brought certain African issues, such as unrest in Angola, Congo, and the Horn of Africa, to the forefront of U.S. foreign policy concerns. On the other hand, public interest in the East-West aspects of the African conflicts has come at the expense of the relevant local political issues.

As in Latin America and Asia, U.S. popular media are commonly accused of insensitivity to Africa's economic and social issues and undue emphasis on communism and East-West issues. Yet the actual level of East-West obsession has not been definitively established. This chapter attempts to ascertain the level of East-West obsession present in the U.S. government, as manifest in the official State Department *Bulletin*, and in the U.S. popular media, as exemplified by *Newsweek* magazine.

VIEWS OF AFRICAN VIOLENCE IN THE EAST-WEST CONTEXT

Since Africa's emergence from colonialism, the shadow of the Cold War has extended over many interpretations of Africa's politics. For the most part, African nations initially maintained close relations with the former colonial powers. Most were thus considered pro-Western, with occasional exceptions. Any destabilization of these regimes therefore was seen to threaten Western interests. Western analysts soon came to regard any political violence as a threat.

Cold War approaches to analysis of African politics persisted well into the 1980s. The purest form of that approach may be found in what Helen Kitchen called the "chessboard" school of international politics.[6] This relatively small group of scholars saw Africa (and Asia and Latin America) solely as a game board for the East-West conflict. They argued that communists were extending their interests by overthrowing reactionary regimes and replacing them with revolutionary allies, and that violence resulted from designs conceived largely in Moscow.[7] A larger group of scholars conceded that domestic factors are at the root of violence but argued that when violence erupts, the East opportunistically intervenes to capitalize on it.[8]

Although these views appear different, they share one common perspective, rooted in a Cold War coloration of the geopolitical map. Both assert that the Soviets advance when African internal politics change.[9]

This chapter investigates the level of East-West coloration in government and media reports on African violence. To what extent are events in Africa tied to superpower conflict? Do the two sources differ, or do the media reflect the government's concerns? Finally, are these trends variable over time, and if so, can the trends be explained?

Earlier research has demonstrated a difference between government and media sources, exemplified by the State Department *Bulletin* and *Newsweek* magazine.[10] Specifically, the *Bulletin* was less variable over time, while *Newsweek* greatly increased its emphasis on East-West issues. The two sources had diverged from a point of commonality in 1957–62 to a point where the popular media source had far more East-West references than the government. This trend emerged even as the superpowers were loosening bipolar tensions in the 1970s.

This chapter extends that data collection into the 1980s to examine new questions arising from the passage of time. Not least of these is the fading of the East-West conflict. Given that the East is no longer a threat, even in the eyes of conservative analysts, attention to the Cold War should subside.[11]

On the other hand, the Cold War approach has the advantage of being simple. When violence arose, media analysts could simply ask which side the U.S. government supported and which side the communists supported. A rigorous examination of domestic factors is a more difficult task. When communicating with the public, simplicity is no small factor, and both government and media could continue to be tempted to use the East-West conflict as a simple model for understanding African violence.

Moreover, there are ideological considerations at stake. During the 1980s the Reagan administration reinvigorated the Cold War approach, especially through the efforts of Undersecretaries of State Elliot Abrams (Latin America) and Chester Crocker (Africa). Public support for rebel movements in countries perceived to be pro-Soviet (the so-called rollback approach) rested on convincing the public of a Soviet threat.

How then, have media and government descriptions of African violence changed over the years?

METHOD

This investigation consisted of a content analysis of articles in two publications, *Newsweek* and the State Department *Bulletin*. The analysis considered all articles on African domestic violence. The number of paragraphs in the article was recorded to give a rough estimate of the size of the story. The number of paragraphs with a reference to an Eastern-bloc country (the Soviet Union and Cuba were almost all of these) and the number of paragraphs with a reference to Marxism (communism, social-ism, reds, but excluding leftism) were also recorded. Finally, because they showed up so often, paragraphs with a reference to Libya were also recorded. While not an Eastern-bloc country, Libya is often considered either a Soviet surrogate or an independent menace.

In short, the research consisted of a word search for each article in the sample. We counted the (1) total paragraphs in the article, (2) number of paragraphs with at least one reference to the East, (3) number of para-graphs with at least one reference to Marxism, and (4) number of para-graphs mentioning Libya at least once.

The simple search for dictionary keywords was done for two main reasons. First, the alternative was to take articles and judge whether or not violence was presented as primarily local or primarily an East-West problem, which raises serious reliability questions. Second, the keyword search has the advantage of locating brief references which may have a strong effect on the reader. For example, some descriptions of violence read like this: "The rebels, brandishing Soviet-made AK-47 rifles, attacked a small village." This sentence contains a strong East-West tag, the gratuitous inclusion of the origin of the rifles.

In such a case, the reference may not have been a direct attempt to define the violence as an East-West issue. After all, there is a difference between presence and control.[12] However, the average reader of a mass publication is unlikely to make that distinction. In the end, the reference raises the East-West issue, irrespective of intent.

The paragraph was selected as a unit of analysis for a couple of reasons. Most importantly, it minimizes the amount of double-counting from an article. If a single sentence contains more than one reference—for example, "the communists hope to establish a Marxist government"—it may be more of a necessity within the sentence construction. Similarly, a follow-up sentence may also contain a reference which simply continues the previous thought. On the other hand, if two references appear in two separate paragraphs, the point is more strongly made. There has been a conscious effort to include the thought in separate sections of the article. Therefore, neither total word counts nor sentences containing references would be adequate for this study. Second, the paragraph is a unit that is fairly uniform, at least among these publications. The *Bulletin* and *Newsweek* have very different layouts, so a unit like the column inch would be inappropriate. Although *Bulletin* paragraphs do appear to be longer than the mass-based *Newsweek*, the difference is not major.

The three time periods chosen for data collection represent different eras in U.S.-Soviet relations. The 1957–62 period was one of Cold War tension, culminating in the Cuban missile crisis in its final year. The 1973–78 period begins Richard Nixon's second term, when detente was launched. The final period, 1982–87, falls entirely within the presidency of Ronald Reagan. More significantly, it begins with the death of Leonid Brezhnev, and includes the brief regimes of Andropov, Chernenko, and the beginning of Gorbachev. It is here that, following a period of intense rivalry, the Cold War receded.

These three periods represent vastly different epochs of modern African history. The first period comprises the major decolonization of the British and French empires. It also represents the earliest initiatives of the Soviet

Union in Africa, including the Congo crisis. The second period follows the consolidation of the new African states and also includes the breakup of the Portuguese colonies. It, too, was a period of expanding Soviet influence, following a retrenchment in the late 1960s.[13] The final period has been characterized as one of consolidation, when Soviet influence has neither increased nor decreased.[14] Decolonization has extended to Namibia, with increasing emphasis on transition from white rule in Zimbabwe and the issue of apartheid. The following propositions guided the research effort:

1. East-West themes in coverage of African violence will be more frequent during a period of U.S.-Soviet conflict internationally and lower during a period of cooperation. The chessboard school would postulate that the Soviets will increase violence in Africa during periods of global tension and decrease violence when relations improve. If either source is influenced by this school, its emphasis on East-West themes will ebb and flow with the freezes and thaws in the Cold War. We would expect, as specific results, a decrease from the first to second periods (reflecting decreased tensions) and then an increase in the third period (reflecting Reagan's renewed anticommunism), but not to the levels of the first period, when the Cold War was at its most serious level.

2. East-West themes in coverage of African violence will be more frequent during periods of increased Soviet activity and lower when there is less activity. This proposition distinguishes the regional from the international arenas. It is based on the assumption that coverage of African violence depends more on the extent of Soviet initiatives in Africa and less on the overall bipolar relationship. From this proposition, we would expect an increase from the first to the second periods, and then a decrease.

3. East-West themes in coverage of African violence will subside over time. The maturation of African nations would imply that violence might come more from domestic pressures than external sources. Moreover, with the Soviet Union looking inward in the 1980s, there should be less reason to view violence as either a product of or a benefit to the Soviets. Evidence for this proposition would be a decrease from the first through the third periods.

4. *Newsweek* and the *Bulletin* will not differ greatly in their attention to East-West themes. Critics of U.S. policy in Africa assert that the news media are subordinate to the U.S. government and that they uncritically mirror its interests. If so, then the two sources will be similar in their coverage of African violence. The null hypothesis reflects this assumption.

One significant methodological problem appeared along the way; specifically, the *Bulletin*'s switch from weekly to monthly publication in the late 1970s. This would theoretically cut the level of coverage fourfold, but in fact the differences are much less dramatic. The actual number of articles was comparable. The total number of paragraphs fell by quite a bit, but *Newsweek*'s totals also declined. In all probability, the change in frequency of publication did not affect results.

There was also one limitation, specifically, the inability to compare results for Cuba and Libya over time. Neither had appeared during the previous periods to any significant extent, but the two appeared frequently from 1982 to 1987. We can compare results between sources during this last time period, but cannot make any longitudinal comparisons.

RESULTS

Table 8.1 contains the basic descriptive data for the chapter. Two sources, *Newsweek* 1973–78 and the *Bulletin* 1982–87 clearly stand out. In both cases, more than half the articles contained at least one Soviet or Marxist reference.

This trend is verified by the data analyses summarized in Table 8.2. However, the differences are not as sharply defined; the *Bulletin* does not

Table 8.1
Proportions for East-West References

	Total Articles (N)	Proportion with E-W reference[1]	Total Paragraphs (N)	Proportion with reference to USSR	Marxism
Newsweek 1957-62	(145)	.46	(1215)	.06	.05
Newsweek 1973-78	(88)	.68	(680)	.18	.08
Newsweek 1982-87	(70)	.49	(452)	.10	.06
Bulletin 1957-62	(50)	.40	(921)	.15	.02
Bulletin 1973-78	(58)	.31	(1035)	.12	.02
Bulletin 1982-87	(51)	.59[2]	(481)	.16	.05

1. USSR or Marxism. 1982–87 figures include Cuba.
2. Includes one article that referred only to Cubans.

Table 8.2
Z-Test for Differences of Proportions: *Newsweek* **versus State**
Department *Bulletin*

	Articles East-West	Paragraphs Soviet Bloc	
Time Period	Higher Proportion (sig)	Higher Proportion (sig)	Higher Proportion (sig)
1957-1962	*Newsweek* (NS)	*Bulletin* (NS)	*Newsweek*(**)
1973-1978	*Newsweek* (***)	*Newsweek* (***)	*Newsweek*(***)
1982-1987	*Bulletin* (NS)	*Bulletin* (**)	*Newsweek* (NS)

NS= not significant
  * p < .05
 ** p < .01
*** p <.001

clearly outdistance *Newsweek* during the most recent time period. Still, there are strong differences among all three time periods.

The two publications were at first similar in their use of East-West terms. Then they diverged, with *Newsweek* dramatically intensifying its East-West coloration. In the 1980s, the two seem to have converged, with the number of references in the *Bulletin* increasing and *Newsweek* decreasing.

Table 8.3 completes the picture by looking specifically at each publication and its change over time. For *Newsweek*, the figures verify a sharp increase from the first to second time periods, and then a drop back to previous levels. There is very little difference between *Newsweek* during the first and third periods.

With the *Bulletin*, the pattern is a bit different. The most recent time period is where the increase took place, while the first two periods are relatively similar. Thus, the *Bulletin* in 1982–1987 contained more references to the East-West conflict than it did at the height of the Cold War. Neither pattern fits the overall conduct of U.S.–Eastern bloc relations over the past thirty years. The *Bulletin* did reflect the spirit of detente in the 1970s. *Newsweek* at best ignored it, at worst served to undermine it.[15] *Newsweek*'s pattern does however, approximate the level of Soviet initiative on the continent. From a point where the Soviets were only beginning to exercise any influence in the area, the 1970s were years of new

Table 8.3
Z-Test for Differences of Proportions over Time,
Intra-Publication Comparisons

Source, Period[1]	Articles East-West		Paragraphs Soviet Bloc		Paragraphs Marxism	
	Higher Proportion (sig)		Higher Proportion (sig)		Higher Proportion (sig)	
Newsweek						
1 vs. 2	Period 2	(***)	Period 2	(***)	Period 2	(**)
2 vs. 3	Period 2	(*)	Period 2	(***)	Period 2	(NS)
1 vs. 3	Period 3	(NS)	Period 3	(*)	Period 3	(NS)
Bulletin						
1 vs. 2	Period 1	(NS)	Period 1	(*)	Neither	(NS)
2 vs. 3	Period 3	(**)	Period 3	(*)	Period 3	(*)
1 vs. 3	Period 3	(*)	Period 3	(NS)	Period 3	(*)

Note: Period 1: 1957–62
      Period 2: 1973–78
      Period 3: 1982–87
NS = not significant
  * $p < .05$
 ** $p < .01$
*** $p < .001$

initiatives and new areas of interest. The 1980s were years of consolidation with no new initiatives but also no significant retrenchment. *Newsweek*'s references increased sharply and then receded over time.

Probably the most striking feature of the data set is the instability of the figures for the three time periods. Even though the two sources were roughly comparable during the first time period, they diverged significantly in the 1970s. At that point, despite the rhetoric of the time, *Newsweek* was including Marxism or the Soviet Union in more than two-thirds of all articles about violence. In contrast, the State Department of the 1970s had slightly decreased the level of East-West reference, significantly so when we consider the paragraph count.

This trend reversed in the 1980s. *Newsweek*'s use of Soviet/Marxist labeling fell from more than two-thirds of all articles to less than half. In paragraph counts, the figure also fell, although not as dramatically. The

State Department, in contrast, increased to a point beyond even the levels of 1957–62. It also reversed its position with *Newsweek*, surging above the latter's density of references.

The *Bulletin*'s results are perhaps understandable as the reflection of the administrations they served. In the 1970s, the Nixon, Ford, and Carter administrations all played up the theme of detente and an increasingly more peaceful international scene. In the 1980s, the Reagan administration breathed anticommunism, even as the international Soviet threat was decreasing.

The best illustration of the latter point came in a speech by Chester Crocker reproduced in the January 1986 *Bulletin*. In that speech, twenty-three separate paragraphs had at least one reference to the Soviet Union, which is easily the highest total in the data set. The subject was violence in the Horn of Africa, which by 1986 posed no more threat to the West than it ever had.

This does not necessarily mean that *Newsweek* is a more accurate source. Their obsession with Soviets and Marxism in the 1970s goes far beyond the themes raised during the Reagan administration. Moreover, the decrease in the 1980s could easily have given the impression that the Soviets were no longer interested in Africa.

LIBYA AND CUBA

There were also some clear differences in sources on Cuba and Libya (see Table 8.4). The former was much more a concern of the State Department, while the latter was more of a *Newsweek* favorite. Table 8.4

Table 8.4
Differences Between *Newsweek* and *Bulletin*, Cuba and Libya, 1982–1987

Country	ARTICLES Higher Proportion (sig)	PARAGRAPHS Higher Proportion (sig)
Cuba	*Bulletin* (***)	*Bulletin* (***)
Libya	*Newsweek* (NS)	*Newsweek* (**)

NS = not significant
  * p < .05
 ** p < .01
*** p < .001

shows that the State Department had a great deal more concentration of references to Cuba than did *Newsweek*, both as a proportion of articles and paragraphs.

The opposite holds for Libya, which was more often cited by *Newsweek* in paragraphs. For total articles, the relationship was not significant. This difference is undoubtedly because of the heavy concentration of Libyan references in individual *Newsweek* articles.

It is curious that Libya shows up so much in the data set. Quadaffy clearly had a hand in coup attempts in the Sudan and the Chadian civil war, but Libya is also mentioned in stories about Ghana[16] and Uganda.[17] Moreover, in the articles where Libya or Quadaffy are mentioned, they appear often; much more often, in fact, than either Cuba or the Soviet Union in any articles involving those countries. Cuba appears much stronger as an East-West player. Although some have advocated that Cuban foreign policy is independent of Moscow, neither of our sources seem to see it that way.[18] All *Newsweek* articles that mention Cuba also mention the Soviet Union or Marxism, and only one *Bulletin* article mentions the Cubans alone. The *Bulletin* occasionally refers to a "Soviet/ Cuban" entity.

SOUTH AFRICA AND APARTHEID

Table 8.5 shows a separate consideration of articles about violence in South Africa in 1982–87. Unfortunately, the paucity of articles poses problems for the stability of our results (the *Bulletin* had only twelve articles on South African violence), so that only a consideration of paragraphs was possible.

The *Bulletin* outdistances *Newsweek* in references to the Soviet Union. The two sources are comparable in references to Cuba, but that is not surprising. Cuba has no military advisors or troops in South Africa, in contrast to other areas. The two sources did not differ in references to Marxism.

A stronger difference resulted from comparing South African and other African articles. Both publications showed differences between South African and non-South African nations. *Newsweek*'s results in this regard were particularly striking. *Newsweek* virtually never mentioned any outside forces. Instead, the struggle was framed as an internal conflict between black nationalist forces and the ruling whites, or among rival black factions. The State Department did much the same. Its articles on South African violence had fewer references to the Eastern bloc than articles on violence in other African states. However, the State Department main-

Table 8.5
South African Violence, 1982–1987 (Paragraphs Only)

COMPARISON OF	Reference to USSR	Reference to Marxism	Reference to Cuba
	Higher Proportion (sig)	Higher Proportion (sig)	Higher Proportion (sig)
Newsweek -*Bulletin*	*Bulletin* (**)	*Bulletin* (NS)	*Bulletin* (NS)
Newsweek (1)	Other African (***)	Other African (NS)	Other African (***)
Bulletin (1)	Other African (**)	Other African (NS)	Other African(**)

Note: (1) Compares articles on South Africa with articles on violence in
  "other African" states.
NS = not significant
  * p < .05
 ** p < .01
*** p < .001

tained a higher level than *Newsweek,* and significantly differed from
Newsweek in references to the Soviet Union.

The latter point was illustrated dramatically by President Ronald Reagan.
The *Bulletin* had only one presidential press conference relevant to South
African violence. President Reagan was asked why the United States had
not included the African National Congress (ANC) in the search for a
peaceful solution in South Africa. The president responded by discussing
the communist origins of the group (*Bulletin,* October 1986). Still, the
overall results from the *Bulletin* showed a lower concern for East-West
issues in South Africa compared with articles on violence in other African
nations.

There are a few possible reasons for this decrease in references. The
mass media may have decided that apartheid is an interesting issue, and
needs neither Quadaffy nor communists to hold readers' interest. Certainly, African-American concerns about dismantling apartheid would add
to that interest.[19] Another possibility is that correspondents and editors see
violence as a direct result of apartheid and do not believe the East-West

conflict to be relevant. The debates over sanctions and the Sullivan principles focus discussion on the internal dimensions of the conflict. Moreover, many see violence as incipient and inevitable in the country. If violence created apartheid, it may well be the way to destroy it.[20] The same trend in the *Bulletin* rests less on readership interest and more on the government's public stance on South Africa. Whatever the Reagan administration's policies may have been (and they were open to question), the official stance was to seek a third position, opposing both the militant antiapartheid approach and the government's often hard-line stance.

This would mean downplaying East-West issues. South Africa has presented itself as a bulwark against communism in Africa in an attempt to subordinate the race issue.[21] However, South Africa is more of an albatross to U.S. policymakers, and the United States may have been trying to distance itself publicly from South Africa.[22] This would mean, among other things, ignoring the anticommunist line.

Public pressure may also have influenced the government's position, as reflected in the *Bulletin*. The administration was under serious pressure from both mass and elite quarters on South African policy. This pressure may have meant less freedom to invoke Cold War images and more of a necessity to handle the question of apartheid directly.

Whatever the source of this development, it is a hopeful sign that both the mass media and the government covered an African issue without mentioning the Soviet Union. The South African example stands out against other areas of coverage of African political violence.

CONCLUSIONS

This chapter began by posing four questions about media coverage on African violence. Following are conclusions regarding the four propositions, plus two additional observations.

1. *Reporting of African violence does not appear to have been influenced by U.S.–Soviet bipolar relations.* Neither source showed any evidence of proposition 1, which asserted that East-West references would increase and decrease with deterioration or improvement of U.S.–Soviet relations. Instead, *Newsweek* showed opposite trends, and the *Bulletin* conformed more to the thinking of the current administration than to the actual state of relations.

2. *Over time, Newsweek more accurately reflected the trends of Soviet influence in Africa. Newsweek*'s increase in the 1970s, while hopelessly exaggerated, nevertheless reflected at least the direction of Soviet influence. In the 1980s, *Newsweek* significantly lowered these references,

which also reflected the slowing or reversal of Soviet gains on the continent. *Newsweek*'s pattern therefore conformed to the expectations of the second proposition. In contrast, the government's trends reflect no known scholarly opinion.

3. *Cold War themes are becoming less prevalent in popular media.* *Newsweek* dramatically lowered its portrayal of African violence as an East-West construction between the second and third time periods. This might be considered limited evidence for the third proposition, except that *Newsweek* only returned to its previous level, rather than reducing its emphasis on the Soviet Union below levels established thirty years ago.

Newsweek at least showed evidence of increasing sophistication regarding the meaning of socialism and Marxism in the African context. One *Newsweek* article on Zimbabwe was careful to point out that calling that country socialist creates a false impression (which unwittingly created an additional East-West reference). This stands in contrast to the Marxist and Soviet-backed labels so readily applied in the 1970s. This does not mean that *Newsweek* now covers violence with much greater care. Their use of Colonel Quadaffy can only be described as excessive. Possibly, that publication has merely shifted its prejudice from the Soviet Union to Libya.

The *Bulletin* did not show any such tendency, but its Cold War obsession may be a temporary disturbance coming from the Reagan administration. Future investigation may clarify this matter. Or future investigation may be irrelevant. The Cold War is not even on the U.S.–Soviet agenda, much less the African agenda. The question is no longer whether the Soviet Union has influence in Africa, but whether it has influence in the Baltic Republics.

4. *Newsweek's approach was consistently at odds with the official U.S. stance. There is strong evidence of an independent media.* After the 1957–62 period, *Newsweek* diverged completely from the *Bulletin*. *Newsweek*'s concentration of Cold War themes increased when the *Bulletin* was decreasing, and vice versa. In East-West themes, *Newsweek* was clearly not mimicking the government's presentation; if anything, it was studiously at odds with it. The evidence is diametrically opposed to the fourth proposition. Specifically, *Newsweek*'s ratios in 1973–78 were so much larger than the *Bulletin*'s that it is hard to imagine the government in control of the reporting. It appears instead that *Newsweek* was, either consciously or unconsciously, subverting the official detente stance of the U.S. government.

If that alone is not persuasive, the results from the 1980s should drive the point home. *Newsweek* showed a precipitous decline in reporting

East-West themes, right in the middle of the Reagan administration. *Newsweek* steadfastly refused to be influenced by the onslaught of anti-communist rhetoric in briefings on Africa. The *Bulletin*, in contrast, was rather accommodating toward this change in emphasis from previous administrations.

5. *The findings verify no particular ideological claims.* Indeed, the results are frustrating to both the right and left. To those on the right, who frequently voice their criticism of the media's liberal bias, *Newsweek*'s 1973–78 results stand as a counterpoint. To leftists, who accuse the media of compliance (if not complicity) with the government, the persistent differences between the public and private sources gainsay such claims. The public has an important role to play in this process.

The coverage of South Africa is particularly instructive on the importance of public concern. As both *Newsweek* and the *Bulletin* devoted more space to the question of apartheid, references to the East disappeared. Interest in that issue has been increasing in the American public, particularly in the African-American community. Thus the concern for apartheid, aside from its intrinsic value, has the positive side-effect of contributing to a more thorough consideration of African politics. In the absence of public interest, those controls cease to function. Correspondents and editors will be tempted to create interest in stories on African violence by bringing in Cubans, Russians, or Colonel Quadaffy. The government will be able to focus interest on external actors and ignore the important domestic political concerns that generate violence.

These results underscore the importance of specific issues that generate such public concern. In 1957–62 the main issue in Africa was decolonization. This was a period of history in which the map of Africa was being redrawn constantly, and the push for independence seemed relentless. Even though there was an increasing Soviet presence, the issue of decolonization superseded East-West rivalry. The 1980s present the issue of apartheid as an issue that frames violence in South Africa. In that sense, 1982–87 is similar to 1957–62. As long as there is a domestic issue of interest to Americans, there is less attention paid to red flags.

Ultimately, the quality of information on African politics may depend on the willingness of Americans to concern themselves with specifically African issues. We can only hope for an increase in that concern. The alternative is continued ignorance.

NOTES

1. Henry F. Jackson, *From the Congo to Soweto: U.S. Foreign Policy Toward Africa Since 1960* (New York: William Morrow and Co., 1982), pp. 283–84.

2. U.S. House of Representatives, Committee on Foreign Affairs, *Africa: Observations on the Impact of American Foreign Policy and Development Programs in Six African Countries*. Report of a Congressional Study Mission (Washington, DC: U.S. Government Printing Office, 1982).

3. Howard E. Wolpe, "The Dangers of Globalism" in *African Crisis Areas and U.S. Foreign Policy*, edited by Gerald Bender, James S. Coleman, and Richard L. Sklar (Berkeley: University of California Press, 1985), pp. 284–90.

4. Jackson, *From the Congo*, p. 289.

5. James S. Coleman and Richard L. Sklar, "Introduction" in *African Crisis Areas and U.S. Foreign Policy*, edited by Gerald Bender, James S. Coleman, and Richard L. Sklar (Berkeley: University of California Press, 1985), pp. 1–25.

6. Helen A. Kitchen, *U.S. Interests in Africa*, Washington Papers 98 (New York: Praeger, 1983).

7. Morris Rothenberg, *The U.S.S.R. and Africa: New Dimensions of Soviet Global Power* (Miami: Advanced International Studies Institute, 1980), p. 1.

8. Kitchen, *U.S. Interests*, pp. 2–3.

9. Robert Legvold, "The Soviet Union's Strategic State in Africa," in *Africa and the United States: Vital Statistics*, edited by Jennifer S. Whitaker (New York: NYU Press, 1978), pp. 166–67.

10. Rodger M. Govea, "East-West Themes in the Reporting of African Violence," *Social Science Quarterly* 64, no. 1 (March): 193–99.

11. Helen A. Kitchen, *Some Guidelines on Africa for the Next President* (Washington, DC: CSIS, 1988), pp. 5–6.

12. Mark V. Kauppi, "The Soviet Union and Africa: The Dynamics and Dilemmas of Involvement," in *The Soviet Impact in Africa*, edited by R. Craig Nation and Mark V. Kauppi (Lexington, MA: D. C. Heath, 1984), p. 232.

13. R. Craig Nation, "Introduction: The Soviet Impact in Africa," in *The Soviet Impact in Africa*, edited by R. Craig Nation and Mark V. Kauppi (Lexington, MA: D. C. Heath, 1984), pp. 2, 4.

14. Ibid., pp. 2–3.

15. Govea, "East-West Themes in the Reporting of African Violence," pp. 193–99.

16. *Newsweek*, January 11, 1982.

17. *Newsweek*, March 8, 1982.

18. William M. LeoGrande, "Foreign Policy: The Limits of Success" in *Cuba: Internal and International Affairs*, edited by Jorge I. Dominguez (Beverly Hills, CA: Sage, 1982), pp. 169–79.

19. See esp. Jackson, *From the Congo*, pp. 121–68.

20. Ibid., p. 289.

21. Patrick Wall, *The Indian Ocean and the Threat to the West* (London: Stacey International, Distributed in the U.S. by the Information Service of South Africa, 1975).

22. William J. Foltz, "United States Policy toward South Africa: Is One Possible?" in *African Crisis Areas and U.S. Foreign Policy*, edited by Gerald J. Bender, James S. Coleman, and Richard L. Sklar (Berkeley: University of California Press, 1985), pp. 32–48.

9

Are We Really the World? Coverage of U.S. Food Aid in Africa, 1980–1989

Jo Ellen Fair

Food is necessary for survival. It is essential to life. But sometimes not enough food abounds to feed all those who are hungry. Whether for reasons of war, poor marketing of agricultural products, drought or rising urbanization, many Africans during the 1980s had difficulty in securing consistent access to food.[1] As a result, several African countries suffered from chronic food shortages throughout the decade. African governments and the West alike often saw food aid as the quick remedy to Africa's ills.[2] Threatened by recurring disruptions to the food supply, Africa's need was great. In this environment of perceived vulnerability and crisis, the media told the story of U.S. food aid sent to Africa during the 1980s.

By 1985, during the height of the Ethiopian famine, the U.S. public was awash in media coverage of food aid to Africa. The media's focus on hunger in Africa was so keen that 89 percent of the 500 respondents to a *Seattle Times* survey knew and could describe something about the famine. Nearly three-quarters of those surveyed said that hunger was among the top three problems facing the world.[3] Without the news media, this awareness of Africa's difficulties seems inconceivable.[4] The media are important not only as transmitters of information but also as creators of images, as producers of certain "ways of seeing" the world.[5] This chapter is an examination of Africa's media image as it was constructed through the coverage of U.S. food aid sent to Africa during the 1980s.

This chapter examines how one of the most influential newspapers in the United States, *The New York Times*, covered food aid sent to Africa between 1980 and 1989 by the United States (through its own government agencies or through international groups or organizations).[6] Through textual and content analyses, it is argued that images of Africa constructed by the *Times*'s coverage of food aid revolved around four primary discourses. They are (1) the discourse of crisis, (2) the discourse of aid donors, (3) the discourse of aid recipients (governments of African countries), and (4) the discourse of the people. Discourses are defined as certain rules and regularities that make up news content, creating or reproducing a structure of meaning.[7] All of the discourses identified in the *Times*'s coverage of food aid ultimately were part of a Cold War interpretation of relations between the United States and the Soviet Union. However, before examining these discourses, we discuss just how often and under what circumstances Africa makes its way into U.S. newspapers or television newscasts.

MEDIA COVERAGE OF AFRICA

News is not merely a collection of facts put together in narrative form. It plays an important cultural role by providing audiences with ways of handling new and recurring issues and problems.[8] To produce the news, media interpret the actions of people and events by selecting and emphasizing certain stories over others. Thus, the way in which the mass media cover Africa contributes to the public's view of the region. The U.S. news media play a key role in providing information to government officials, decision makers, as well as to the awaiting public.[9] Walter Lippmann once noted that "the only feeling that anyone can have about an event he [she] does not experience is the feeling aroused by his [her] mental image of that event."[10] Given that Africa is not experienced by most Americans, what can we say about U.S. media coverage of Africa and Africa's subsequent image?

Generally, research on media coverage of Africa suggests that Africa, if not the least covered region of the world, is one of the most seldom covered.[11] Of course, getting the story out of Africa is not easy. Reporters must contend with sources reluctant to speak for fear of their own safety, difficult travel conditions, censorship, inadequate communication facilities that make transmitting stories at times nearly impossible.[12] And for media organizations to maintain a correspondent in Africa involves large financial commitments.

But when the media do cover Africa, stories often conceive of Africa in a very narrow focus. Stories are largely event-based and crisis-oriented.[13] Most commonly, media coverage is of an Africa enmeshed in a series of political and military imbroglios and ethnic violence.[14] Moreover, relations between East and West—the Cold War framework—often inform this crisis coverage, as violence and conflict in Africa are seen as the site for struggle between the superpowers.[15] Thus, for Africa to be part of "all the news that's fit to print," as the motto of *The New York Times* says, it seems that news stories must include three elements: events, crisis, and superpower conflict.

Indeed, food aid stories presented in *The New York Times* from 1980 to 1989 contained these essential items. Food aid stories were newsworthy because they could be pegged on particular events or activities of important people; these included the visits of aid officials or rock stars to relief camps and the unloading of grain from port. And though these stories were part of larger, historical processes of political-social inequalities,[16] as well as environmental and climatic changes,[17] new stories would focus on the immediate crisis of hunger and deprivation, pitting, for instance, aid contributions of the United States against those of the Soviet Union. What remains important is not just how the *Times* covered food aid, but how the *Times* helped to construct certain images of Africa as revealed through the discourses of African governments as aid recipients, of aid donors, of the African people themselves, and of crisis. Together these discourses were interpreted in terms of relations between the United States and Soviet Union.

NEWS AS SOCIAL PRACTICE IN THE FORMATION OF DISCOURSES

News stories are socially determined. They are produced within an environment in which individual journalists and their organizations determine events, occurrences, or activities as newsworthy on the basis of both highly personal rationale and organizational imperative. Certain events—the mainstay news stories—are chosen over others for coverage because journalists and the media outlets they work for have different, sometimes conflicting events needs.[18] As a result, the media construct social reality in a variety of ways. They do not merely reflect a single reality through a set of facts reported in a news story. Rather, the media structure and define reality by selecting certain facts, emphasizing certain events, and giving stories a certain tone.[19] In essence, the media, as social institutions, are part of "the more active labor of making things mean."[20]

The news media help to make meaning through professional practices that create discourse. Discourse is defined as conventions and rules that structure the content of news stories, linking the content or text to larger bodies of social knowledge. In this process of the formation of discourse, the media do not act alone in the way in which they produce and present knowledge. As Peter Bruck notes, "The news media deploy their discourses within a net of determinations produced by politics, science, education, religion, and other institutions of knowledge production."[21]

What is important about this net of determinations is that the media use the discourse of other institutions, repackaging it for reuse in their own stories.[22] And in doing so, the media are likely to produce discourses that borrow from or even contradict each other. Despite what Bruck sees as an unevenness in the way the media are able to construct knowledge or social reality, he argues that the result of the media's creation of discourses is invariably the same: Media, through their content, reproduce certain dominant notions of reality.[23]

Because the purpose of this chapter is to explore how Africa's media image was created through coverage in *The New York Times* of U.S. food aid sent to Africa from 1980 to 1989, the appropriate method is one that facilitates looking at how meaning is produced and one that attempts to identify the processes of definition and their connections to social institutions. Textual analysis was used to locate and examine news discourses of food aid presented in the *Times*.[24]

There is now within media studies an extensive literature based on this sort of analysis, particularly analysis of news. A wide range of studies examines how the definition of news determines what will be seen as newsworthy and meaningful, which events and peoples will not be seen, and the connections of those definitions to social structures.[25]

Textual analysis involves first what Stuart Hall calls "a long preliminary soak," whereby the investigator thoroughly reads each and every news story on U.S. food aid printed in the *Times* from 1980 to 1989 (a population of stories, rather than a sample).[26] The investigator notes, for example, the content of stories, the sources interviewed, and the context in which reporters place their stories. This soak usually involves more than one reading of the population of stories. The preliminary soak has two purposes: First, it is used to help the researcher discover whether certain hypothesized discourses exist. Second, it allows the researcher to select representative news stories to analyze in greater detail.

The detailed analysis of selected stories seeks to understand why the content is the way it is. In Hall's terms, the goal of this analysis is to identify "a framework of ideas and beliefs" the media produce.[27] The researcher takes note not only of recurring themes and ways of writing about U.S. aid sent to Africa but also exceptions to the general pattern. The purpose of this segment of the analysis is to attempt to go beyond manifest content and begin to explore over time implicit patterns, emphases, and the images media have about audiences when they present news stories in a particular way.

Thus, a textual analysis of the coverage of U.S. food aid in *The New York Times* revealed four news discourses: (1) the discourse of crisis, (2) the discourse of aid givers, (3) the discourse of aid recipients, and the (4) discourse of the people. These discourses are part of a larger Cold War framework in which the *Times* placed U.S. food aid to Africa largely in the context of superpower relations. These categories of discourses are not mutually exclusive. Discourses are informed by each other and overlap, representing different ways news stories can produce meaning.

THE COLD WAR FRAMEWORK AND FOOD AID DISCOURSES

As the role of the United States in international affairs has evolved and expanded, foreign assistance has become an integral part of U.S. foreign policy, used to court friends and spurn foes. Foreign aid sent to Africa—whether it be military, economic, or humanitarian—is, of course, no exception.[28] Since their inception, food aid programs under Public Law 480[29] have been used both to support humanitarian concerns and to further political interests, namely to stop the spread of communism.[30]

During the Reagan administration foreign assistance took on rather dramatic political overtones. The U.S. government, slow to react to African countries' appeals for economic aid, simply neglected the urgency of Ethiopia's request for humanitarian aid because of the country's Marxist form of government and alliance with the Soviet Union.[31] Perhaps reflecting Washington's priority of protecting its security interests in the region, military aid given by the United States during the 1980s far outdistanced other aid forms sent to Africa.[32] Thus, in the ideological environment of the 1980s, Africa was a site for superpower struggle for influence.

Given this atmosphere, *The New York Times* used the Cold War as its framework to present and interpret discourse about U.S. food aid sent to Africa. The Cold War framework is defined as "the great struggle between the free world and communism."[33] This battle between East and West served to define "the limits of 'responsible' political discussion, and pervaded the reporting of virtually every event that took place outside the borders of the United States."[34] And coverage of food aid in Africa was no exception.

Because of the pervasiveness of the Cold War framework, it seems natural rather than ideological. By counterpoising the United States and the Soviet Union as forces of good and evil, the framework provides journalists with both the questions and answers in which events can be understood and explained.[35] Because the media repackage the discourse of other social institutions largely through the interviewing of sources for stories, news organizations can (and do) reproduce dominant views of social reality. In the case of U.S. food aid, U.S. government officials—who as participants in the superpower struggle often voiced anti-Soviet rhetoric—served as primary sources to *Times* reporters.[36] Moreover, nearly 55 percent of the 134 stories examined (N = 73) were datelined in the United States, perhaps further indicating the nexus of sources with whom reporters worked.[37] It comes as no surprise, then, that news stories about food aid in Africa reduced the continent to a site where U.S.-Soviet relations were played out.

The reduction of Africa to a counterpoising of the free world and the communist world is found in the discourses of crisis, aid givers, aid recipients, and the people. Not all the discourses are equally represented in the *Times* coverage of food aid. Yet, together these discourses present a particular way of seeing Africa through the coverage of food aid. The discourse of crisis appears throughout the decade of news coverage. It peaks during the 1984–85 coverage of famine in Ethiopia and the Sudan, during which the *Times* ran 102 of 134 food aid articles.

The discourse of crisis largely was one of urgency, emergency, catastrophe, and the prediction of deaths. As was pointed out earlier, times of crisis are often the only occasions in which the media cover Africa. News stories used terms such as *grim, agony of famine, famine stricken, famine engulfed, fear of food crisis, food emergency, catastrophic shortage, scenes of horror, battling famine, war against famine, hunger's toll, hunger threat,* and *continent of misery* to express the deprivation caused by food shortages and the need for food aid. The food crisis in Africa was defined primarily by U.S. government officials, Westerners in international organizations, and Western relief groups operating in Africa. The most frequent reason stated in news stories for food aid was because of famine[38] (81 mentions, 47 percent), which was equated not with its historical meaning of hunger[39] but with death through starvation. Predictions and counts of death were common, particularly during 1984–85, and comparisons to earlier food shortages (such as the 1972–74 Ethiopian drought) were frequent.

The *Times* covered the food aid needs of 23 African countries, centering on Ethiopia (73 mentions) and the Sudan (25 mentions).[40] In this discourse of crisis, the *Times* saw food aid as the moral duty of Westerners to halt the crisis by relieving the suffering of others. In response to a question posed in an editorial concerning why the United States should give food aid to a "Marxist regime [Ethiopia] that gets $2.5 billion in weapons from the Soviet Union," the *Times* said: "For Western donors to retaliate by cutting relief would punish a whole people to spite their government. The decent response is to keep the food flowing to both Ethiopia and the insurgent areas" (January 19, 1985). Thus, within the discourse of crisis, the appropriate course of action for the United States to relieve the emergency was to donate food, an action, the *Times* pointed out, the Soviets could not or would not undertake.

Tied to the discourse of the crisis are the discourses of aid givers and aid recipients. They are linked because each appropriates materials from the other. The actions of aid givers and aid recipients (African governments) as reported in the *Times* are key to the sense of urgency or crisis. The discourse of aid givers focuses on the actions of U.S. government officials, Western relief workers, international agency staffers, and pop culture figures such as singers and actors. Coverage of their actions and their words make up this discourse. Yet, the words of official sources often went unattributed. One article suggested the reason was fear that their dealings with governments might be impaired or relief efforts controlled. This fear, however, is illustrative of the "us" (donors) and "them" (recipients) environment of the African food aid context.

In the *Times*, aid donors were humanitarians. They were the forces of good. "Western conscience dictates that people should not be allowed to starve," one correspondent wrote (November 29, 1984). By contrast, the *Times* assailed recipient African governments for making food political. Quoting an unnamed U.S. aid worker, the *Times* explained that governments inflated food aid needs to divert additional food to urban constituents (December 3, 1984). U.S. aid giving, it seemed, was above the politics of Africa. This point is particularly evident in the *Times*'s coverage of the U.S. reaction to Ethiopia's charges that delays in food pledges were to blame for the devastating impact of the famine.

Ethiopia's accusation that the United States had stalled food aid met with singling out of the country in terms of what was seen as wrong with Africa. What was wrong is that too many African countries were associated with socialism/communism/Marxism. Aid-receiving countries falling into this camp were always identified as such, and stories frequently went on to describe the country's poor agricultural system or government inefficiency. (The most frequently reported constraint in reaching the U.S. food aid goal in Africa was government inefficiency or mismanagement, with 46 mentions or 34 percent.)[41]

Ethiopia was a special case in which the *Times* was particularly critical. *Times* coverage of U.S. food aid sent to Ethiopia used U.S. government

officials (largely unnamed) to criticize the Mengistu regime as an ungrate-
ful, corrupt Soviet ally that placed little priority on feeding its people. As
one headline summed up this position: "[U.S.] Relief Official Accuses
Ethiopia of 'Biting the Hand that Feeds It' " (December 13, 1984).[42]
According to the *Times* sources, Ethiopia's famine was caused by the
country's failed Soviet-inspired collective farming system, corruption,
and mismanagement. The *Times*'s evidence of Ethiopia's low priority on
feeding its people was to cite figures (varying from $3 million to $200 million in news stories) for the celebration of the tenth anniversary of the
revolution that brought Mengistu to power.

This coverage of U.S. food aid sent to Ethiopia represents the movement
of crisis, aid giver, and aid recipient discourses set in a Cold War framework. Each discourse informs the other. As the unfolding crisis was
defined in news stories, the persona of aid giver and aid recipient took
form. It is through the discourse of crisis that the urgent need for human-
itarianism—for food aid—even to governments that were not U.S. allies
became apparent. Once the urgency for food aid was established, the
discourse of aid giver and aid recipient delineated the boundaries of
struggle between East and West in which Africa was a part, but in which
Africans played a small role.[43]

The discourse of the people appears less frequently than the other three.
This discourse of the African poor, of the hungry and of the refugees, is
really about them, not by them. The discourse of the people is one in which
the neediest of the needy were seldom heard, though their photos were
often taken.[44] Of the 134 stories about U.S. food aid sent to Africa, only
a handful of stories used as sources the common person, Africans uncon-
nected to governments or relief agencies.

When the ordinary person does appear in a news story, it is more than
likely in a feature story. Farmers are one such group who did appear in
Times coverage of food aid. This coverage focused largely on how African
farmers were unable to produce enough food, nor import the necessary
agricultural technology from the West to increase their food production
because of constraints put on them by their Marxist governments. In other
feature stories, the *Times*'s use of ordinary persons as sources seemed to
ground the story in an exoticized Africa distant from the West. For
example, one village woman said to live in "a low gumdrop-shaped hut,"
explained, the *Times* correspondent said, "cryptically" why she could no
longer maintain her nomadic way of life. Perhaps more logically than
cryptically, the woman said, "All the animals died because of the drought.
. . . We are here because of the drought. For three years' duration, there

was a drought. We don't have any sheep or goats, and we can't do anything now even if the rains come" (December 27, 1985).

More commonly, news stories assumed the African's perspective, with phrases such as "the people hope it will rain" or "the people are hungry." For the most part, the discourse of the people is one in which Africans appear in the background only to be described or have their situation described for them by Western aid officials or relief workers. For example, women were described as "stick figures" (December 29, 1984) and children seen as "shrunken little old men with no bellies, almost no flesh" (November 10, 1984) or food shortages as tragic and the inability to get aid into certain regions as hopeless or distressful.

Coverage of the people in food aid stories represents Africans as aid dependent and helpless, with little or no control over ensuing food shortages. It is part of the Cold War framework to the extent that coverage used African farmers to explore the inadequacies of agricultural policies in countries with Marxist governments. More indirectly, because the Cold War framework informed news coverage by providing a guiding perspective on African reality, news stories were not likely to draw on the experiences of the ordinary African.

CONCLUSIONS

In 1985, American pop singers proclaimed, "We Are the World." The song, along with Live Aid, Fashion Aid, and dozens of other private relief efforts, signaled a Western awareness of the dramatic nature of poverty and deprivation caused by food shortages. The *Times*'s coverage of the U.S. food aid sent to Africa to relieve those shortages was wide-ranging, examining U.S. food aid in twenty-three countries. But in some ways, the *Times* seemed to suggest that we—the United States—really are the world. In coverage of food aid from 1980 to 1989, the four discourses were part of a Cold War framework in which Africa was merely a context for East and West opposition. Africa was a site of moral victory for the United States. The implication for Africa's media image—or more broadly, the construction of social reality about Africa—is that Africa becomes a secondary player in events that occur within its own boundaries. Africa is reduced to just another trouble spot or basket case where Soviets and Americans vie for power. And Africans are precluded from defining events that affect them and from positioning Africa on its own terms within the world community.

NOTES

1. P. Gill, *A Year in the Death of Africa* (London: Paladin, 1986); R. Hopkins, *The Politics of Food Aid and Food Security in Africa* (paper presented to the annual meeting of African Studies Association, Atlanta, November 1989.

2. A. de Waal, *Famine That Kills* (Oxford: Oxford University Press, 1989); R. Hopkins, *The Politics of Food Aid.*

3. "American Public Opinion Data," *African Hunger* (Louisville, KY: Opinion Research Service, 1985).

4. Subcommittee on Africa of the Committee on Foreign Affairs, House of Representatives, *Emergency Famine Relief Needs in Ethiopia and Sudan* (Washington, DC: U.S. Government Printing Office, 1986); M. H. Glantz, "Drought and Economic Development in Sub-Saharan Africa," in *Drought and Hunger in Africa*, edited by M. H. Glantz (Cambridge: Cambridge University Press, 1987), pp. 37–58; and L. M. Li, "Famine and Famine Relief: Viewing Africa in the 1980s from China in the 1920s," in *Drought and Hunger in Africa*, pp. 415–34.

5. P. Dahlgren and S. Chakrapani, "The Third World on TV News: Western Ways of Seeing the 'Other,' " in *Coverage of International News*, edited by W. C. Adams (Norwood, NJ: Ablex, 1982), pp. 45–65.

6. The influence of the *Times* has been widely noted by scholars and journalists alike. The newspaper is important to U.S. journalism in terms of the kind of readership it has (elites, leaders of opinion, decision makers in governments, journalists, academics, and individuals in business), as well as its ability to set news agendas for regional and local media. See C. Kadushin, J. Hover, and M. Tichy, "How and Where to Find Intellectual Elite in the United States," *Public Opinion Quarterly* 35 (1971): 1–18; C. Weiss, "What America's Leaders Read," *Public Opinion Quarterly* 38 (1974): 1–22; J. Merrill and H. Fisher, *The World's Great Dailies* (New York: Hastings House Publishers, 1980).

7. Stuart Hall, "Introduction," in *Paper Voices: The Popular Press and Social Change*, by A. C. H. Smith, E. Immirzi, and T. Blackwell (Totowa, NJ: Rowman and Littlefield, 1975), pp. 11–24; J. Hartley, *Understanding News* (London: Routledge, 1988).

8. P. Elliott and P. Golding, "Mass Communication and Social Change: The Imagery of Development and the Development of Imagery," in *Sociology and Development*, edited by E. de Kadt and G. Williams (London: Tavistock Publications, 1974), pp. 113–36; Stuart Hall, "The Rediscovery of 'Ideology': Return of the Repressed in Media Studies," *Culture, Society and the Media*, edited by M. Gurevitch, T. Bennett, J. Curran, and J. Woollacott (London: Routledge, 1988), pp. 56–90.

9. Kadushin et al., "How and Where," pp. 1–18; Weiss, "What America's Leaders Read," pp. 1–22; Merrill and Fisher, *The World's Great Dailies.*

10. Walter Lippmann, *Public Opinion* (New York: Harper Colophon Books, 1965), p. 9.

11. O. Stokke, "The Mass Media in Africa and Africa in the International Mass Media—An Introduction," in *Reporting Africa*, edited by O. Stokke (Uppsala: Scandinavian Institute of African Studies, 1971), pp. 9–25; G. Gerbner and G. Marvanyi, "The Many Worlds of the World's Press," *Journal of Communication* 27 (1977): 52–61; S. Peterson, "Foreign News Gatekeepers and Criteria for Newsworthiness," *Journalism Quarterly* 56 (1979): 116–25; C. Pratt, "The Reportage and Images of Africa in Six U.S. News and Opinion Magazines: A Comparative Study," *Gazette* 26 (1980): 31–45; G. C. Wilhoit and D. Weaver, "Foreign News Coverage in Two U.S. Wire Services," *Journal*

of Communication 33 (1983): 132–48; J. B. Weaver, C. J. Porter, and M. E. Evans, "Patterns in Foreign News Coverage on U.S. Network TV: A 10-Year Analysis," *Journal of Communication* 61 (1984): 356–63; W. A. Hachten and B. Beil, "Bad News or No News? Covering Africa, 1965–82," *Journalism Quarterly* 62 (1985): 626–31; and R. L. Terrell, "Problematic Aspects of U.S. Press Coverage of Africa," *Gazette* 43, no. 2 (1989): 131–54.

12. M. A. Fitzgerald, "The News Hole: Reporting Africa," *Africa Report* (July–August 1989): 59–62.

13. B. Kirtz, "Covering Foreign News Is Different Now," *Editor and Publisher* 38 (March 31, 1989): 65.

14. See C. Pratt, "The Reportage and Images of Africa in Six U.S. News and Opinion Magazines: A Comparative Study," *Gazette* 26 (1980): 31–45; G. C. Wilhoit and D. Weaver, "Foreign News Coverage in Two U.S. Wire Services," *Journal of Communication* 33 (1983): 132–48; P. O. Agbese and C. W. Ogbondah, "The U.S. Press and Political Change in the Third World: The Coverage of Military Coups," *Political Communication and Persuasion* 5 (1988): 33–47; and R. L. Terrell, "Problematic Aspects of U.S. Press Coverage of Africa," *Gazette* 43, no. 2 (1989): 131–54. For anecdotal evidence, see M. Rosenblum, *Coups and Earthquakes* (New York: Harper Colophon Books, 1981); D. Lamb, *The Africans* (New York: Random House, 1982); and E. Harriman, *Hack: Home Truths about Foreign News* (London: Zed Books, 1987).

15. R. M. Govea, "East-West Themes in the Reporting of African Violence," *Social Science Quarterly* 64, no. 1 (1983): 193–99; J. E. Fair, "The Analysis of Foreign Assistance Coverage in Five U.S. Publications" (Master's thesis, Indiana University, 1984).

16. de Waal, *Famine That Kills.*

17. Glantz, "Drought and Economic Development," pp. 37–58.

18. R. A. Hackett, "Decline of a Paradigm? Bias and Objectivity in News Media Studies," *Critical Studies in Mass Communication* 1, no. 3 (1984): 236.

19. Stuart Hall, "Introduction," in *Paper Voices*, pp. 11–24.

20. Stuart Hall, "The Rediscovery of 'Ideology': Return of the Repressed in Media Studies," in *Culture, Society and the Media*, 64.

21. Peter Bruck, "Strategies for Peace, Strategies for News Research," *Journal of Communication* 40 (1989): 118.

22. Ibid., pp. 117–18.

23. Ibid., pp. 108–29.

24. A content analysis—the quantitative account of frequency of various items in manifest news content—also was undertaken for this study. The content analysis confined itself to coding the following categories: name of aid recipient country; stated reasons for aid needs; mention of problems/constraints in reaching food aid goals in recipient country; type of news article; dateline/story origination; type of reporter covering story; type of sources used in story.

25. G. Tuchman, *Making News: A Study in the Construction of Reality* (New York: Free Press, 1978); Stuart Hall et al., *Policing the Crisis: Mugging, the State, and Law and Order* (London: Macmillan, 1978); and Hartley, *Understanding News.*

26. Stuart Hall, "Introduction," in *Paper Voices*, p. 15.

27. S. Hall, *Policing the Crisis*, p. 83.

28. C. Lancaster, "Africa's Development Challenges," *Current History* 84, no. 501 (1985): 145–49, 183, 189; P. Schwab, "Political Change and Famine in Ethiopia," *Current History* 84, no. 502 (1985): 221–28; and J. Shepherd, "Ethiopia: The Use of Food

as an Instrument of U.S. Foreign Policy," *Issue: A Journal of Africanist Opinion* 14 (1985): 4–9.

29. S. B. Epstein, "Food for Peace, 1954–1986: Major Changes in Legislation," *CRS Report for Congress* (Washington, DC: U.S. Government Printing Office, April 1987), p. 6.

30. Ibid., pp. 7–8.

31. J. Shepherd, "Ethiopia: The Use of Food as an Instrument of U.S. Foreign Policy," *Issue: A Journal of Africanist Opinion* 14 (1985): 4–9; Schwab, "Political Change and Famine in Ethiopia"; and Li, "Famine and Famine Relief."

32. J. Shepherd, "When Foreign Aid Fails," *Atlantic Monthly* (April 1985): 41–46; and Lancaster, "Africa's Development Challenges."

33. D. C. Hallin, "Cartography, Community and the Cold War," in *Reading the News*, edited by R. K. Manoff and M. Schudson (New York: Pantheon Books, 1987), p. 135.

34. Ibid.

35. R. Astroff and A. Kiste, *"French Voters Were Taken by Surprise When They Elected Mitterand": Discursive Hierarchies and the Construction of Crisis* (paper presented to the Conference on Media and Crisis, Laval University, Québec, October 1990, p. 7.

36. The 134 *Times* food aid articles found and coded for the content analysis were examined for the type of sources interviewed in the news stories. For the news source category, news stories were multiple coded for up to three sources per news item. Of the 209 sources coded, journalists consulted U.S. sources (both government and nongovernment) the most frequently (N = 113, 54 percent). In 73 of the 113 cases (65 percent or 35 percent of the total), only U.S. government officials appear. Officials from international organizations appeared 32 times (15 percent). Africans were the voice in discussing their own problems about 20 percent of the time, with officials from aid recipient countries in Africa and nongovernment sources appearing about 20 times each.

37. By contrast, African countries were the site of story origination in 45 stories (about 34 percent).

38. Reasons for aid giving were multiple coded, with up to three reasons. The total number of reasons stated was 173.

39. de Waal, *Famine That Kills*, pp. 9–32.

40. Countries were multiple coded, with up to four countries per article.

41. Mentions of problems/constraints in reaching foreign aid goals were multiple coded, with up to three problems. The total number was 135.

42. Interestingly, the *Times* devoted news space to the question of whether the United States should send food aid to Marxist countries in Africa. These stories represent how meaning constructed in discourse are fluid and do not set out one single ideological position. The raising of the issue of the United States aiding a Marxist country contradicts the dominant discourse of aid givers as humanitarians.

43. In 1985, coverage of food aid increasingly began to turn away from Africa. More and more, aid stories became personalized stories, focusing on the efforts of celebrities, politicians, and schoolchildren to aid African countries, despite their political leanings.

44. Robert Chambers argues that often the poorest of the poor remain unseen because of spatial, professional, project, person, diplomatic, or seasonal biases that make their poverty go unperceived. See Robert Chambers, *Rural Development: Putting the Last First* (London: Longman, 1983), pp. 1–27.

10

African-American Press Coverage of Africa

Charles A. Bodie

In 1987, members of the African-American press assembled in Detroit for the annual convention of their professional body, the National Newspaper Publishers Association (NNPA). It was the 160th anniversary of the founding of the black press, and they dedicated its program to the earliest black paper, *Freedom's Journal*, launched in 1827 by John B. Russwurm and Samuel E. Cornish.[1] Much of the convention talk centered on economic problems within the press. Little interest was shown in an issue that Russwurm and Cornish had pondered: the responsibility of journalists of African descent toward Africa. Because of this recent anniversary and the attention that Africa commands from Americans in the 1980s and 1990s, an analysis of this issue is particularly appropriate.

Having started their enterprise in an era of ascendant racism, Russwurm and Cornish felt a special obligation to lift the veil of ignorance surrounding Africa. "Useful knowledge of every kind and everything that relates to Africa," they noted in their first issue "shall find a ready admission into our columns; and as that vast continent becomes daily more known, we trust that many things will come to light, proving that the natives are neither so ignorant nor stupid as they have generally been supposed to be."[2] *Freedom's Journal* lasted only a few months, but it left a guide for the black press to follow. How this press has dealt with Africa in recent years provides the focus of this chapter. After surveying its record on this matter, the chapter examines recent trends over four selected years after 1960 and then suggests some possible future directions.

Emerging in the late nineteenth century, when printed news about

African-Americans was largely confined to crime reports in the white press, the successors to *Freedom's Journal* helped to fill the information gaps and bolstered racial pride. The focus was largely on community activities, a tradition that still continues. Before World War I, their coverage of international affairs was thin and mainly confined to Africa and the Caribbean region. In more recent years, this coverage has increased considerably, while the geographic focus has remained the same. Publishing operations were small, and access to foreign news was limited. Between 1865 and 1915, most of the 1,976 papers that started in this period disappeared. In the pages of those that survived, Africa was treated as an afterthought. There were infrequent, ambiguous, and sometimes uncomfortable references to degraded savages, ancient nobility, and people oppressed by colonial rule. The tension that resulted from the conflicting images was not unique to the press. It characterized the discomfort toward Africa in African-American thought at large, as well as the bias of news sources available at that time.[3]

The growth of black urbanization and literacy, and the expansion of a black middle class stimulated a higher newspaper circulation in the 1920s. The Chicago *Defender*, the Pittsburgh *Courier*, the Baltimore *Afro-American*, the New York *Amsterdam News*, and Marcus Garvey's *Negro World* were the leading weeklies. Aside from the *Negro World*, with its global orientation, these papers still published mainly community news. But interest in Africa was growing. World War I had weakened colonialism, and such movements as the Harlem Renaissance and Marcus Garvey's United Negro Improvement Association (UNIA) nourished ancestral pride. Papers reported more often about colonial unrest, oppression in South Africa, and meetings of the Pan-African movement. They included material from the recently formed Associated Negro Press that circulated a small amount of African news, from Africans traveling in the United States, and by dispatches reprinted from other sources.[4] The *Negro World* was exceptional in its reporting on Africa. A Jamaican journalist by training, Garvey saw his weekly as an organ of propaganda for the UNIA. His editors supported rebellious activities in Europe's colonial territories and called on blacks around the world to unite. A number of governments labeled the publication seditious and suppressed it.[5]

Conflicting images endured in the mainstream black press. In at least one case, however, a pro-African approach improved circulation. After Robert Vann of the Pittsburgh *Courier* discerned black anger among his readership toward the Italian invasion of Ethiopia in 1935, he sent writer Joel A. Rogers to the front. Rogers became the only war correspondent in Ethiopia sent by a black weekly, and the first newsman, black or white, to interview deposed Emperor Haile Selassie. His dramatic reports about heroic Ethiopian soldiers boosted the *Courier*'s circulation by around 25,000 copies.[6]

The African story came into its own after World War II, with the spread of independence on the continent, well-publicized United Nations sessions in New York, and the American Civil Rights movement in the 1950s and 1960s. The Associated Negro Press, alert to these changes, made reciprocal agreements to exchange dispatches with African papers and devoted about a fifth of its output to African news. Another news supplier was the NNPA. By the 1950s, some leading papers contained weekly digests of African news, and occasionally correspondents were sent to Africa on temporary assignment.[7] At the same time, because of tighter financial pressures, editors found themselves reexamining their foreign coverage. Among the smaller papers, African stories were less frequent. Others with more capital maintained their former level of coverage, which even increased in the Baltimore *Afro-American*.

The following analysis of three leading papers, the New York *Amsterdam News*, the Norfolk *Journal and Guide*, and the Baltimore *Afro-American*, demonstrates these trends.[8] It is based on a count of African-related items, measurement of the column space devoted to them and the distribution of references to newsmaking nations. The period studied embraces two significant biennia in recent African affairs. In the first one, 1967–68, the devastating Nigerian civil war occurred. In the second, 1975–76, Southern Africa was in the forefront of world news. After Portuguese rule was withdrawn in 1974, a civil war ensued in Angola. In Rhodesia tense negotiations for black rule took place, while in South Africa surface calm exploded in 1976 with the Soweto massacre, followed by months of spreading massive student demonstrations.

As Table 10.1 shows, the *Afro-American* offered the largest number of African stories overall. Its treatment was erratic, however, swinging from a low of 14 items in 1968 to a high of 385 in 1976. It also published relatively longer articles, averaging annually from 14.2 to 17.5 column inches. The sample also reveals a lower incidence of crisis reporting, compared to the white media.[9] On an annual average basis for each paper, crisis reporting amounted to a range of 21 to 28 percent.[10] Most items dealt with such issues as economic development, internal administration, cultural change, and the exchange of visits between American and African leaders. Readers learned about the opening of an airport in Zambia, the loan policies of Kenyan banks, and how Ghanaians assigned names to people.[11] Another feature of the coverage was its broad geographical latitude. The *Journal and Guide*, the smallest of the three papers, carried

Table 10.1
Total Annual African Coverage

Newspaper	Years	No. Items	Column inches	Average Column Size
Afro-American	1967	92	1,484	16.1
	1968	14	245	17.5
	1975	329	4,694	14.2
	1976	385	6,033	15.7
Amsterdam News	1967	69	1,340	19.4
	1968	40	535	13.3
	1975	48	818	17
	1976	67	1,143	17.1
Journal and Guide	1967	40	413	10.3
	1968	22	199	9
	1975	20	228	11.4
	1976	37	537	14.5

news about seventeen nations over the four years. The *Amsterdam News* spotlighted thirty-seven, the *Afro-American* forty-four.[12]

Editors had the choice of a number of news sources. The *Journal and Guide* and *Afro-American* acquired much of their African news from United Press International, a relatively large expense for such capital-thin companies. Other available news suppliers were the National Black News Service, the NNPA, and Novesti, a Russian service. The *Amsterdam News* benefited from contacts within New York City's African community, and one of its lead reporters, Nigerian-born Simon Anakwe, wrote both news dispatches and a wide-ranging weekly column, "Africa Today."[13] Papers also collected news from stringers, many of them African-born.

Prohibitive costs kept editors from stationing their own reporters full time in Africa. However, after the death of Emperor Haile Selassie in 1975, James Hicks, the executive editor of the *Amsterdam News*, flew to Ethiopia and sent back a series of reports. During the same year, John H. Murphy III, president of the *Afro-American*, joined other black journalists on a trip to Ghana to examine that nation's political and economic progress.[14] In 1976, Carlos Russell, a correspondent with the *Amsterdam News*, visited Uganda to evaluate the rule of Idi Amin, while two staff members of the *Afro-American*, Raymond Boone and Moses Newson, traveled to Helsinki and Havana respectively to interview spokesmen for the Movement for the Popular Liberation of Angola (MPLA), the Angolan political party that had won that nation's civil war.[15]

How well did the sampled papers cover the big stories? This analysis reveals that although no consistent correlation existed between stories and extent of coverage, a large story usually elicited more attention. In the late sixties, the most tragic event was Nigeria's civil war. It lasted from 1967 to 1970 and was triggered by the breakaway to its eastern province, Biafra. Attempts by the federal government to regain this area resulted in widespread destruction and a high loss of life, estimated at between 500,000 and 2 million people.[16] Readers learned little of this in the *Journal and Guide*, which offered no editorial reaction and only several brief UPI news items, including an appeal to relieve widespread starvation in Biafra.[17] In the *Afro-American* a total of twelve items about the war appeared, mostly on military activities. Its editorial page was silent, and the paper's regular commentator on Africa, Charles Howard, avoided the Nigerian tragedy in his column.[18] The *Amsterdam News*, with reporter Simon Anakwe, offered the fullest coverage and comment. Anakwe prepared the news dispatches and the reflections in his column from a pro-Biafran position. The paper's editorials conveyed a general sadness about this internecine conflict and urged immediate outside mediation, at first by American black leaders, and later by the United Nations.[19]

As Table 10.1 reveals, during 1975–76 only the *Afro-American* showed significant increase in overall African coverage. In the *Amsterdam News*, the increase was only slight; it declined in the *Journal and Guide*. The chief region of concern was Southern Africa, where the key stories were about oppression versus freedom rather than Africans fighting Africans. For many African-Americans, the struggles for liberation in Angola, Rhodesia, and South Africa evoked memories of their own fight for racial justice in America. When the Republican administrations in Washington linked Southern African issues to strategic American interests, strong black concern was further aroused, both in the press and in other arenas.[20]

The main target of the criticism was Henry Kissinger, at first national security adviser, then secretary of state and, above all, architect of an unpopular Republican Cold War policy. At the beginning of the Nixon administration, Kissinger insisted that America should back its NATO partner, Portugal, in its war against the Angolan rebels. As a result, the administration sent additional assistance that included covert military aid. After the Portuguese abandoned their colony in the following year, the aid continued, now directly to pro-Western rebel forces fighting soldiers of the Marxist-oriented MPLA. Kissinger's "tar baby" policy, as it was derisively termed, drew loud protests and triggered congressional hearings.[21]

Here was a story made to order for the African-American press, but no consistent coverage surfaced in the sampled papers. The *Journal and Guide* ran nothing at all on Angola in 1975, the year of heaviest fighting. In 1976, there was one UPI news item, several columns, and an editorial that delivered the paper's lone statement on the issue: "The civil war in Angola and other African countries," it said in part, "is due to the rivalry of colonial powers for supremacy in the rape of Africa for their personal economic aggrandizement, always at the expense of the natives."[22] The *Amsterdam News* did scarcely better. In 1976, it aired the controversy over efforts by Roy Innis, head of the Congress of Racial Equality, to recruit mercenaries to join pro-Western rebels. It also printed an article by Congressman Charles Diggs of Michigan, who argued against American involvement in the civil war.[23]

In comparison, the *Afro-American* delivered a torrent of words on military activities, Kissinger, and Angola's future. Dispatches from news services were frequent. It ran front-page stories prepared by its staff critical of both American intervention and that of South Africa, whose troops entered Angola against the MPLA in late 1975.[24] Besides denouncing America's general opposition to liberation movements in the Third World, editorials labeled Kissinger's approach in Angola a "mad folly." The U.S. government, they charged, was hypocritical to condemn Russian advisors and Cuban troops on the side of MPLA forces in Angola in view of its own covert aid to anti-MPLA factions and the stationing of American troops around the globe. "Instead of crying about Russian and Cuban involvement," an editorial advised, "the U.S. should become involved in helping whatever government is in power to solve some of its problems."[25]

Following the military success of the MPLA, the Baltimore paper campaigned in 1976 for the United States and United Nations to recognize the group as the legitimate government of Angola. Staffers joined other black journalists for interviews with the MPLA, first in Helsinki and later in Havana. After spending time with the Angolans, Moses Newson wrote of being favorably impressed by "these freedom-loving realistic people . . . now moving into the tough business of nation-building." When American officials stalled on recognizing the MPLA in the months ahead, the paper continued its campaign, adding to the swelling chorus of criticism of Kissinger's Angolan policy.[26]

By the middle of 1976, with black rule imminent in Rhodesia and Mozambique and with South Africa in a state of war with youthful protestors, press attention shifted toward other areas of Southern Africa, especially toward the hated land of apartheid. Over the years, coverage of South Africa had outranked that of other countries on the continent (see

Tables 10.2 and 10.3). With its long history of racial separation, it had been an affront to nonwhites around the world. Its troops had entered Angola. The Pretoria government had resisted international calls to lift its mandate rule over South West Africa, now the independent nation of Namibia. Then, in mid-1976 it revealed the naked power of apartheid policy by reacting brutally to student demonstrations.[27]

On June 16, school children in the overcrowded township of Soweto demonstrated against mandatory study of the Afrikaans language. They were met with police guns and dogs. The resulting massacre was a sharp jolt to black Americans. On television the scenes of dead and injured youth, flailing police batons, and snarling dogs revived memories of Southern brutality of summers past. This event aroused mass student protests in South Africa that lasted through the rest of the year and resulted in further casualties. Black leaders in the United States were galvanized into new attacks on America's relationship with South Africa as a close ally and corporate partner.[28] All three papers, led by the *Afro-American*, issued news dispatches and editorial comment.[29] Still angry over the Angola fiasco, they attacked U.S. foreign policy in South Africa as morally bankrupt and irrational. And with the Pretoria government at war with its black majority, papers turned up their heat on South Africa.

The *Afro-American* published a story on the country in nearly every issue, spotlighting, among other matters, its "plunder" of Namibia, the pettiness of apartheid laws, protests among black miners, and the likelihood of a racial upheaval.[30] In an abundant spate of copy on police violence against demonstrators, the paper vividly detailed the rioting, while photographs depicted the dead and injured. "[T]he Soweto explosion," one editorial cautioned, "is a brutal, bloody reminder for the world that time is running out on the status quo and 'good face' program in South Africa." In one of his syndicated columns, Roy Wilkins, president of the National Association for the Advancement of Colored People, warned that because of their own oppressive blanket of self-censorship, South African "whites will continue to live in a fool's paradise. They will know what causes future Sowetos but they may not say so."[31] As for future American policy, editors listened warily when Secretary of State Kissinger issued public comments. After he called in September for the end of apartheid "in a reasonable time," the *Afro-American* suspected a possible American deal with South Africa's Prime Minister John Vorster. Would Kissinger offer continued American support of the regime for an indefinite period if Vorster stopped backing the white government in Rhodesia and surrendered control over South West Africa? The paper adamantly opposed any compromises with South Africa. For the rest of the year, it grew more

Table 10.2
Percentages of Selected Nations as Newsmakers, 1967, 1968

	N = References	% of References			
		Congo/ Zaire	Nigeria	Rhodesia	South Africa
1967					
Afro-American	92	13	10	5	12
Amsterdam-News	69	1.5	26	1.5	2.9
Journal and Guide	40	10	12.5	5	35
1968					
Afro-American	14	7	21	0	14
Amsterdam-News	40	0	53	0	5
Journal and Guide	22	4.5	18	9.1	18

N = the base number, the total number of African-related items in each paper for that year

Table 10.3
Percentages of Selected Nations as Newsmakers, 1975, 1976

	N = References	% of References			
		Angola	Mozambique	Rhodesia	South Africa
1975					
Afro-American	329	7.5	2.4	3.6	11
Amsterdam-News	48	2.1	4.2	0	8.3
Journal and Guide	20	0	15	25	0
1976					
Afro-American	385	13	2	8.1	14.5
Amsterdam-News	67	4.5	1.5	9	39
Journal and Guide	37	16.2	0	5.4	37.9

N = the base number, the total number of African-related items in each paper for that year pessimistic about the chances of bringing about substantive reform in South Africa through American pressure.[32]

What does this analysis say about the recent relationship of the black press and Africa? Considering the changes since World War II in American society and in African politics, it is not surprising that newspapers revealed a shift in tone. The earlier ambivalent attitude toward the continent had disappeared. Pride, engendered by the new context of African independence movements, had replaced shame and romantic idealization. In the new reality, black Africans were attempting to chart their own courses. When the new context delivered upbeat news, papers were quick to report it. "Tanzania Takes First Steps Towards Economic Freedom," an *Afro-American* headline trumpeted in 1967. But pride did not blind editors to the momentous problems of nation-building. Crisis headlines were also given play, news of corruption aired.[33] By the 1960s, with more abundant news sources, editors could inform readers on a broad range of topics.

Racial pride and the availability of news shaped the position of black editors toward crisis reporting. As noted earlier, crisis stories were less frequent than in the white press. Overall story content reflected an apparent desire to achieve balance rather than highlight bad news. When they reported the latter, African-American papers tended to view it as the bitter fruit of colonialism and racism. Africa was beset, in fact, with neocolonialism, they insisted. Columnist Charles Howard hammered this theme often in the 1960s. He blamed army coups on the Western "lust" for Africa's natural resources. He derided American foreign aid as a form of "economic colonialism." In Howard's view, much of the violence in Africa amounted to "white folks fighting over black folks' money."[34] The idea of American neocolonialism came under increasing attack during the Kissinger era at the State Department. According to the sampled papers, his misconceived African policy subordinated the interests of Africans to Cold War concerns. Large allocations of military aid created prolonged warfare and led to stalemate in the case of Angola. In an essay published in the *Amsterdam News*, Lewis Clayton Jones bitterly concluded that U.S. policy amounted to "let[ting] Africans kill each other."[35]

Considering their economic problems, the fact that a few papers such as the *Afro-American* and *Amsterdam News* devoted extended column space to these stories is itself remarkable. No black paper has been a picture of health over the past thirty years. This medium operates in an arena of high mortality with low capital, high turnover of staff, and aging equipment. Social changes and developments in publishing have also threatened it. For one, the process of integration has added competition. As the dominant white media increased minority hiring, black publishers found it more difficult to hold their own reporters. And as coverage of the nonwhite world improved in the white media, the African-American public was given more choices for information—choices further enlarged by magazines, radio, and television. Meanwhile, the flight of middle-class readers from the inner cities to the suburbs has undercut the traditional financial base of many black papers. In the face of these threats, editors revealed an impressive commitment to African coverage by their willingness to run lengthy articles rather than succumb to cost-cutting measures.[36]

Future trends do not encourage optimism that this coverage will continue. Fighting rough economic seas, a number of papers have foundered. Others survive by adjusting their sails. In 1987, the *Journal and Guide* filed for bankruptcy after being held by a succession of recent owners. At the *Afro-American*, following a state of editorial drift, a new management took over in 1988 with ideas of redesigning content. In 1990, the *Amsterdam News* was still publishing in New York as the leading black paper of the city, though its circulation was only half what it was in the 1950s.[37] Among editors at large, much discussion centers on the need for more investigative reporting and analysis rather than offering news available in the white press. Their priorities are still on community matters, an outlook that may further reduce African coverage.[38] More and more of this coverage will likely come from magazines and the electronic media. Whether these news sources will inform African-Americans in the manner of papers such as the *Afro-American* of the mid-1970s remains to be seen.

NOTES

1. Mark Fitzgerald, "The black press celebrates its 160th birthday," *Editor & Publisher* 120 (June 27, 1987): 14–15.

2. Quoted in Herbert Aptheker, ed., *A Documentary History of the Negro People in the United States* (New York: Citadel Press, 1951), p. 84.

3. Armistead Scott Pride, "Negro Newspapers: Yesterday, Today and Tomorrow," *Journalism Quarterly* 28 (Spring 1951): 179–88. For information on the coverage of Africa in the black press, see Charles A. Bodie, "The Images of Africa in the Black American Press, 1890–1930" (Ph.D. diss., Indiana University, 1975), esp. chaps. 1 and 4.

4. Bodie, "The Images," chap. 4. On the Associated Negro Press, see Lawrence D. Hogan, *A Black National News Service: The Associated Negro Press and Claude Barnett, 1919–1945* (Rutherford, NJ: Fairleigh Dickinson University Press, 1984).

5. In the United States, the *Negro World* was censored in a government report, though not banned. Tony Martin, *Race First: The Ideological and Organizational Struggles of Marcus Garvey and the Universal Negro Improvement Association* (Westport, CT: Greenwood Press, 1976), pp. 91–100.

6. Andrew Buni, *Robert L. Vann of the Pittsburgh Courier: Politics and Black Journalism* (Pittsburgh: University of Pittsburgh Press, 1974), pp. 244–48. The Ethiopian conflict is considered a "watershed event" in the black press by Henry Lewis Suggs. See

Suggs, *P. B. Young, Newspaperman: Race, Politics and Journalism in the New South, 1910–1962* (Charlottesville: University of Virginia Press, 1988), pp. 116–17.

7. Richard L. Beard and Cyril E. Zoerner II, "Associated Negro Press: Its Founding, Ascendancy and Demise," *Journalism Quarterly* 46 (1969): 50–51; Armistead S. Pride, "Emergent Africa and the Negro Press," *The Nation* 177 (November 7, 1953): 370; and "Ethel Payne's Lead Story," *Washington Post* (June 14, 1982), pp. C1, 6.

8. These papers were selected both for their likelihood of African reporting and for being representative of the African-American press. In the period studied, the *Amsterdam News*, with a national and local edition, had a weekly circulation of about 60,000; the *Afro-American* with a national and four local editions, about 120,000; the *Journal and Guide* with only one edition, about 29,000.

9. One study of three white papers randomly sampled on news of Ghana and Tanzania between 1965 and 1982 revealed a crisis reporting average of about 40 percent. See William A. Hachten and Brian Beil, "Bad News or No News? Covering Africa, 1965–1982," *Journalism Quarterly* 62 (Autumn 1985): 626–30.

10. The following crisis themes were adopted from a list by James L. Larson: unrest and dissent; war, terrorism, and crime; coups, assassinations, and disasters. See Larson, *Television's Window on the World: International Affairs Coverage on the U.S. Networks* (Norwood, NJ: Ablex, 1984), p. 45.

11. *Afro-American* (August 12, 1967): 16; (May 3, 1975): 16; and *Journal and Guide* (October 18, 1975): 2.

12. Small regions were not left out. Even French Somaliland, Burundi, and the Seychelle Islands received attention. See *Afro-American* (August 12, 1967): 16; (May 3, 1975): 16; and *Journal and Guide* (October 18, 1975): 2.

13. Anakwe usually profiled a different nation each week. After May 1967, he wrote increasingly on the Nigerian conflict. See *Amsterdam News* (July 1, 1967): 16; (July 22, 1967): 17; (September 30, 1967): 17; (December 23, 1967): 17; (March 9, 1968): 15; and (October 12, 1968): 9.

14. *Amsterdam News* (September 3, 1975): 1, 5, 10; (September 24, 1975): 1, 3, 5; (October 1, 1975): 10; *Afro-American* (December 6, 1975): 16; (December 13, 1975): 16; and (December 20, 1975): 16.

15. *Amsterdam News* (November 13, 1976): 10; (November 20, 1976): 11; (December 4, 1976): C9; *Afro-American* (February 14, 1976): 10; (March 6, 1976): 1, 2; and (March 12, 1976): 1, 12.

16. On Nigeria's civil war, see T. C. McCaskie, "Recent History of Nigeria," in *Africa South of the Sahara 1990*, 19th ed. (London: Europa Publication Ltd., 1990), p. 765.

17. *Journal and Guide* (June 15, 1967): 2; (June 22, 1967): 3; (September 9, 1967): 2; (December 30, 1967): 3; and (August 17, 1968): 7.

18. For examples of *Afro-American* coverage, see (June 10, 1967): 20; (June 15, 1967): 11; (December 2, 1967): 1. Howard's columns include (June 1, 1967): 20; (September 30, 1967): 20.

19. For news coverage in the *Amsterdam News* see (June 3, 1967): 2; (September 7, 1967): 27. Editorials include (July 1, 1967): 16; (May 27, 1967): 16. For Anakwe's columns, see (July 22, 1967): 17; (September 9, 1967): 17; and (September 30, 1967): 17.

20. For a discussion of African-American interest in Southern Africa during the 1970s, see Henry F. Jackson, *From the Congo to Soweto: U.S. Foreign Policy Toward Africa Since 1960* (New York: William Morrow and Company, 1982), chap. 4.

21. Ibid., chap. 2.

22. *Journal and Guide* (January 10, 1976): 6; (April 10, 1976): 8. In her column

written in Washington, D.C., Alfreda Madison wrote about the congressional hearings on U.S. African policy in 1976. See (January 10, 1976): 8; and (April 3, 1976): 9.

23. Readers of the *Amsterdam News* in 1975 found neither news coverage of Angola nor editorial comment. Only two columns addressed the conflict. See (December 13, 1975): 5; and (December 20, 1975): 5. As for 1976, see (January 16, 1976): 5; (March 6, 1976): 5; and (March 27, 1976): 1, 12.

24. For examples of news dispatches in the *Afro-American* see (August 16, 1975): 16; (August 23, 1975): 16; (September 13, 1975): 16. Managing editor, Moses Newson wrote several front-page news stories critical of U.S. policy. See (December 27, 1975): 1, 2; and (March 12, 1976): 1, 12.

25. *Afro-American* (January 3, 1976): 4; (January 10, 1976):4; (March 13, 1976): 4; and (May 22, 1976): 4.

26. *Afro-American* (March 6, 1976): 1, 2, 16; (March 12, 1976): 1, 2, 16; (April 3, 1976): 4; (May 22, 1976): 4; (June 5, 1976): 4; (September 18, 1976): 16; and (December 4, 1976): 4.

27. For a summary of recent South African history, see Jackson, *From the Congo*, chap. 7.

28. Ibid., pp. 244–47.

29. *Journal and Guide* (July 24, 1976): 1; (August 21, 1976): 1; (August 28, 1976): 1, 9; (December 4, 1976): 1, 8; *Amsterdam News* (June 26, 1976): 4; (August 25, 1976): 4; (August 26, 1976): 1, 4, 5, 6; and (November 27, 1976): 4.

30. For example, see *Afro-American* (January 3, 1976): 21; (April 10, 1976): 16; and (May 29, 1976): 1, 2.

31. For examples of news coverage, see *Afro-American* (June 19, 1976): 1, 2; (July 3, 1976): 1, 2; and (August 14, 1976): 1, 6. For editorial reaction and comment from columnists such as Roy Wilkins and Vernon Jordan, see (May 29, 1976): 4; (June 26, 1976): 4; and (September 4, 1976): 4.

32. *Afro-American* (September 11, 1976): 4; (October 16, 1976): 4; and (November 6, 1976): 4.

33. *Afro-American* (April 22, 1967): 20; *Journal and Guide* (August 9, 1975): 1, 2; *Amsterdam News* (January 6, 1968): 2.

34. *Amsterdam News* (April 8, 1967): 20; (July 1, 1967): 20; (July 24, 1967): 20; (September 30, 1967): 20; (October 14, 1967): 20; (November 4, 1967): 20; (December 2, 1967): 20; (December 23, 1967): 16; and (December 30, 1967): 20.

35. *Amsterdam News* (December 20, 1976): 7.

36. From 1945 to 1969 the following declines were reported: the *Courier*, from a national circulation of approximately 257,000 to 48,798; the *Defender*, from 202,000 to 69,778; the *Afro-American*, from 137,000 to 119,902; and the *Journal and Guide*, from 64,368 to 29,313. By 1970 two new circulation "giants" had arrived, *Mohammed Speaks* (at least 400,000) and the *Black Panther* (110,000). See L. F. Palmer, Jr., "The black press in transition," *Columbia Journalism Review* 9 (Spring 1970): 31, 32; Henry La Brie III, "The Black Press," *Editor & Publisher* 117 (March 31, 1984): 12–15.

37. On the decline of the *Journal and Guide*, see Suggs, *P. B. Young*, pp. 187–91; *Washington Post* (October 17, 1987), p. C5. On the *Afro-American* see *Washington Post* (November 14, 1988), pp. WB5, 6. On the *Amsterdam News* see *New York Times* (August 17, 1987), pp. B1, 2.

38. On the recent trends in the African-American press, see La Brie, "The Black Press," pp. 12–15; Mark Fitzgerald, "Threatened with Extinction?" *Editor & Publisher* 119 (August 30, 1986): 11–12.

11

New York Times Coverage of Africa, 1976–1990

Hassan M. El Zein and Anne Cooper

The New York Times ranks as one of the best papers in the world, not just in the United States. John Merrill and Harold Fisher count it among the planet's fifty "great dailies."[1] As the platinum bar of American journalism, the *Times*'s prestige has long rested partly on its highly regarded foreign coverage.

As Merrill and Fisher state, "The quality and completeness of the *Times*'s international coverage is directly traceable to eyewitness reporting by its large foreign staff."[2] In 1990, the *Times* had thirty-one correspondents—nine of them women—working out of twenty-six foreign bureaus. In addition, the paper's coverage is the product of about twenty staff members on the foreign desk in New York, and the resources of all the major wire services. In 1990, the *Times* received its twenty-fourth Pulitzer Prize for foreign correspondence—none of which, however, was won for African coverage.

This chapter tries to determine whether the *Times*'s reputation for overall excellence in foreign correspondence carries through to the African continent, where the *Times* has four bureaus: Cairo in the north, Nairobi in the east, Johannesburg in the south, and Abidjan in the west. By scrutinizing fifteen years of *Times* content, we judge how four correspondents are handling the job of covering fifty-one countries.

The *Times*, with a circulation in 1990 of about 1,057,000, sells fewer copies than *USA Today* or *The New York Daily News*. What the *Times* says, however, has greater impact than any U.S. newspaper.[3] *Times* correspondents are "accorded treatment equal to the U.S. ambassador's," while "public figures avoid direct challenges to *Times*'s judgments" because they fear its power.[4] Moreover, to a great extent, the *Times* sets the agenda for America's media. The Associated Press, *Time, Newsweek*, ABC, CBS, and NBC—all headquartered in New York, the U.S. communications capital—rely heavily on *The New York Times*. Indeed, the *Times* and CBS work together on conducting polls. At CBS and NBC headquarters, "research files are based largely on *Times* clippings," meaning field reporters know that "their product will be checked by editors against the *Times*'s product at headquarters."[5]

The *Times* serves as the hometown newspaper for Northeast decision makers in many fields, including the representatives of 166 nations stationed at New York's United Nations headquarters. The New York Times News Service sends some *Times* stories farther afield, reaching half the readers in the United States. And the ubiquitous New York Times Index has a further rippling effect in spreading the *Times*'s influence. Finally, *Times* stories have a global reach when they appear in *The International Herald Tribune*, owned by *The Washington Post* and *The New York Times*. The *Tribune*'s facsimile transmission facilities permit printing at eight sites, from which copies are distributed to 164 countries. In 1986, according to a *Tribune* brochure, the average household income of readers was $82,700, of whom 38 percent had post-university graduate degrees.

Of the *Times*'s thirty-one foreign bureaus, only thirteen are in the Third World, where more than 70 percent of the planet's population live. This imbalance and other issues related to the power of Western mass media began to concern some Third World leaders in the 1960s. By the end of the 1960s, the Third World had the numerical power to bring such concerns regarding mass media to a public forum.

In 1970, the first resolution regarding mass media appeared on the agenda of the United Nations Educational, Cultural and Scientific Organization (Unesco). (See Table 11.1.) Then in 1972, the Soviet Union and Byelorussia introduced a resolution requesting the director-general to prepare a declaration on "the fundamental principles governing the use of the mass media." Only the United States voted against it, establishing a pattern whereby "the Soviet Union capitalized on [Third World] dissatisfaction."[6] The arguments on the resolution and other matters that ensued came to be called the New World Information Order (NWIO) debate. One result was an intense research focus on the reporting of news from the Third World, including Africa, in the mass media of the United States.

Table 11.1
The New World Information Order Debate, 1970–1990

1970	Unesco 16th General Conference, Paris The first resolution regarding mass media is placed on the agenda.
1972	Unesco 17th General Conference, Paris The first resolution on the "use" of mass media is presented.
1974	Unesco 18th General Conference, Paris Amadou Mahtar M'Bow of Senegal is elected new director-general.
1976	Unesco 19th General Conference, Nairobi MacBride Commission appointed; IAMCR multi-country media study requested. (First Unesco meeting in Africa.)
1978	Unesco 20th General Conference, Belgrade Resolution on "contribution" (not "use") of mass media is passed.
1980	The MacBride Commission report, *Many Voices, One World*, is released.
1981	Western media representatives, meeting at Talloires, France, issue declaration supporting free flow of ideas.
1984	The United States withdraws from Unesco
1985	Unesco 23rd General Conference, Sofia, Bulgaria The United Kingdom and Singapore withdraw from Unesco; absence of these three members costs Unesco one-third of its budget.
1987	Unesco 24th General Conference, Paris M'Bow steps down; Federico Mayor of Spain is elected director-general, vowing to deemphasize NWIO.
1989	Unesco 25th General Conference, Paris
1990	State Department report affirms U.S. decision to stay out of Unesco. United Kingdom also affirms decision, but will reassess situation in one year.

RELATED STUDIES

When the 1976 Unesco General Conference at Nairobi deadlocked over the Soviet/Byelorussian resolution, it passed other resolutions that eventually resulted in two projects: a report by a special commission and a multimedia, multicountry content analysis of foreign news coverage that included *The New York Times*. The study, which analyzed two weeks' media coverage in 1979, found that *The New York Times* devoted 39 percent of its general news pages to foreign stories. Among U.S. papers, the *Times* ranked just below *The Washington Post* (42 percent) and ahead of *The Minneapolis Tribune* (30 percent), *The Los Angeles Times* (25 percent), and *The New York Daily News* (19 percent).[7]

A more recent study by Michael Emery also ranked the *Times* just below *The Washington Post*. However, differing definitions, procedures, and time frames resulted in a much smaller percentage devoted to foreign news: 3.3 percent. For the period November 6, 1987, to January 6, 1988, *The Christian Science Monitor*, with 15.1 percent, ranked head and shoulders above the *Times* and *The Washington Post* (5.4 percent). To its credit, the *Times* carried many more foreign stories (1,021) than the down-sized *Monitor* (579). The *Times* had by far the largest correspondent corps among the ten papers studied.[8] Emery commends the *Times* for offering "the most evenly distributed" foreign news, by having the most stories not dealing with the hot spots of the moment.[9]

Of the many arguments and assertions of the NWIO debate, two lend themselves well to research: (1) that news of the Third World is infrequently reported and (2) when reported, it is laden with conflict and crisis. In the words of a North African active in the debate, Mustapha Masmoudi of Tunisia, the Western media "present these [Third World] communities—when indeed they do show interest in them—in the most unfavorable light, stressing crises, strikes, street demonstrations, putsches, etc., or even holding them up to ridicule."[10]

The New York Times fares well when one considers overall Third World coverage. W. A. E. Skurnik found that more than half of the paper's total foreign news coverage was about the Third World.[11] But what about Africa specifically? Of six newspapers that Anthony Bonnah-Koomson studied during 1977–88, *The New York Times* gave the most—501—separate mentions of African countries south of the Sahara in news stories.[12] *The Washington Post* was a close second, with 492 mentions over twelve years; and *The Los Angeles Times* was third with 454 mentions.

But end-product studies tell only part of the story. How does the news of Africa get selected or rejected on its way to American audiences? Cleveland Wilhoit and David Weaver took a random sample of a five-day constructed week from stories filed by Associated Press reporters working in Africa south of the Sahara during 1981. This process yielded 44 dispatches from nine countries. When AP's New York editors chose stories to send out on the regional wire to client media, only five countries remained in the pool: Nigeria, Ethiopia, Tanzania, Zimbabwe, and South Africa. However, after a sample of Indiana editors chose stories to actually put in their newspapers, only *one* country remained: South Africa.[13]

Do gatekeepers at elite newspapers select differently from editors at smaller Indiana newspapers? In the six elite newspapers Koomson studied during 1977–88 only six countries received more than 5 percent of the news items: Zimbabwe, 14.2 percent; Ethiopia, 8.1 percent; Angola,

7.1 percent; Kenya, 5.5 percent; Uganda, 5.5 percent; and Mozambique, 5.2 percent.[14] Why such unevenness?

Jeff Charles, Larry Shore, and Rusty Todd used three noncontent variables—trade, telecommunications traffic, and population—to try to explain *New York Times* coverage of eighteen Southern African nations for the first six months in 1960, 1965, 1970, and 1975. The authors found strong correlations between trade and news coverage (.84) and population and news coverage (.72).[15]

American journalism seems to have a penchant for negativism. Jack Haskins, who calls American readers "bad news bears," concluded that negativity, disaster, or "bad" news "appears to be overselected from the real world."[16] Since 1950, bad news has continued to represent about one-third of news content, with good news also representing about one-third.[17] Barbara Hartung and Gerald Stone found that bad news dominated page one, but that good news predominated on the inside pages of seven of the eight California dailies they studied.[18]

Applying these principles to Africa, Koomson found 54.7 percent of reported events to be noncrisis oriented, and 45.3 percent to be crisis oriented.[19] Similarly, William Hachten and Brian Beil found 40 percent of African stories to be related to crisis events.[20] Using Haskins' figure of about 33 percent negative news as a norm, some overselection of negative news from Africa does seem to occur. But without a real-world referent, it is hard to say whether negative events are being overselected in the case of Africa, or whether a large number of crises are in fact occurring. Wilhoit and Weaver provided that referent in the research on the gatekeeping "funnel" that stretches from Africa to Indiana.

Their study found that stories "reporting violent conflict were twice as likely to appear in the regional wire news about Africa than in trunk news."[21] In other words, the 44 dispatches from reporters in the field covered various topics—diplomatic relations, racism, independence movements, and conflict. However, the editors in New York overselected negative news items to send on to their U.S. clients. Thus the charge of Masmoudi and other critics about Africa's "unfavorable light" does appear to have some validity.

Drawing on the findings of these previous studies, African coverage of *The New York Times* over a period of fifteen years is analyzed next to see if the NWIO debate affected content. The study explores the following questions:

1. Has the volume of stories about Africa increased or declined over the past fifteen years? Has this news of Africa taken up a greater or smaller portion of the foreign news hole?

2. Which countries are highly visible, moderately visible, and invisible?

3. How much African news is crisis oriented? Has the proportion of such news increased or decreased over fifteen years?

4. What kind of news from Africa will find its way onto page one? Crisis news? Or other topics?

METHOD

Bernard Berelson defined content analysis as "a research technique for the objective, systematic and quantitative description of the manifest content of communication."[22] This study analyzed the content of twelve issues of *The New York Times* from each of three years—1976, 1981, and 1985—and issues from January to June 1990.[23]

We started with 1976 because Africa's prominence in the NWIO debate grew especially strong that year. Following the election of Amadou Mahtar M'Bow of Senegal as Unesco's director-general, African voices were accorded more attention. A symbol of African strength was the choice of Nairobi, not Paris, as the site for the 1976 Unesco general assembly. The year 1981 was chosen as the time when the Western backlash against Third World (including African) demands regarding media coverage gained the strength of a movement. A meeting in Talloires, France, that year produced a declaration supporting the free flow of ideas. The year 1985 was chosen as the depth of the chasm between the First and Third Worlds. On the heels of Ronald Reagan's reelection in November 1984, the United States withdrew from Unesco. The United Kingdom and Singapore did likewise in 1985.

In 1987, African nations fought hard to keep M'Bow, the first African to hold a top U.N. post, as Unesco's director-general. However, Unesco's executive board, prompted by the Soviets (who control six of its fifty votes), chose instead to nominate Federico Mayor of Spain. Despite Mayor's reform efforts, the Bush administration decided, in a report released April 16, 1990, to stay out of Unesco.[24] The year 1990 is a good time to reassess the NWIO, since the First/Second/Third World axis which gave it birth is ceasing to exist. Mayor has made it clear that "the only thing in dispute is the wording of the [NWIO] eulogy."[25]

After pulling the sample issues, coders followed these guidelines:

1. Unit of analysis: the news story, including photographs, headlines, and graphics. As in most similar analyses, coding was confined to the news pages, eliminating sports, business, and lifestyle sections.

2. Unit of measurement: column inches in a six-column newspaper format, with a conversion factor used for four and eight columns.[26]
3. Placement: front-page position, which means that gatekeepers accorded prominence to the story, was compared with position on any other news page.
4. Nation: a total of fifty-one nations as set forth in the *Hammond Ambassador World Atlas* (1982) was used to define Africa.
5. Content categories: ten categories, adopted from those used by James Larson, were developed.

Crisis news includes (1) unrest and dissent, (2) war, terrorism, and crime, (3) coups and assassinations, and (4) natural and man-made disasters. Noncrisis news includes (5) political-military, (6) economic, (7) technology-science, (8) environment, (9) human interest, and (10) miscellaneous.[27] A reliability test of thirty randomly selected articles yielded an 80 percent agreement between one test coder and the main coder, and an 83 percent agreement with a second test coder.

RESULTS AND DISCUSSION

Because data for only half of 1990 was available at this writing, and thus is not comparable to the full-year data for 1976–85, the 1990 results are discussed in the text, not displayed on tables.

1. *Volume/proportion of African news.* Table 11.2 shows no clear, steady increase or decrease in the number of stories during 1976–85, but rather a zig-zag pattern. The percentage of the international news hole varied, but stayed between 15 and 20 percent. Table 11.2 also reveals that story length increased steadily, good news for readers who want more information.

Table 11.2
Proportion of Total African News out of Total International News Hole in *The New York Times*

		(Column-Inch)			
Year	*N*	*AFN col/inc*	*INTN col/inc*	*Percent*	*Ave. Length AFN Story col/inc*
1976	52	573.57	3176.46	18.06	11.03
1981	41	582.87	3871.87	15.05	14.22
1985	57	928.21	4808.08	19.30	16.28

N = total number of stories
AFN = African news in column inches
INTN = international news in column inches

Table 11.3

New York Times Coverage of Africa by Country: Number of Stories and Length in Column Inches, 1976–1985

Country	N	1976 col/inc	N	1981 col/inc	N	1985 col/inc
1. Angola	11	106.29	2	30.24	0	
2. Egypt	8	41.98	11	214.86	10	214.65
3. S. Africa	9	124.17	3	60.34	30	499.54
4. Kenya	4	102.29	1	13.44	1	37.48
5. Rhodesia	9	71.53	0		0	
6. Eritrea	1	6.62	0		0	
7. Mauritania	1	7.56	1	13.86	0	
8. Ivory Coast	1	18.72	0		0	
9. Sudan	1	24.65	2	26.46	2	46.34
10. Namibia	1	1.26	4	45.36	0	
11. Rwanda	1	18.28	0		0	
12. Madagascar	1	2.20	0		0	
13. Ethiopia	1	3.78	0		5	74.34
14. General	3	44.24	0		0	
15. Algeria	0		2	17.67	0	
16. Senegal	0		2	19.32	0	
17. Zimbabwe	0		1	2.10	0	
18. Libya	0		6	118.22	3	19.32
19. Morocco	0		3	11.76	1	3.78
20. Central Africa	0		1	4.20	0	
21. Uganda	0		1	1.68	1	10.08
22. Seychelles	0		1	3.36	0	
23. Nigeria	0		0		2	7.14
24. Mozambique	0		0		1	3.78
25. Ghana	0		0		1	11.76

N = number of stories

For the first six months of 1990, the trend of increased story lengths continued; indeed, the average story doubled in size (from 11.03 inches in 1976 to 22.07 inches in 1990) over fifteen years. In 1990, the percentage of the news hole devoted to Africa stayed within the 15 to 20 percent range, at 16.2 percent.

2. *Visible/invisible countries.* Table 11.3 shows that during 1976–85, a total of only twenty-five countries received any coverage—less than half of the fifty-one that comprise Africa. But just a handful of those got the lion's share of attention. Notwithstanding some variation year by year, the high-profile countries (those with a total of more than five stories) are Angola, Egypt, South Africa, Kenya, Rhodesia (Zimbabwe), Sudan, Namibia, Ethiopia, and Libya.

In 1990, South Africa was by far the most visible nation, with seven stories appearing in just six months. Tunisia, where the Palestine Liberation Organization has its headquarters, ranked second. Liberia and Libya ranked third. The only other countries mentioned, with one story each, were Ethiopia, Morocco, Uganda, and Zimbabwe.[28]

3. *Negative/crisis news.* Table 11.4 shows a remarkable surge in crisis news. The year 1976 registered a crisis orientation of 53.8 percent of stories—somewhat higher than the findings of Hachten and Beil[29] of 40 percent and Koomson of 45.3 percent.[30] However, the proportion zoomed upward substantially in 1976, with 73.2 percent crisis stories. Then it escalated again, to an amazing 87.7 percent crisis orientation in 1985.

That trend reversed itself in the first half of 1990; the nineteen stories on Africa veered visibly away from crisis topics. Indeed, the 1990 figures of 57.1 percent crisis and 42.1 percent noncrisis topics hark back to those for 1976, a reversal of the bad news trend that peaked in 1985. The high profile of political change in South Africa, including an entire page of stories (no ads) on February 14 titled "South Africa's New Era," accounted for the noncrisis emphasis.

In no year does the catchphrase "coups and earthquakes" apply, because no coup stories and few natural disaster stories appeared.[31] The negative stories were almost entirely reports on unrest/dissent and war/terrorism/crime.

Table 11.4
Distribution of Crisis and Noncrisis Themes of African News in
The New York Times

	1976			*1981*			*1985*		
	col/inc	*N*	*Percent*	*col/inc*	*N*	*Percent*	*col/inc*	*N*	*Percent*
Crisis Themes									
1. Unrest & Dissent	200.96	20	35.04	282.76	20	48.51	556.20	37	59.92
2. War, Terrorism, Crime	31.24	4	5.45	140.09	9	24.03	212.50	10	22.89
3. Coups & Assassinations	—	—	—	—	—	—	—	—	—
4. Disasters	18.31	4	3.19	2.52	1	0.43	57.54	3	6.20
		53.8%			73.2%			87.7%	
Non-Crisis Themes		46.2%			26.8%			12.3%	
5. Political-Military	219.60	20	38.29	157.50	11	27.02	61.97	5	6.68
6. Economics	34.34	2	5.99	—	—	—	—	—	—
7. Environment	44.47	1	7.75	—	—	—	—	—	—
8. Technology-Science	—	—	—	—	—	—	—	—	—
9. Human Interest	24.65	1	4.30	—	—	—	40.00	2	4.31
10. Miscellaneous	—	—	—	—	—	—	—	—	—
		N = 52			N = 41			N = 57	

N = number of stories

Table 11.5
Distribution of Crisis and Noncrisis Themes of African News on
Page One

	1976		1981		1985	
	col/inc	*Percent*	*col/inc*	*Percent*	*col/inc*	*Percent*
Crisis Themes						
1. Unrest & Dissent	34.73	70.02	50.01	57.35	97.60	61.76
2. War, Terrorism, Crime	3.17	6.39	37.19	42.65	52.40	33.16
3. Coups & Assassinations	—	—	—	—	—	—
4. Disasters	—	—	—	—	—	—
	80%		100%		90%	
Non-Crisis Themes	20%				10%	
5. Political-Military	11.70	23.59	—	—	8.03	5.08
6. Economics	—	—	—	—	—	—
7. Environment	—	—	—	—	—	—
8. Technology-Science	—	—	—	—	—	—
9. Human Interest	—	—	—	—	—	—
10. Miscellaneous	—	—	—	—	—	—
	N = 6		N = 5		N = 10	

N = number of stories

4. *Page one coverage.* Africa did not find its way onto *The New York Times*'s front page very often, but when it did, the headlines almost always told of unrest, war, terrorism, or crime (see Table 11.5). The year 1985 proved the most newsworthy for the continent, with ten front-page stories appearing in the sampled issues. Only two noncrisis stories (both about political/military matters) made page one in the 1976–85 period. The high percentages of crisis stories were 80 in 1976, 100 in 1981, and 90 in 1985. In light of Hartung and Stone's discovery about the negative tone of most front pages, the finding about Africa is not surprising, although pronounced.[32]

In 1990, only one story from the continent made page one, about the prospects for the end of white rule in South Africa, accompanied by a photograph of Nelson Mandela returning to Soweto (February 14). This noncrisis story fell into the political/military category.

CONCLUSIONS

The press, wrote Walter Lippmann, "is like the beam of a searchlight that moves restlessly about, bringing one episode and then another into vision."[33] *The New York Times*—with its four African bureaus, its large news hole, and its tradition of excellence in foreign coverage—represents the best day-by-day coverage of Africa readily available to U.S. readers. The depth of its coverage, judging from story lengths that increase year by year, deserves praise. But this best of searchlights seems magnetized, pulled consistently back and forth between a handful of countries; it shines occasionally on some others, but leaves the rest of the continent in the dark.

For the years 1965–82, Hachten and Beil compared the events in Ghana and Tanzania as recorded in *Keesing's Contemporary Archives* with coverage in *The New York Times* and two other newspapers. They found that more than half the coverage occurred in 1965, even though events continued apace in these nations.[34] This study corroborated their findings. In fifteen years, in our sampled issues, only one story appeared about Ghana and none about Tanzania.

Ghana and Tanzania "disappeared" in the late 1960s. Zimbabwe/Rhodesia "disappeared" in the late 1970s. In 1976, Rhodesia was the second most visible country, after Angola; but after that, as Zimbabwe, no more stories appeared until one cropped up in a sampled issue of 1990. However, most countries (about half of the continent) have never had even this kind of brief turn in the spotlight.

The quality of coverage when the spotlight does shine on a country is important. Based on this study's findings, more economic, environmental, science, and human interest news ought to be reported. In the realm of political news, the tide has clearly turned for South Africa, which may result in more political coverage of other nations on the continent. But we need to remember that a country whose troubles make the news has at least secured a place on the media agenda. Many nations' troubles (let alone triumphs) do not break the news glass ceiling because gatekeepers deem those nations unimportant.[35]

The sin of commission pales in importance when compared with the sin of omission. Hachten and Beil state that the invisibility of many African countries "is far more serious and disturbing than the outdated polemics of Masmoudi and other proponents of a New World Information Order."[36]

When *The New York Times* conveys invisibility, readers go without information. Beyond this loss for individuals, invisible countries themselves may suffer because of the *Times*'s reach, and who the *Times* reaches. An incomplete picture of Africa could influence collective decisions, such as those regarding public and private investment.

If American readers have trouble relating to foreign concerns, Andrew Torchia reminds us that reporters also have to work at "overcoming the barriers to understanding that, after all, make us correspondents so foreign."[37] What can an elite newspaper do so that its reporters, gatekeepers, and, eventually, readers find news about Gabon and Malawi as "newsy" as news about Libya and Liberia? Some modest proposals:

• Add another correspondent, preferably in an interior nation, to bring the total to five (ten countries per bureau).

• Choose desk editors who have lived and worked in Africa and who will not easily dismiss regions wholesale due to unfamiliarity.

• Train future journalists—especially desk editors—for sensitivity to overseas issues.

• Educate news consumers to demand more quantity and variety in Africa coverage.

With twenty years of hindsight, we have learned that NWIO criticism did not have much effect on how elite newspapers cover the news. Since 1976, we have not seen *The New York Times* devote a progressively greater proportion of the news hole to Africa; devote a progressively smaller proportion of the news hole to crisis news from Africa; or put progressively greater emphasis on economic, science, and human interest news. In any case, Unesco's conscious effort to bury the NWIO makes the point moot.[38] The demands of subscribers, much more than critics from overseas, will bring change, if change is to come.

NOTES

1. John C. Merrill and Harold Fisher, *The World's Great Dailies: Profiles of 50 Newspapers* (New York: Hastings House, 1980).

2. Ibid., p. 223.

3. Carol Weiss, "What America's Leaders Read," *Public Opinion Quarterly* 38 (1974): 1–22.

4. Russ Braley, *Bad News: The Foreign Policy of The New York Times* (Chicago: Regnery Gateway, 1984), p. 571.

5. Ibid., p. 570.

6. C. Anthony Giffard, *Unesco and the Media* (White Plains, NY: Longman, 1989), p. 20.

7. Annabelle Sreberny-Mohammadi, "The 'World of the News' Study," *Journal of Communication* 34, no. 1 (1984): 121–38.

8. Michael Emery, "An Endangered Species: The International Newshole," *Gannett Center Journal* 3, no. 4 (1989): 151–64.

9. Ibid., p. 162.

10. Mustapha Masmoudi, "The New World Information Order," in *Current Issues in International Communication*, edited by L. John Martin and Ray Hiebert (New York: Longman, 1990), p. 312.

11. W. A. E. Skurnik, "A Look at Foreign News Coverage: External Dependence of National Interests?" *African Studies Review* 24, no. 1 (March 1981): 99–112.

12. Anthony Bonnah-Koomson, "News of Africa South of the Sahara in Six U.S. Newspapers, 1977–1988." (Ph.D. diss., Ohio University, 1991).

13. G. Cleveland Wilhoit and David Weaver, "Foreign News Coverage in Two U.S. Wire Services: An Update," *Journal of Communication* 33 (Spring 1983): 145.

14. Koomson, "News of Africa."

15. Jeff Charles, Larry Shore, and Rusty Todd, "The New York Times Coverage of Equatorial and Lower Africa," *Journal of Communication* (Spring 1979): 152–53.

16. Jack Haskins, "What We Know about Bad News," *Third World Annual Communication Symposium: A Proceeding*, Vol. 3 (Knoxville: College of Communication, University of Tennessee, 1980), p. 157.

17. Ibid., pp. 152–57.

18. Barbara Hartung and Gerald Stone, "Time to Stop Singing the Bad News Blues," *Newspaper Research Journal* 1 (February 1981): 21.

19. Koomson, "News of Africa."

20. William Hachten and Brian Beil, "Bad News or No News? Covering Africa 1965–1982," *Journalism Quarterly* 62, no. 3 (1985): 626–30.

21. Wilhoit and Weaver, "Foreign News Coverage," p. 145.

22. Bernard Berelson, *Content Analysis in Communication Research* (Glencoe, IL: Free Press, 1952), p. 18.

23. The first step in sampling was to select a week within each month. This was done systematically, choosing the first week in January, the second week in February, the third in March, and so forth. The second step selected days of the week by random sampling. The six days of the week, Monday through Saturday, excluding Sunday, were presented on folded papers to a person who was asked to pick one number, which randomly determined the day to be selected for the specific week. The Sunday paper was excluded because it was a much larger issue including different sections that required greater in-depth reporting and treatment of news and features hardly comparable to the effort spent on the daily issues and as such fell beyond the scope of analysis in this study.

The days chosen from the year 1976 were Saturday, January 3; Monday, February 9; Thursday, March 18; Saturday, April 24; Tuesday, May 4; Wednesday, June 9; Monday, July 19; Thursday, August 26; Friday, September 3; Saturday, October 9; Saturday, November 20; and Monday, December 27.

For the year 1981, the chosen days were Thursday, January 1; Thursday, February 12; Tuesday, March 17; Thursday, April 23; Thursday, May 7; Saturday, June 13; Wednesday, July 15; Tuesday, August 25; Thursday, September 3; Wednesday, October 14; Monday, November 16; and Thursday, December 31.

And the days chosen for the year 1985 were Monday, January 7; Friday, February 8; Tuesday, March 19; Monday, April 29; Thursday, May 2; Thursday, June 13; Saturday, July 20; Friday, August 30; Monday, September 2; Thursday, October 10; Monday, November 18; and Tuesday, December 24.

The days chosen for the first half of 1990 were Wednesday, January 3; Wednesday, February 14; Thursday, March 29; Friday, April 27; Tuesday, May 8; and Tuesday, June 12.

24. Robert Pear, "U.S. Won't Rejoin UNESCO, Deriding Agency as Inept," *New York Times* (17 April 1990), p. 1.

25. Arthur Ross and Edward C. Luck, "The Man Struggling to Reform UNESCO," *Christian Science Monitor* (27 October 1989), p. 19.

26. Microfilm photocopies were reduced, and the researchers had to use a formula to ensure that the column inch on the microfilm equated to the space of the actual column inch in the real issue of *The New York Times*. The number of columns on a page also differed. The 1976 issues used an eight-column format, while some of the issues in 1981 used a four-column format. However, the standard format adopted after 1981 by the paper was the six-column format. A formula was adopted to justify the uniformity of measurement of the width of the newspaper.

27. James Larson, *Television's Window on the World* (Norwood, NJ: Ablex, 1984), p. 45.

28. The following events accounted for the high profile of various countries in the years under study: In 1976, Angola dominated the news from the continent. Following its independence from Portugal in 1975, the country suffered from internal crises and racial tensions. In Rhodesia, the independence movement made that country the second most covered, along with South Africa, also in the news for freedom demonstrations and unrest.

On October 6, 1981, President Anwar al Sadat of Egypt was assassinated in Cairo, followed by the confirmation on October 13 of Vice President Hosni Mubarak as Sadat's successor. By early November, more than 700 people were officially cited as having been arrested. The trial of the assassins opened November 21. In addition, Egypt's relations with Israel kept the nation in the news. Libya came into the limelight in 1981 when a conflict with the United States developed over territorial waters in the Mediterranean. On August 24, American Sixth Fleet fighters intercepted Libyan aircraft on forty-five occasions. Quadaffy accused the United States of aggression.

In 1985, South Africa moved to center stage. President P. W. Botha announced a state of emergency in thirty-six districts, mainly covering black townships in the Transvaal and eastern Cape provinces. There were widespread demonstrations against apartheid, especially serious in June and July. In September, blacks at seven mines went on strike over pay issues. Ethiopia also received coverage in 1985 because of the devastating famine. Coinciding with stories of suffering and of relief efforts, news about an airlift of more than 7,000 Ethiopian Jews to Israel was revealed in early 1985.

As the new decade opened, South Africa came center stage again with the release of Nelson Mandela in February 1990. News from South Africa became largely political, involving speeches and negotiations. Elsewhere on the continent, however—notably in Ethiopia and Liberia—rebel incursions made for crisis news.

29. Hachten and Beil, "Bad News or No News?"

30. Koomson, "News of Africa."

31. Mort Rosenblum, *Coups and Earthquakes* (New York: Harper, 1981).

32. Hartung and Stone, "Time to Stop Singing," p. 21.

33. Walter Lippmann, *Public Opinion* (New York: Macmillan, 1922, repr. 1961), p. 364.

34. Hachten and Beil, "Bad News or No News?" pp. 626–30.

35. Charles, Shore, and Todd, "The New York Times Coverage," pp. 152–53.

36. Hachten and Beil, "Bad News or No News?" p. 629.

37. Andrew Torchia, "Assignment: Africa," *Columbia Journalism Review* (May/June 1981): 41.

38. Ross and Luck, "The Man Struggling," p. 19.

III

The Southern African Story

12

Inkatha: Notions of the "Primitive" and "Tribal" in Reporting on South Africa

Lisa Brock

INKATHA AND THE MEDIA

Since early 1984, a sweeping and far-reaching challenge—unprecedented in its continuity and resilience—to the white minority government of South Africa has been underway. Well-coordinated antiapartheid actions and police repression of them reached such intensity by the summer of 1985 that a state of emergency was declared by the government. In Natal Province, members of the organization known as Inkatha, based on the scattered land sites of the Bantustan Kwazulu, began to attack members of the newly formed multiethnic and multiracial United Democratic Front in August 1985. The South African *Weekly Mail* commented, "An unprecedented wave of terror is sweeping the Durban townships of Umlazi and KwaMashu where hordes of armed warriors are purging the townships of United Democratic Front sympathizers."[1] *The Weekly Mail* estimated that three people were killed by the "impis" (feared nineteenth-century Zulu soldiers) in late September.[2]

There has been a correlative rise in Inkatha attacks and in mass antiapartheid activity since the summer of 1985. On the one side, antiapartheid forces have garnered solid international support and protest has become more widespread inside South Africa, even in the traditionally conservative Bantustans. This has compelled the apartheid government to make unparalleled reforms. On the other side, an estimated seven thousand people have been killed in Natal since 1985, most of them members or sympathizers of established antiapartheid organizations and most killed in clashes with Inkatha.[3] In the middle of the summer of 1990, Inkatha was permitted by the government to hold a rally in the Transvaal Province, an area with traditionally no Inkatha support. Since that time, killings have increased in the Transvaal, especially in the township of Soweto, as well as in Natal.[4] The ten days between August 17 and August 26, 1990, saw an estimated five hundred people killed in Soweto.[5]

News coverage of the killings involving Inkatha peaked in the United States after the release of Nelson Mandela in February 1990. In a review of television coverage by ABC, CBS, and NBC from January to May 1990, there were no stories about the Natal violence, per se, in January. In February and March there were ten stories per month, and in April there were twelve stories. This coverage should be viewed against a decrease in coverage of Mandela since the period of his initial release. Natal stories in February were one-tenth of South Africa coverage while they were one-fourth of the stories in March. In *Newsweek* between March 1990 and August 1990, five out of the six stories on South Africa were about the conflict in Natal. Television news reports of fighting in the Transvaal were almost daily between August 17 and August 26.

A content analysis of the three major television news networks, the top three news journals (*Newsweek, Time*, and *U.S. News and World Report*), as well as twelve most widely read newspapers (representative of different regions in the United States) reveals the specific concepts commonly used to describe the conflict between Inkatha and what appears to be African National Congress (ANC), United Democratic Front (UDF), and the Congress of South African Trade Union (COSATU) members and supporters. First, news reports have largely portrayed the conflict between Inkatha and antiapartheid activists as "black-on-black violence," "tribal violence," or "factional fighting." Inkatha's leader, Gatsha Buthelezi, is often depicted as "chief of South Africa's 7 million Zulus." Actual combat is often presented only as violence. Events are described as "bloodbaths" and spates of "senseless killings." Natal has been named "the valley of death" in which these "Zulu wars" are being waged.[6] The following passage is from *Time* magazine:

The slaughter began with an incident all too familiar in South Africa's seething black urban townships. Returning from a Sunday drinking session in a local shebeen, or pub, a noisy group of Xhosa migrant workers from the grim, single sex hostels of Tokoza township clashed with a crowd of Zulu rivals. Insults were traded, weapons brandished. When the dust settled, a man lay dead. Some said the victim was a Zulu killed by Xhosas, others a Xhosa killed by Zulus. In the end it hardly mattered: the murder unleashed tribal-based animosities that date back centuries and have claimed 4,000 people over the past three years. . . . [R]oving bands of Zulus set houses on fire and attacked fleeing residents with guns, spears, and butcher knives. Whole villages fled in terror as Zulu impis went on the warpath kicking up dust with their traditional war dances and waving sticks, pangas and stabbing spears.[7]

The presentation of the complex situation in South Africa as "tribal" is striking. Indeed, Inkatha is an organization made up of people of Zulu descent and one of its stated goals, among many, is to preserve Zulu heritage.[8] However, its stated membership is argued at approximately one million of South Africa's six to seven million people of Zulu descent. Its roster is impressive but it clearly does not have the ethnic mandate. Moreover, there is evidence that Buthelezi as head of state of Kwazulu and chief of its police has secured Inkatha membership by making it impossible to get a job or travel visas in Kwazulu without an Inkatha membership card.[9] It is also known that much of the fighting in Natal has been Zulu against Zulu.[10] Witnesses have testified that Inkatha has been assisted by the South African police in attacking antiapartheid activists. In fact, the most recent reports indicate that Inkatha members are actually being trained by South African military units in a camp near Swaziland. Reports also imply that South African backed forces from the region— RENAMO (Mozambique National Resistance Movement), UNITA of Angola, and the special police counterinsurgency unit operating in Namibia, Koevet (literally, "crowbar")—have been integrated into Inkatha ranks.[11] In July 1991, *The Weekly Mail* printed government documents that clearly revealed that Buthelezi and his Inkatha Freedom Party had consistently received money from the South African government over the previous few years.

Buthelezi has taken important political positions markedly different than those of the ANC. He has been willing to work within the apartheid Bantustan system as chief of Kwazulu. He has lobbied widely against sanctions in the international arena.[12] He asserts that he and his organization stand against armed struggle, uphold a free enterprise system, and he has been quoted as saying that he believes in some form of ethnically constructed future South Africa.[13] The ANC, the UDF, and COSATU have advocated the right of armed struggle against apartheid, have encouraged sanctions and nationalization of certain aspects of the economy, and strive for an integrated and nonracial South Africa.[14] Inkatha's disputes with the ANC, UDF, and COSATU are clearly more ideological and political than they are ethnic.[15]

Second, media use of a racial armature—if blacks fight other blacks, then it is factional or "black on black"—is similarly pointed. Do reporters presume there should be total ideological unity among Africans and differences are aberrations? The recent ideological discord in Eastern Europe and the Soviet Union were never once, to my knowledge, coined as "white on white" violence by American media sources. Groups in Europe were viewed as angry citizens fighting a government that they perceived as undemocratic. The internal clashes were portrayed as struggles between those who supported the unpopular leaders and those who did not, or between those who had opposing views about the future direction of the new governments. Why has South Africa, which is at a similar historical crossroads, been depicted so differently? Indeed, apartheid is a racial system and so racial paradigms are likely. However, it is also an economic, political, and social system. The press would do well to see apartheid as a political system in which race is a tool of repression.

Similarly, even though the ethnic components were visible in struggles in Eastern Europe and did receive media attention, they were not defined by the press as tribal. Neither did we get the level of graphic descriptions of bloodbaths and violence. Use of these terms in association with the use of tribal and without thoroughly situating it within political struggle, is boldly analogous to descriptions one finds in late-nineteenth-century depictions of European colonial confrontation with African societies or of Native American struggles with pioneers over land.

The root causes of the violence, rather than isolated sensational terms, would better explain the fighting. Migrant labor, the core of apartheid, has torn families apart and left large segments of the South African population in poverty. Unemployed and undereducated youths are often left to their own psychological and physical defenses. These social conditions often breed gangs and persons who may engage in misdirected violence. It can also hurl the least strong into arrant desperation and rank opportunism. The media have generally failed to link violence to poverty, unemployment, or gangs. Neither have they compared "tribalism" to ethnic or racial scapegoating which has been common in multiethnic industrialized countries.

It appears acceptable in the American media to view Africans, as well as many other non-Western peoples, as groups who live in tribes and/or individuals whose worldviews are prescribed by tribal definition. William Artis, in an examination of news stories of the 1960s Nigerian-Biafran war, found what he termed a *tribal fixation* in American press interpretations.[16] Additionally, in a review of abstracts for six major daily newspapers— *The New York Times, The Wall Street Journal, The Atlanta Constitution Journal, The Boston Globe, The Christian Science Monitor* and *The Los Angeles Times*—I found the words *tribe* or *tribal* employed to describe native Americans, Africans, Asians and other peoples of non-European descent in 235 out of the total of 250 times that it was used between January 1989 and April 1990. Thirteen of the other fifteen times it was used to describe the British rock band "The Tribes."[17]

THE "TRIBAL" CUSTOM AND ETHNIC REALITIES

Interpretations by individual media personnel—staff reporters, editors, and news producers—are reflective of long-established Western custom. Morton Fried notes that the term *tribe* itself is "rooted in the general lexicon, and entrenched in the technical vocabulary of anthropology and other social sciences."[18] It emerged at the turn of the century as the conventional description in the West of non-Western societies. Before the French Revolution, *tribe* and *nation* had been interchangeable to define groups who had a common ancestry, history, language, and culture, and usually lived in a common territory.[19] The development of modern nations in Europe and the United States during the eighteenth and nineteenth centuries with their concomitant industrial capitalism led the League of Nations after World War I to redefine *nation* as "nation-state" with territorial titles being more important than common ancestry.[20] Because Africans at that time had been defeated by Europe and had no internationally recognized claims to land, the term *tribal* continued to be utilized to describe their societies whose boundaries did not coincide with colonial territories. This became customary in spite of a lack of consensus among scholars about what characteristics actually distinguish a "nation-state" from a "nationality," or an "ethnicity."[21]

To the term *tribe* were added notions informed by colonial expansion, social Darwinism, eugenics, biological racism, segregation, and anthropologists' studies of "primitive" societies. *Tribe* evolved not simply as a word in the American vocabulary but as a concept with companion images. African tribes were first seen through the eyes of early explorers and missionaries who sent back pictures and diaries of the "dark continent" to magazines such as *National Geographic*. Even when sympathetic or paternalistic, these versions portrayed Africa as an uncivilized continent.[22] A passage from the accounts of a naval expedition in Africa during World War I illustrates this view: "These particular Nile blacks are shiftless, vain, noisy, and warlike. Their villages are clusters of grass huts, like gigantic beehives. These savages own fine herds of cattle and flocks of goats, but they use the cattle for currency. So many cows buy a wife. They drink the milk, but it is very unwise for a white man to do so."[23] Victorian ideals of the over-sexualized African meshed with the myth of the "Black rapist" in the American mind.[24] Significantly, one of the first photographs printed of an African in a popular American magazine was that of a bare-breasted Zulu woman in the 1896 issue of *National Geographic*. Its publication was controversial. It was "the first picture of a bare-breasted woman in the magazine."[25] The biological racists of the period exploited such images to bolster their deductions that people of African descent were inferior.

The African as primitive and all people of African descent as inferior became associated with the primordial characteristics of tribes. The primordial societies lacked advanced political systems and were presumed barbarous.[26] Their motives were more instinctual than rational and very little that they did was perceived as calculated or long range. The 1878 *Encyclopedia Britannica* definition of the Negro for decades influenced the thinking of Americans. Following is part of this definition and a quote of Walter Francis Wilcox, chief statistician of the U.S. Census Bureau in 1911:

Nearly all observers admit that the Negro child is on the whole quite as intelligent as those of other human varieties, but that on arriving at puberty all further progress seems to be arrested. . . . The intellect seemed to become clouded, animation giving place to a sort of lethargy, briskness yielding to indolence. We must necessarily suppose that the development of the Negro and white proceeds on different lines. . . . It is more correct to say of the Negro that he is nonmoral than immoral. All social institutions are at the same low level, and . . . seem to have made no perceptible advance except under the stimulus of foreign influences.[27]

The mental constitution of the negro is . . . normally good-natured and cheerful, but subject to sudden fits of emotion and passion during which he is capable of performing acts of singular atrocity, impressionable, vain. . . . [A]fter puberty sexual matters take the first place in the negro's life and thoughts.[28]

Tarzan and cowboy-and-Indian movies helped fuel and popularize this image of people of non-European descent. In the movies, Indians warred against pioneers because they were savages not because their land had been appropriated. Similarly, when Africans rose up in Kenya with the Mau Mau revolt, they were initially painted as blood-thirsty savages in the media, killing just to be killing, not as anticolonial guerrillas who had made a conscious decision against British colonialism. That the media continues to utilize the *tribal* concept to describe events in Africa should be challenged. The term is not a neutral one. The term continues to conjure up deep-seated, stereotypical, and incorrect images of the African reality.

In fact, blanket use of the term *tribe* in the African context has fallen into such disfavor with anthropologists and political scientists that *ethnic-*

ity is now the preferred term, and there is no general consensus on the evolution or role of ethnicity in Africa. The boundaries of today's African states were created in the colonial era without regard to ethnic cohesion. During the 1960s, the Organization of African Unity (OAU) supported the retention of colonial frontiers as boundaries of the independent states. The policy was based on the belief that new nationalisms ignited during the anticolonial struggles had replaced ethnic identities. Civil and regional conflicts and border disputes have illustrated that ethnicity when combined with socioeconomic issues can impose itself. The OAU continues to wrestle with this policy today.[29] Further, scholars are pointing out that ethnicity today in Africa is not the unadorned result of cultural inertia.[30] During colonial rule, ethnic clusters were pitted against each other via access to education, employment, or in pursuit of other privileges, and traditional ruling lineages were often propped up within colonial administrations.

The term *tribal* is particularly unsettling when engaged in the South African context. Both African nationalism and ethnic distinctions were transformed and entrenched by white rule. The formation of the African National Congress in 1912 as the first sustained multiethnic organization on the continent is evidence of national consciousness. The steady integration of the African majority into a centralized economy kindled that political process. South African governments and private industries, in an effort to diffuse class and racial unity, have tried to sharpen ethnic distinctions in the workplace, in the townships, and in the Bantustans. Ethnic considerations were used as a tool in organizing the labor force into job categories. Migrant laborers from one ethnic group, working as scabs, were often used to undercut wages of more permanent workers. Ethnic distinctions continue to be made by industries, even in the housing arrangements of migrant laborers.

South African nurturing of all potential divisions has guaranteed the continued flow of profits from the migrant labor system and sustained the operation of white minority rule. Since the early part of the century, South African administrations have promoted ethnic organizations. Zulu identity, for example, was given new life during the 1920s and the 1930s. After being defeated in 1879, the Zulu royal lineage was encouraged to form new Zulu associations in Natal to push "traditional" values. According to Shula Marks, such organizations, although not all their members, acted as bulwarks against radical movements. In fact, there were two ANCs and two Industrial and Commercial Workers Unions (ICUs) during the 1920s in Natal. One Natal ICU branch was largely a Zulu organization.[31] Buthelezi situated his Inkatha as heir to these earlier organizations.

Creation of the Bantustans was the most grand of all schemes by the South African government to manipulate ethnicity and undermine unity. It not only served to physically separate the African majority but also created leaders and bureaucrats who have an economic stake in maintaining ethnic structures. Buthelezi, as chief of Kwazulu, some analysts say, is currently in fear of losing his power base if the ANC should set the direction for a post-apartheid South Africa. Violent conflict may be one way for him to secure a place at the negotiating table. Ethnicity in today's South Africa is in large part a consequence of three hundred years of white minority policy.

A CONVERGENCE OF AGENDAS?

Current characterizations of Inkatha and the conflicts in Natal and the Transvaal as tribal raise important questions. In their attempt to capture the news—which they fondly view as objective—the media are perpetuating ahistorical and stereotypical notions. One word can have great impact when that word is rooted in a body of historical, social, and cultural thought. It takes on added significance when that pattern has been based on racial or ethnic degradation. Walter Lippmann said that "the news is not a mirror of social conditions but the report of an aspect that has obtruded itself."[32] Based on this view, some reporters may defend their reporting on Inkatha. They may argue that fighting has increased in South Africa at the very time that a post-apartheid future is being negotiated. Inkatha has thrust itself onto the scene at the very time when a clear field is most needed. It is therefore news.

But the concept *tribal* does little to explain Inkatha excesses since 1984. Therefore, why has it been utilized? Who decides which words, phrases, and images are to reflect the entire scope of unfolding social processes? Phil Harris points to the development of Western news agencies that have come to dominate the international news industry.[33] He found that news agencies emerged in much the same way as other capital enterprises in the nineteenth and twentieth centuries. They competed for markets but agreed on well-defined spheres of influence. Today, these monopoly agencies— Associated Press, Reuters, and United Press International—control much of the flow of information throughout the world. Information, to them, has always been a commodity to be packaged, marketed, and sold. Their goal is to reach the widest audience possible. Harris contends that "the majority of the world's news media rely on the definitions of reality provided by these few Western news agencies."[34]

Curious about the depth of western dominance, Unesco convened a conference in Berlin in 1978. With more than thirty countries present, representatives discovered that Western countries hoard technology, maintain information monopolies, and control the generation and dissemination of information. Participants from developing countries reported that it was very difficult for them to influence the amount of news coverage given their areas or the types of news stories produced by Western agencies.[35] They had even less control over the ways in which their nations were depicted in Western news coverage. Paul Harrison and Robin Palmer noted that "despite the fact that we can receive live television pictures from anywhere in the world there is often less informed coverage today than there was two decades ago."[36] Gil Onwochei determined that "African news stories were predominantly about wars, political unrests and natural disasters."[37] Anthony Ayeni detailed in a content analysis of ABC news coverage of Nigeria between 1974 and 1983 that "certain subject matters covered were stereotypical in the choice of news stories aired, indicating a negative coverage."[38]

The Western media create the images, the phrases, the paradigms that encapsulate African affairs. Because most operate as capitalist industries, they are concerned first with marketing the news. Making use of well-established American images is a time-tested marketing technique. Like the myth of the Old West, or Grant Woods's "American Gothic," a "tribal" and "uncivilized" Africa has a comfortable place in American lore. Massaging such notions is probably easy, convenient, and marketable. "Go with what you know" is the rule of thumb. Yet, the media can and do become image makers. They can create the "Latino pusher," the "Black male thug," and as Edward S. Herman and Gerry O'Sullivan have recently illustrated, they can create the "Arab terrorist."[39] Joanmarie Kalter indicates that image making is accomplished partly through exclusion of stories that would contradict the standard perception.[40]

Why has the image of tribal warfare in South Africa become the most persistent image from South Africa since the release of Nelson Mandela? Reesom Haile, among others, argues convincingly in his study of coverage in the United States that news is generated in the national interest. Global political and economic interests are served by having certain news reflected in the Western media.[41] The economies of all Western countries, which are dominated by banks and industries, are thoroughly integrated into the South African economy. Large capital investments date back to the late 1880s when the gold mining industry was floated. Multinational capital flow continued unabated until the recent sanctions and divestment movement led to some interruption. Most Western economies, however, remain tied to South Africa. Is it to the benefit of multinationals and

Western governments, which included industrialized South Africa, to have this period in South Africa understood as a country at tribal war with itself?

Portrayals of Buthelezi as a Zulu chief and the struggle between Inkatha and antiapartheid activists as tribal clearly serve the policy objectives of the South African government. This image bolsters the faulty arguments for a continuation of the homeland policy. It also lends credence to the minority rights proposal currently under discussion by the National Party. Under this arrangement, blacks would not be designated as a majority but as a group of national minorities whose political status would weigh equally against the white minority.[42] Most recently the white government of de Klerk has floated a constitutional proposal that would base elections at the local and national levels on equal representation of the top three parties. For instance, if in a given province the National Party won 15 percent, the Conservative Party 10 percent, and the ANC 75 percent, all three parties would have equal power. Even the presidency would not be the prerogative of the majority, but rather a coalition based on the same model.

The South African government also gains from publicity of the fighting in Natal and now in the Transvaal, especially if much of it is viewed as random and ethnically based. It raises doubts in the international community about the capabilities of black rule. For those who are against change, it gives them an excuse to stall. For those who are sympathetic, but ignorant of South African history and influenced by Western racism, it may sway their previously held positions. These Americans may normally be against apartheid but the chaos of tribal bloodshed seems as much, if not more, of a travesty. The South African government benefits most by undermining support among this segment.

The media prominence of Buthelezi has been beneficial to the West as well. Over the last few years, Buthelezi has been pushed to the fore as a leader acceptable to the interests of the apartheid government, multinationals, and some Western administrations. His views against sanctions and the armed struggle and in support of privatization have permitted newspapers sympathetic to the National Party such as the *Citizen* to characterize Buthelezi as a friendly leader.[43] Similarly, Western leaders such as Ronald Reagan, George Bush, and Margaret Thatcher met with Buthelezi long before they were prepared to meet and speak with the ANC. They have consistently attempted to establish him in the press as a leader of equal stature to Nelson Mandela. However, the motivations of Buthelezi have yet to be seriously examined by the media in light of recent information that he has been on the payroll of the apartheid government.

The image of tribal warfare reflects a convergence of market policy of news makers with the interest of powerful corporations, white South African leaders, and Western racial mythology. Whether individual staff reporters realize it or not, the image of a tribal South Africa is not objective reporting. The images of irrational, tribal, primordial inclinations, however, do provide the smoke and mirrors. Comparisons between increased violence in South Africa and other national liberation movements at similar junctures in their histories have yet to be made. Inkatha, its origins, and implications have yet to be seriously examined.

NOTES

1. *Weekly Mail* (Johannesburg), September 13–19, 1985.

2. Ibid.

3. *Report of the Indicator Project of Social and Development Studies* (Durban: University of Natal, March 1989), cited in *New York Times*, March 5, 1989. Allister Sparks, "S. Africa's Inkatha Dealt Setback: Buthelezi Confidant Resigns High Post in Zulu Organization," *Washington Post*, June 2, 1990.

4. "Factional Violence Intensifies Near Johannesburg: Toll at 156," *Philadelphia Inquirer*, August 17, 1990.

5. ABC, CBS, and NBC news networks reported consistently during this period. Five hundred was the figure on "McNeil/Lehrer News Hour," August 24, 1990.

6. Phrases derived from a detailed review of *Television News Index and Abstracts* prepared by Vanderbilt University from January to June 1990 and a review of twelve top circulating newspapers and the three top circulating news journals during the same time. For example, headlines: Christopher Wren, "Neutrality Has Its Dangers in the Blood Feuds of a South Africa Province," *New York Times*, April 22, 1990; "South Africa: Black vs. Black Torture," *Newsweek*, April 30, 1990; "South Africa: A Black vs. Black Bloodbath," *Newsweek*, August 27, 1990; "Rival Zulus Renew Fight in South Africa: Toll Mounts," *Washington Post*, March 29, 1990; "Death Toll at 37 in Fighting between Black Factions," *Boston Globe*, March 31, 1990; "Wave of Black-on-Black Violence in South Africa More than Skin Deep," *Atlanta Journal*, April 7, 1990; "Natal's Valley of Death Goes On," *Washington Post*, April 8, 1990.

7. Guy D. Garcia, "Roar of the Lions," *Time*, August 27, 1990.

8. Asha Rambally, editor, *Black Review, 1975–1976* (Lovedale: Black Communities Program, 1977), p. 47.

9. Tom Lodge, *Black Politics in South Africa since 1945* (New York: Longman, 1983), pp. 350–51; Mzala, *Gatsha Buthelezi: Chief with a Double Agenda* (London: Zed, 1988), p. 130.

10. John F. Burns, "Black vs. Black in Natal: Future at Stake," *New York Times*, January 21, 1988; and "The Zulu Wars Are Back Again," *Economist*, January 16, 1988.

11. "South Africa Now," Television Interview with Thandi Gquebele, September 2, 1990; "Report Blames S. African Police," *The Plain Dealer*, September 2, 1990; South Africa Now, "Special Report: The Hidden Hand," October 4, 1990; Cable News Network, "Special Report: The Violence in South Africa," October 22, 1990.

12. Ned Temko, "Different Tactics to End Apartheid Behind Tribal Violence in S. Africa," *Christian Science Monitor*, October 29, 1987.

13. Mangosuthu G. Buthelezi, "Letter to the Editor," *New York Times*, February 13, 1988; Rod Nordland, "South Africa's Zulu Wars," *Newsweek*, January 11, 1988.

14. Francis Meli, *A History of the ANC: South Africa Belongs to US* (Harare: Zimbabwe Publishing House, 1988); John Battersby, "S. Africa Balances Equality, Growth," *Christian Science Monitor*, May 31, 1990. "Mandela Still Opposes End to Sanctions," *Baltimore Sun*, June 8, 1990.

15. For a review of the way that Inkatha views itself see Wessel, De Kock, *Usuthu, Cry Peace, The Black Liberation Movement Inkatha and the Fight for a Just South Africa* (Cape Town: The Open Hand Press, 1986). For a detailed history of the political differences, see Mzala, *Gatsha Buthelezi*.

16. William Artis Jr., "The Tribal Fixation," *Columbia Journalism Review* (Fall 1970): 48–49.

17. University Microfilm International, Newspaper Abstracts ONDISC (computer file) Ann Arbor, MI: January 1989–April 1990.

18. Morton Fried, *The Notion of Tribe* (Menlo Park, CA: Cummings Publishing Company, 1975), p. 1.

19. Phillip White, "What Is Nationality?" *Canadian Review of Studies in Nationalism* XII, no. 1 (1985): 1–23.

20. Robert Isaak, "The Nation-State and International Organization-Wilson," in Robert Isaak, ed., *Individuals in World Politics* (North Scituate, MA: Duxbury Press, 1975), pp. 111–45.

21. For a discussion of some of the issues, see Fred W. Riggs, "What Is Ethnic? What Is National? Let's Turn the Tables," *Canadian Review of Studies in Nationalism* XIII, no. 1 (1986): 111–23.

22. For a good illustration of images popularized through travel diaries see Henry Savage Landor, "Across Widest Africa," *National Geographic Magazine* XLII, no. 4 (October 1922): 694–705; Felix Shay, "Cairo to Cape Town, Overland," *National Geographic Magazine* XLVII, no. 2 (February 1925): 1 passim.

23. Frank J. Magee, "Transporting a Navy through the Jungles of Africa in War Time," *National Geographic Magazine* XLII, no. 4 (October 1922): 140–41.

24. See Patrick Brantlinger, "Victorians and Africans: The Genealogy of the Myth of the Dark Continent," 185–222; and, Sander Gilman, "Black Bodies, White Bodies: Toward an Iconography of Female Sexuality in Late Nineteenth-Century Art, Medicine, and Literature," 223–62 in Henry Louis Gates, ed., *"Race," Writing and Difference* (Chicago: University of Chicago Press, 1986). For a discussion of the myth of the black rapist, see Angela Davis, *Women, Race and Class* (New York: Random House, 1983).

25. Charles McCarry, "Three Men Who Made the Magazine," *National Geographic* (September 1988): 287–313.

26. See definitions of *tribe* in *The Century Dictionary and Cyclopedia* VII (New York: Century Company, 1904); and the *Oxford English Dictionary* XII (Oxford: Oxford University Press, 1933).

27. *Encyclopedia Britannica* XVII (New York: Charles Scribner's Sons, 1878).

28. Robert Fikes, "Commentary: Racist Quotes from Persons of Note," *Journal of Ethnic Studies* 16, no. 3 (Fall 1988): 163.

29. See Onyeonoro S. Kanamu, "Secession and the Right of Self-Determination: An O.A.U. Dilemma," *The Journal of Modern African Studies* 12, no. 3 (1974): 355–76.

30. See Archie Mafeje, "The Ideology of Tribalism," *Journal of Modern African Studies* 11, no. 2 (1971): 253–61; Owen J. M. Kaling, "Colonial Rule, Missionaries and Ethnicity in the North Nyasa District, 1891–1938," *The African Studies Review* 28, no. 1

(1985): 57–72; and Leroy Vail, ed., *The Creation of Tribalism in Southern Africa* (London: James Curry, 1989).

31. Shula Marks, "Patriotism, Patriarchy and Purity: Natal and the Politics of Zulu Ethnic Consciousness," *The Creation of Tribalism in Southern Africa*, Leroy Vail, ed. (London: James Curry, 1989), pp. 215–40.

32. Walter Lippmann, *Public Opinion* (New York: Macmillan, 1954), p. 341.

33. Phil Harris, *Reporting Southern Africa* (Ghent: Unesco, 1981).

34. Ibid., p. 22.

35. Unesco, *Report and Working Papers of the International Conference toward a New World Information Order: Consequences for Development Policy* (Institution for International Relations, Bonn, West Germany, December 4–6, 1978).

36. Paul Harrison and Robin Palmer, *News Out of Africa: Biafra to Band Aid* (London: Hillary Shipman Limited, 1986), p. 4.

37. Gil Onwochei, "U.S. Television Coverage of Africa: Geopolitical, Economic, and Strategic Policy Implications" (Ph.D. dissertation, University of Oklahoma, 1987), p. xiv.

38. Anthony Ayeni, "Content Analysis Study of ABC News Presentations on Nigeria as an Example of Third World News Coverage, 1974–1983" (M.A. thesis, North Texas State University, 1986), p. 38.

39. Edward S. Herman and Gerry O'Sullivan, *The "Terrorism" Industry: The Experts and Institutions that Shape Our View of Terror* (New York: Pantheon Books, 1989).

40. Joanmarie Kalter, "The Untold Stories of Africa, Why TV is Missing Some Big Ones," *T.V. Guide*, May 24, 1986, 4–12.

41. Reesom Haile, "Africa on Television: U.S. Network Coverage of African Affairs, 1977–1980" (Ph.D. dissertation, New York University, 1987).

42. Christopher Wren, "South African Talks Yield Outlines of an Agreement on Basic Political Changes," *New York Times*, May 11, 1990.

43. For sympathetic reporting on Buthelezi see: "Kwazulu Police Killed at Umzali," *Citizen* (Johannesburg), July 4, 1990; "Woman Hacked to Death," *Citizen*, July 5, 1990.

13

Beyond Black and White: An Overview of Nonracialism and the Image of Racial Polarization in South Africa

Julie Frederikse

The American media image of the South African conflict centers around a polarized racial dynamic: an exotic black mass, torn by conflicts, versus a small minority of white people, largely united, with a culture not too different from "ours." Yet most of those involved in the struggle to change South Africa would dispute this construct. The black-versus-white image has been shaped by a range of factors: South African government censorship and U.S. policy considerations, the media's own ideological constraints, and perceived audience interest, to name but a few. An influence that is less often considered is the history of race-related strife in U.S. society, which has given rise to a general tendency for Americans to view conflict situations through the prism of race relations rather than class conflict. Based on extensive interviews with political activists, this chapter details South African political complexity and provides needed challenge to that prevailing media image.

HISTORICAL CONTEXT

A wide variety of terms have described African demands for an end to colonial and minority domination: *self-determination, majority rule,* and *independence.* South Africans have enriched this vocabulary, adding a new word to describe their call for a unitary, democratic state with equal rights for all; they are demanding that the new South Africa be a "nonracial" democracy. This demand is the common ground that unites a wide range of forces for change, whose primary goal is a completely restructured society in which people are not differentiated according to racial criteria, but enjoy rights as equal citizens in one united country. South Africans have redefined the enemy, as a system—not as members of particular racial or cultural groups.

The popular media image of South African society is based on a crude understanding of the particularly legalistic repression instituted by the white party that came to power some forty years ago: the policy of apartheid, Afrikaans for "separateness." A longer view of South African history belies this image, showing instead considerable interdependence between black and white.

There was no inherent racism in traditional African society. Settler farmers on the frontier often paid tribute to African chiefs, and cohabitation was not uncommon. In early contacts, shipwrecked Portuguese sailors were integrated into Xhosa communities and English traders became Zulu chiefs. Without the means to exploit, whites embraced blacks as equals; when not threatened with dispossession, blacks welcomed whites.

It took the large-scale investment of international capital in the late nineteenth century and the need to destroy independent African societies to provide a work force for the mines, to create a single racially stratified society in South Africa. Such accommodation as had existed on the frontier was shattered by rapid industrialization. Whites, who mainly owned the means to produce wealth, needed blacks to work for them at wage levels well below the rate required to support workers and their families. Whites needed an ideology to defend this exploitative labor form. These forces gave rise to a philosophy of racial superiority and a battery of racial laws to enforce it. Resistance to racial oppression has been as varied and complex as the society that engendered it. A key distinction to emerge was that between the liberal tradition, rooted in nineteenth-century British missionary culture, and a popular democratic tradition that grew out of the black working-class organizations of the early twentieth century. The central concern of the liberal tradition was to draw a small minority of the oppressed into an alliance with the elites, with change to come from the top down.

The popular democratic tradition in South Africa can be seen as an alliance of all the oppressed. As workers began to organize against the race-based system, they joined forces with others who supported the same basic demands for change from below. This popular democratic tradition gave rise to a mass movement that has dominated South African resistance politics. Throughout the movement's history nonracialism has been a central theme.

THE RISE OF AFRICAN NATIONALISM

Mining catapulted South Africa into the industrial age. The cheapest way for the mine owners to get the minerals required vast numbers of unskilled workers using labor-intensive methods; both profits and the higher white wages derived from the extreme exploitation of black workers. But not all white workers embraced the racial division of labor. A section of white labor broke with the mainstream in the early 1900s and demanded a unity of the working class that transcended racial barriers. They formed the International Socialist League (ISL) in 1915, the first political group to attempt to organize nonracially. In 1917, blacks and whites joined together to launch the Industrial Workers of Africa, South Africa's first independent trade union.

This glimmer of nonracialism in the early twentieth century was overshadowed by the firmly established, if not always stable, political alliance between white labor and capital. The promotion of whites as supervisors of less skilled black labor facilitated the emergence of a labor aristocracy in league with industry and government against the blacks below them. Members of the ISL who formed the Communist Party of South Africa (in 1921), as well as those involved in the nonracial trade unions, began to realize that the country's problems could not be understood solely as conflict between social classes, that relations between the races were also vitally important.

The incipient nonracialism of the working-class socialist movement was rivaled by a joint venture of white liberals and black elites. European missionaries who came to South Africa in the late eighteenth century saw the assimilation of a faithful black middle class as the best means of ensuring the stability of the society defined by race. A group of mission-educated black professionals and traditional chiefs founded the South African Native National Congress (renamed the African National Congress in 1912). They envisioned no restructuring of the economy, nor even challenging racial differentiation. This approach accepted the multiracial nature of a segregated society rather than proposing a radical nonracial alternative.

World War II—a period of accelerated industrialization and urbanization in South Africa—gave rise to a new generation of militant political leaders who founded the African National Congress (ANC) Youth League. With the election of Youth Leaguers to the ANC's national executive committee, and its adoption of the militant Programme of Action in 1949, the bold new ANC gained confidence. Initially the young radicals resisted cooperation with nonAfricans and suspected whites of being Communist infiltrators, but these fears were allayed by the ANC's efforts to inculcate its policy of nonracialism. In an interview, Stanley Mabizela, an ANC member since the 1950s and now a member of its national executive committee, recalled his first exposure to the ANC's nonracialism. "We did query the policy of nonracialism. We were young and we said, 'Why can't we fight and drive the whites away?' But our elders in the organization were very patient people. They told us the history of the ANC and took pains to explain why the ANC must be nonracial. It was something which was not very easy to accept at the beginning, because of immaturity, because of youthfulness."

RESISTANCE AMONG SOUTH AFRICA'S MINORITIES

While the new militancy in the ANC emanated from the growing cooperation between young African intellectuals and workers, those minority groups classified under South African law as colored, Indians and whites were also part of the political rejuvenation of the war years. The Indians, initially imported from India in 1860 as indentured farm labor, were the first oppressed group to mount an effective nonmilitary challenge to the government. Mahatma Mohandas Gandhi inspired Satyagraha—passive resistance to discriminatory legislation—during the twenty-one years he spent in South Africa. This tradition was then overtaken by the accommodationist policies of the Indian business class, until the World War II period spurred a radicalization of Indian resistance politics that paralleled that of the ANC Youth League.

A new spirit of cooperation between Indians and Africans was symbolized by a pact signed in 1947 between the ANC and the Indian Congresses. Less than two years later this unity faced its most serious test, when fighting between Indians and Africans broke out in the major city of Natal Province, Durban. Indian-African cooperation weathered the storm, and the solidarity forged in the 1940s provided a platform for continued nonracial unity between the two communities throughout the 1950s.

The so-called colored shared a community of interests in part because they were defined as a separate community by government policy. The descendants of indigenous Khoikhoi, San, and Bantu peoples, imported Asian and African slaves, and European settlers developed an identity that existed solely in contrast with the other race groups: less privileged than the whites, but better off than the Africans. Government "colored preferences" policies ensured that the coloreds remained in this buffer, precluding any sense of either solidarity with other blacks or equality with whites. Nonracialism in the colored community evolved out of a rejection of this arbitrary ethnic category based on the notion of miscegenation of supposedly pure races. However, as South African poet Dennis Brutus notes, there were historical constraints on the politicization of the colored community. "The history of the coloureds was totally different from the Africans and the Asians. They only lost the franchise in 1956 [when the Nationalist government removed colored voters from the Cape common roll]. There was always the promise of the white dominant group that the coloreds would be treated as an appendage. So out of that comes a certain reluctance to take on the system." Although World War II was fought against fascism, few whites made the link between Nazi persecution of Jews in Europe and the oppression of blacks in their own country. A group called the Springbok Legion tried to organize soldiers in a way that related their war experience to the situation back home. Fred Carneson was among the South African troops who served the Allied Forces and was also active in the legion.

You see, when you look at the problem of bringing the whites across, as an abstract theoretical thing you can see all sorts of bloody problems. But given the right climate, we were able to do an enormous amount of work in a progressive direction amongst them. For instance, when the government was scared to arm the Africans and the coloreds and the Indians in the face of the opposition from the right-wing and antiwar elements, amongst the soldiers you could get across the line that "Look, why shouldn't they be armed? Let's get this bloody thing over." So you'd be bringing in the colour issue around concrete things.

Any wartime political gains were reversed by the Suppression of Communism Act of 1950. That law not only banned the Communist Party but it also unleashed a ruinous offensive against all nonracial organizations. Communists regrouped underground, noting that the abortive effort to woo whites had once again vindicated the view that its most viable base was among the black workers.

THE CONGRESS ALLIANCE AND
THE PAC BREAK-AWAY

Afrikaner nationalists consolidated their unity in the postwar period with a campaign that manipulated white anxieties over growing black labor militancy. The new policy of apartheid promised to solve these problems for whites, but behind the promise lay the reality of *volkskapitalisme* (people's capitalism): the economic empowerment of the Afrikaner middle classes at the expense not only of blacks but also of their poorer white partners in the cross-class alliance. The most serious challenge to the ruling National Party came from the rejuvenated ANC, led by former Youth Leaguers such as the late M. B. Yengwa, who commented, "African nationalism was, as we saw it, a uniting force toward overthrowing white oppression. As we developed our own philosophy of African nationalism, we discovered that we had common goals—it didn't matter whether you are black or white. In other words, we evolved toward nonracialism. I think you can't fight against racism and then substitute racism." The Congress Alliance was led by the ANC, embracing the Indian Congress, the Colored Peoples Congress, the white Congress of Democrats, and the South African Congress of Trade Unions. The 1955 Congress of the People produced a document that enshrined nonracialism as ANC policy: the Freedom Charter proclaimed, "South Africa belongs to all who live in it, black and white, and no government can justly claim authority unless it is based on the will of the people." Still, the nonracialism of the Congress Alliance was not without opposition. In 1959 Africanist dissidents formed a smaller rival party, the Pan-Africanist Congress (PAC), which opposed the involvement of whites and communists in the alliance.

BLACK CONSCIOUSNESS

The ANC and the PAC were banned by the government in 1960, and both organizations responded by declaring an armed struggle. By the mid-1960s, virtually all political leaders had been imprisoned, banned, or hounded out of the country, and thus began a period of South African history that has come to be known as "the lull." The PAC was inactive, while the ANC's military campaign in this period brought limited success—its importance lay in symbolizing that the struggle was alive and continuing from outside. This was a time of analysis and reassessment, and one of the key debates concerned the position of non-Africans in the ANC. The controversy that erupted made a consultative conference imperative to resolve the issue once and for all. The consensus at the 1969 meeting in Morogoro, Tanzania, was that non-Africans should be integrated into the ANC's External Mission and serve for the first time as full members of the ANC, but that only Africans could be elected to its top policy-making body.

In the late 1960s and early 1970s, black students inside South Africa struck an angry blow against the frustration and impotence of the lull. A young student from the Eastern Cape named Steve Biko led a walkout of blacks from the white liberal-dominated student organization, heralding the demise of the era of fear and submissiveness and the embrace of a psychology of liberation: "Black Consciousness." The rebellious founders of the South African Students Organization (SASO) rejected the label of "nonwhite" and pioneered the unity of African, colored, and Indian peoples as blacks against the white oppressor. Pandelani Nefolovhodwe, a SASO member from its inception, was active at the all-black University of the North. He said, "At that stage we were in a state where we were searching for our own identity. We had to liberate ourselves from this psychological oppression, and to do so the argument was that you have got to be away from the people who on a daily basis infuse you with an idea of their superiority." Black Consciousness evolved over time beyond its initial social and cultural focus; by the mid-1970s, a critique which stressed economic issues was beginning to emerge. This development sowed the seeds of an eventual rift between the more left-wing youth and Black Consciousness veterans. Nkosazana Dlamini was among the SASO activists who embraced nonracialism and joined the banned ANC. He remembered, "It was very clear to me from the beginning that Black Consciousness was not going to bring the government down. From a historical point of view, it was clear that no amount of talking and no amount of conscientizing people will do that. I would say it was like a growing child: you need to crawl before you can walk." In 1977 the government banned the Black Consciousness movement, issuing the first organizational restrictions since the 1960s. Many analyzed this delayed state response—nearly a decade after Black Consciousness first emerged—as evidence that it was the decline of the philosophy that had prompted the bannings. What Pretoria would not tolerate was the incipient recon- nection with the history that had gone before it. But the bans came too late, for the new trend toward nonracialism was now firmly entrenched and the revival of the Congress tradition had already begun to eclipse Black Consciousness. ANC underground structures were rebuilt during this period and those involved in this clandestine process were both black and white. Tony Holiday, a white journalist, worked with blacks in secretly producing and distributing ANC literature: "This was the period when the movement reconstructed. Young people were coming in and there were all those challenges, but in a certain sense there was a thread. People think the thread snapped—I'm trying to say it may have looked very thin, but it was there, and it was unbreakable." The explosion in South Africa's largest black township of Soweto on June 16, 1976, was sparked by a range of factors, from mandatory instruction in Afrikaans to the advent of majority rule in neighboring Mozambique and Angola. As the unrest spread throughout the country over the next few months, seasoned ANC members offered advice and support to the inexperienced student activists. Sacky Madi was a member of the Soweto Students Representative Council who was recruited to the ANC after the uprising. Madi said,

Within the ANC I learned that nonracialism should be a concept in the revolution. If I remember well, they never sat down and said, "Now we are discussing nonracialism," but the point was, okay, if you are saying South Africa belongs to both black and white, people used to ask the question, "Then who is our enemy?" That was when experienced ANC stalwarts would come up and explain exactly what we mean in the ANC by nonracialism, that the ANC is a movement of all genuine freedom fighters, black or white. Those who are opposed to racial discrimination and the apartheid system are welcome to participate in the ANC.

Jeremy Cronin, a university lecturer who worked underground producing ANC literature in Cape Town from 1974 to 1976, said that his arrest and interrogation by the Security Police—fellow whites—showed how difficult apartheid's supporters found it to come to grips with the concept of nonracialism. He recalled,

One of the first questions they asked me was, was I Jewish? Because that would have explained things to them. And I had quite a lot of fun evading the question, keeping them guessing and refusing to see the importance of it. And a second question they asked me was, was I born a communist? Because, I presume, if you're a racist the biological explains everything to you. It's all rather difficult to work out if you're white. Then they were quite anxious to use our trial to demonstrate that there were white communists behind the June 16th uprisings, the old story that blacks are contented until whites come along—white politicos with their own motivations who stir up an otherwise contented black grouping, Moscow's agents and that sort of thing.

Of the Black Consciousness activists who fled South Africa, most eventually joined the ANC. Others remained nonaligned, and a few linked up with the PAC. The majority of Black Consciousness supporters who stayed in South Africa after the 1977 crackdown eventually endorsed nonracialism. The transformation was most profound for those arrested, tried, and sentenced to serve time on Robben Island. Patrick Lekota was sentenced to imprisonment with eight other Black Consciousness leaders, and while on the island he came to support the ANC. Lekota said,

In our formative years, politically, we saw the struggle strictly in terms of one race versus another race because we were deprived of the wealth of the heritage of struggle which others who had gone before us had already amassed. Then we were arrested, with men who were blacks like ourselves, and it was precisely from among those men that some of them took the witness stand, side by side with the Security Police, and condemned us and sent us to jail. Tony Holiday, who happened to have been arrested at the same time we were on trial in '76, stuck to his opposition to apartheid to the end, and the black man he was arrested with abandoned him and testified against him. And then there were men like Bram Fischer, who at the time was serving a life sentence [for ANC and Communist Party work] and died a prisoner because he did not approve of what his own people were doing to us. There was also Beyers Naude, an outstanding Afrikaner who had reached very high positions within the Dutch Reformed Church and the Broederbond [Afrikaner Brotherhood]—he had been ostracized by his own people they had actually banned and restricted him.

Now I felt it was high time that one really reflected carefully as to whether the struggle in this country was a struggle of those who were committed to justice— never mind the colour of their skin—and those who were committed to injustice. Even if there were not white people participating in the struggle, we would still say it is wrong to judge anyone by the colour of his skin.

NEW ORGANIZATIONAL FOUNDATIONS

A wave of strikes in Durban in early 1973—the biggest since World War II—signaled the end of a decade-long lull in activity among ever-growing numbers of black urban workers. The reinvigoration of the labor movement sparked by those strikes gained valuable support from white intellectuals. Alec Erwin left academia to teach workers and then joined the trade unions. He said,

The change in historiography that was initiated in the seventies—looking at South Africa not just in terms of race, but looking at the economic structures that evolved, why migrant labour was so important to gold mines and how it totally reshaped the society—made is clear to me that the only way, in the long run, that this was going to change was through worker organization. White intellectuals were accepted in the organization for what they could offer—it became clear that in the wider arena, racism is not the answer, that we should take a nonracial position.

New organizational foundations were laid in the late 1970s and early 1980s, rooted in the segregated communities but committed to a nonracial future. Students once again took the lead, as veterans of the 1976 uprising now armed with both concrete experience of struggle and counsel from the elders—including ANC leaders released from prison. The result was the first public black-white student cooperation since the Black Consciousness era. The new spirit was symbolized by a leaflet announcing a rally jointly organized by students from black high schools, black universities, and white universities. It proclaimed:

A resistance rally has been organized by the three major student groupings in South Africa. Together they form the nonracial student movement in this country. While it has been necessary to organize separately because of the practical and ideological effects of apartheid, we are all striving for a South Africa based on a single, united and democratic future. Our vision is encapsulated in the Freedom Charter. We call on all students to attend the rally so that we can build nonracialism in the process of our struggle.

For the government, the revival of mass political organization was a worrying sign. Even more alarming was the sporadic yet ever-increasing ANC guerrilla activity. In 1983, the state responded to these mounting pressures with a constitution aimed at reforming but not abolishing apartheid. Coloreds and Indians were to be represented in two new chambers of Parliament, with whites continuing to dominate and Africans still locked out.

This attempt to thwart the budding nonracial alliances by co-opting minority groups into the ruling bloc failed. Instead, it prompted the formation of the most powerful legal antiapartheid body since the ANC in the 1950s: the United Democratic Front (UDF) formed in 1983. Western Cape activist Saleem Badat analyzed the government's fear of nonracialism, drawing on his own experience of interrogation while in detention:

The Security Police would ask, "How can you work with whites?" I don't know if it was fear in terms of us making cracks in the ruling class, or whether it was just an inability to cope with the fact that blacks and whites were mixing on equal terms and working and living together. The main emphasis during interrogation was: "You know changes are coming. We can come together—you as Indians, and maybe the coloreds as well. We whites can come together, but these blacks will never be able to come together—never, never."

The perennial debates over ethically based mobilization and the nature of white involvement in mass-based organization resurfaced in this period. The racial overtones of the Black Consciousness era were lacking in the early to mid-1980s; criticism was linked instead to an attack on the class base of UDF affiliates like the revived Indian Congresses and white and liberal groupings.

The strongest criticism of mobilization across ethnic lines came from a new alignment of political groups that took form near the time that the UDF was launched. A wide range of organizations and political approaches came together in the National Forum Committee (NFC), united by their opposition to the UDF and the ANC. The NFC rejected any "unprincipled" alliances that might dilute the revolutionary content of the struggle. UDF activists argued that the struggle for nonracial democracy required the widest possible antiapartheid base—in which workers and their allies are strong enough to support the building of socialism. Western Cape youth activist Rehana Rossouw explained why she supports a broad front approach:

It's the whole question of attacking and destroying apartheid on all fronts. We're fighting for a nonracial South Africa—we don't want the problem of having to build nonracialism after the revolution or after negotiations or after whatever's going to happen. And it's important for us to show people that our organizations are nonracial, to show that we aren't going to do to white people what they do to us, that we're just as prepared to work with them now as we will be in a new society. Why do we have women's organizations? There are certain sectors of the community that need to be organized as a sector, in order to ensure that when freedom comes we'll be able to have as many people supportive of us as possible.

The end of 1985 saw the formation of the largest labor federation in the country's history, the Congress of South African Trade Unions (COSATU). Nonracialism was one of its founding principles; at its first annual conference, COSATU formally adopted the Freedom Charter as its lodestar. Billy Nair, a trade unionist who spent twenty years on Robben Island for ANC activities, was elected as a Natal UDF executive upon his release, and worked closely with COSATU.

If you look at it from a purely tactical point of view, the idea is to strip the ruling class of all props that it has. Take the churches, for instance, a formidable force, the vast majority of whose members are workers, peasants and so on. Therefore to exclude the church would be suicidal for the working class. As a parallel, take the patriotic movement that developed during the last world war against Hitler and Mussolini—the forces were wide-ranging. The church played a very important role in those popular fronts. The ruling class actually wants allies desperately—hence the tricameral parliament and so on. The very shifts that are taking place in ruling class circles are indicative of the correctness of our line, the nonracial policies we are espousing.

The government's escalating attacks on unions toward the end of the decade deepened the spirit of cooperation in the labor movement. In 1989 COSATU called a Workers' Summit where all workers—and no union officials—were invited to speak. Many affiliates of the National Council of Trade Unions (NACTU), a smaller federation which opposed COSATU's policy of nonracialism, defied their executive's decision not to attend and sent representatives to meet with their counterparts in COSATU. The message from NACTU's workers was clear: opposition to nonracialism was not seen as an uncompromising point of principle, even by those with a Black Consciousness or Africanist background. In the drive toward worker unity, support for nonracialism was simply accepted as the dominant trend.

NONRACIALISM SHAPES THE FUTURE

In 1985 the ANC formally adopted nonracialism at all levels: from the grass roots to its top policy-making body. At its National Consultative Conference held in Kabwe, Zambia, the decision was taken to open the national executive committee (NEC) to people of all races. After new elections, the NEC consisted of twenty-five Africans, two coloreds, two Indians, and one white. Long-time ANC activist and South African Communist Party leader Joe Slovo was the first white voted onto the NEC. Slovo commented:

Up to about 1984, '85, I was one of the strongest opponents within the movement of opening up the ranks of the ANC's NEC to minority groups. This has been discussed since 1965. I opposed it then because the ANC was enormously weakened after 1960. It didn't exist inside the country: it was like a tender plant, in a way, that had to take root and grow. And at that stage, had the ANC decided to open up its ranks, it would have faced such a salvo from right and left, from Black Consciousness, from Africa, that it would have been damaging to the ANC. One changed one's attitude towards that question when the ANC was transformed from a purely agitational opposition into an alternative power, which it started becoming from about 1984. With the massive sort of welling-up of sympathy and support for the ANC, it then became strong enough to risk the kind of flak which inevitably would be hurled at it. What I'm trying to say is that you've got to analyze policy in relation to a context. Things change.

By the beginning of the 1990s, the new broad front had never been broader. Sections of society that had long been firmly anchored within the ruling bloc were dislodged and engaged in mass actions against the state. In this period, the struggle for a nonracial, democratic South Africa entered a new phase.

The ever-broadening campaign for a nonracial future, now known simply as the Mass Democratic Movement (MDM), gathered extraordinary momentum in 1989. A hunger strike organized in the prisons and supported by activists and professionals succeeded in freeing detainees. A defiance campaign brought the de facto unbanning of restricted people and organizations. Executions of political prisoners and censorship of the media decreased in response to unrelenting pressure. A local battle to desegregate a whites-only Johannesburg secondary school drew all races into a nationwide campaign: "All Schools for All People." In all these campaigns, nonracialism had never been more manifest, whether in the composition of crowds or the articulation of aims. The wave of mass demonstrations in 1989 took popular protest out of the black townships and into the white city centers. Black and white protesters joined together in open city campaigns in Johannesburg, Cape Town, Durban, and Port Elizabeth, defying apartheid in residential areas, buses, hospitals, schools, and beaches.

The success of the broad front strategy suggested a tactic unthinkable only a short time ago: recruiting support from within the repressive arm of the state itself. Changing conditions inspired the confidence to venture into enemy territory. In late 1989, a colored police lieutenant won popular acclaim for denouncing police brutality, demonstrating how an "enemy of the people" could join the people's camp. A black former security police-man confessed to his involvement in the assassinations of political activists; then a white former police captain admitted he had commanded a secret military death squad, fled the country, and announced that he had joined forces with the ANC.

These unprecedented developments unfolded against a background of rising rural resistance. Demands for the reintegration of the homelands into a unitary nonracial South Africa and the rejection of ethnically based separation sparked general strikes and coups throughout the homelands in early 1990. In one striking incident in the Bophuthatswana homeland, police burned their uniforms to protest the killings of demonstrators at a peaceful rally.

In February 1990, the South African government succumbed to political and economic pressure: President F. W. de Klerk unbanned the ANC, PAC, and SACP and released Nelson Mandela. Blacks were jubilant. For whites—aside from the increasingly isolated right wing—initial shock turned to anxious optimism. The South African struggle had entered a new phase, marked by the first talks aimed at negotiating a democratic future. The momentum was clearly irreversible: the long-cherished ideal of a nonracial South Africa was beginning to shape a new political reality. In the words of Nelson Mandela, addressing a mass rally in Durban, February 25, 1990:

We are committed to building a single nation in our country. Our new nation will include blacks and whites, Zulus and Afrikaners, and speakers of every other language. ANC President-General Lutuli said, "I personally believe that here in South Africa, with all of our diversities of colour and race, we will show the world a new pattern for democracy. I think that there is a challenge to us in South Africa, to set a new example for the world." This is the challenge that we face today.

In contradistinction to the prevailing media image of South African politics, historical trends show a coherent pattern of nonracialism. It is thus clear that the tradition of nonracialism has been the most pervasive and enduring ideological tendency throughout South Africa's history, and that it continues to dominate all rival trends. If the media persists in depicting the complex South African conflict simply as one pitting black against white, the American media will continue to misrepresent the origins and lessons of this vitally important tradition.

NOTE

This chapter includes quotations from Nelson Mandela speaking at a rally and from interviews with the following.

Saleem Badat, UDF, in York, England, 1987

Dennis Brutus, poet, in Washington, D.C., 1987

Fred Carneson, Springbok Legion, ANC, in London, 1986

Jeremy Cronin, ANC, in Capetown, 1985

Nkosazana Dlamini, ANC, in London, 1987

Alec Erwin, COSATU, in Durban, 1985

Tony Holiday, ANC, in London, 1986

Patrick Lekota, ANC, Black Consciousness Movement (BCM), in Johannesburg, 1983

Stanley Mabizela, ANC, in Dar es Salaam, 1986

Sacky Madi, Soweto Students Representative Council, ANC, in Dar es Salaam, 1986

Billy Nair, UDF, in Durban, 1985

Pandelani Nefolovhodwe, BCM, SASO, in Johannesburg, 1985

Rehana Rossouw, UDF, in Harare, 1987

Joe Slovo, ANC, SACP, in Harare, 1988

M. B. Yengwa, ANC, in London, 1986

14

Television News from
the Frontline States

Chris Paterson

Throughout the 1980s, as American and European television cameras have focused on South Africa, the other nations of Southern Africa—the Frontline states—have received little coverage, in spite of the critical role their collective title implies. In the United States, the nations of Zimbabwe, Angola, Botswana, Zambia, and Mozambique, along with the smaller nations of the region, are often thought of as poor, if not starving, Marxist countries, in some cases at war with our friends, the forces of democracy. Although this image borders on fantasy, television continues to present it to an audience assumed to be uninterested in African realities. U.S. television has, since its inception, delivered to its viewers such a distorted and simplistic view of Africa that American ignorance of African geography, politics, and culture is hardly as bewildering as African visitors often find it to be.

Television has been the most popular source for news in America since the late 1970s.[1] Even so, there has been little study, much less criticism, of how the TV news monopolies—the American and British networks, and their major international sources for news pictures, VisNews and Worldwide Television News (WTN)—go about selecting, gathering, and disseminating those news stories that determine our image of distant regions such as the Frontline states.

This article examines some of the problems that have made television coverage of the Frontline countries far less than adequate. It is undoubtedly apparent throughout this anthology that news coverage of Africa is by no means easy. Within the broader African context of a uniquely controlled and mobilized indigenous media, monitored and nervous foreign journalists, and sensitivity to anything smacking of Anglo-American media imperialism, we look at how the U.S. networks have reported the Frontline states and how the region has contributed to and reacted to that coverage.

NETWORK COVERAGE OF THE FRONTLINE

Querying American TV viewers about what stories they have recently seen concerning the majority-ruled countries of Southern Africa would yield a strong indication that coverage is lacking, but a more systematic approach is needed to encourage improvements in the flow of television news from the region. To this end, this chapter employs content analysis to quantify and review network coverage of the Frontline countries. No previous academic studies of television's international coverage have been specific to Southern Africa, but more general studies of TV coverage of Africa and of the developing world have been unanimous in their condemnation of the television news industry.

In a 1984 study of Third World television coverage, Anne Messerly Cooper noted that there is extensive overcoverage of a few Third World countries, such as Egypt or Libya, and the remaining countries are virtually omitted. Cooper found that seventy-nine Third World countries received less than 1 percent of all Third World coverage.[2] According to researcher James Larson, it is not uncommon for U.S. television to completely ignore huge sections of the globe, even if they are embroiled in massive conflicts. "Events like the brutal killings in Cambodia from 1975 to 1979 or the Indonesian invasion of East Timor in 1978, and the mass murder which ensued, were scarcely noticed by U.S. network news," Larson wrote.[3] The dearth of coverage of the wars in Mozambique and Angola bolster Larson's point.

Larson's survey showed that references to sub-Saharan African countries between 1972 and 1981 accounted for just 5.6 percent of all international coverage by the U.S. networks (foreign coverage takes about half of the average newscast). Just 2.2 percent was about the Frontline countries discussed in this article. At least two other studies of TV coverage of Africa have yielded similar figures.[4] Two doctoral dissertations and a *TV Guide* magazine study examined the quantity and nature of sub-Saharan African coverage by the networks during 1984 and 1985, the period of severe famine throughout Africa. The studies generally determined that news about Western relief efforts dominated coverage, Ethiopia was the focus of famine stories, South Africa dominated nonfamine reports, and interview subjects were usually non-African. All of these researchers concurred that U.S. coverage reinforced basic stereotypes of Africa, especially the notion of Africa as a helpless victim dependent on Western aid, and reinforced images of American power and good will.[5] A detailed multinational study of European news coverage of the famine came to similar conclusions, accusing each national broadcaster of ignoring the real issues to sing the praises of whatever relief efforts their country was making.[6]

The content analysis of U.S. network news conducted for this study examined substantial instances of news coverage of the Frontline countries between 1981 and 1989, and reviewed that coverage in the specific contexts of various common criticisms. All reports that included news pictures from the Frontline countries were examined.[7]

The study showed that only 117 stories were filmed or taped in the Frontline countries during the eighties. In time devoted to the Frontline countries, that is less than 1 percent of network foreign coverage. That breaks down to an average of twenty minutes of U.S. coverage per year during the eighties, or less than seven minutes per year for each network. As Table 14.1 shows, the networks differ considerably by quantity, in this case expressed in total seconds of Frontline coverage. NBC has consistently demonstrated a greater interest in the Frontline states than its competitors, though hardly a welcome interest. Table 14.2 demonstrates that NBC's coverage has been heavily skewed toward issues of conflict and crisis.

Table 14.1
Yearly Coverage by Network

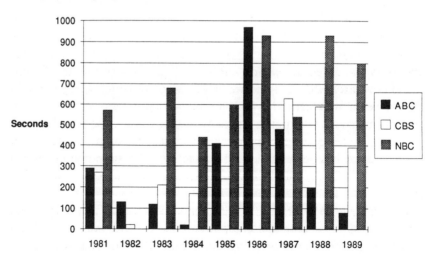

Table 14.2
Thematic Content by Network

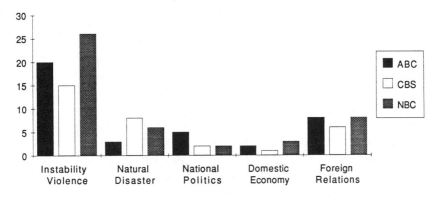

Given the average length of a network newscast, traditionally between twenty-two and twenty-three minutes, spread over the course of a year, we can conclude that seven minutes of Frontline coverage amounts to roughly .0009 of U.S. network news coverage.[8] Certainly that seems meager, especially for a region with such traditionally newsworthy features as East-West conflict, military aggressions from a regional bully, enormous concentrations of refugees, and spectacular economic successes and failures. On a population basis alone, it seems odd to give nearly 100 million people, roughly one-fiftieth of the world's population, .0009 of America's collective attention.

Beyond determining the quantity of Frontline coverage, news stories on the Frontline countries were also coded by thematic content, a standard practice for drawing conclusions about the topics on which television is concentrating. The themes used in this study are instability and violence; natural disaster; foreign relations; domestic economy; national politics; and human interest (of which there were only two stories). Famine stories—an inevitable element of African news coverage—were categorized as natural disasters, even though they are often the result of violence (though rarely are they reported as such).

The thematic content data has been further divided into two broad categories—crisis (comprising instability/violence and natural disaster) and noncrisis stories. The crisis dimension is important to assess the credibility of the common charge that crisis issues dominate Western news coverage of the Third World, and to determine how much of a tendency television news has, by its very nature, to concentrate on such visually exciting stories. This variable is especially relevant to African coverage.

Table 14.3
South Africa and U.S. Orientation

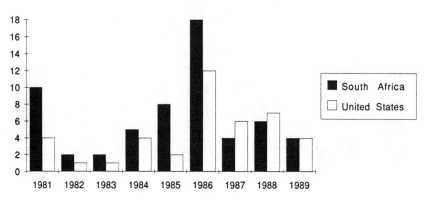

Larson found that crisis coverage made up an average of 27 percent of network foreign coverage, but 38 percent of African coverage. Table 14.2 shows thematic content for all stories over the nine-year period. With 67 percent of the stories concentrating on themes of crisis, the data powerfully demonstrate the network's tendency to report the Frontline from the crisis perspective.

The second subjective variable developed for this analysis is useful in the specific context of the Frontline countries. People from these countries often express the opinion that they are presented to the Western public only in the distorted terms of their significance to the affairs of South Africa or the United States. They are not, so the argument goes, presented as the independent, self-determining nations they indeed are. Although South Africa may be the major story from the region, the Frontline governments insist that neither it nor the United States should be a major part of Frontline news coverage. Table 14.3 shows that 59 stories, half of the 117, were presented as part of the South African story. Over a third were presented in relevance to the United States (including stories concentrating on East-West relations), reinforcing the contention that the U.S. networks report their stories largely from a national, rather than international, perspective. The data also show a seemingly concurrent relationship between United States and South African story orientation, suggesting that in the eyes of the U.S. networks, South African and U.S. interests are analogous.

The network tendency to follow the U.S. government agenda is exemplified by the fact that Angola's U.S.-backed rebel leader, Jonas Savimbi, has been interviewed by U.S. television more than any other prominent regional figure. Another important point regarding the choice of interview subjects is that only 42 percent of network interviews conducted in the Frontline countries appear to be with black Southern Africans. It is not surprising then that Americans should have little concept of the Frontline countries as models of majority rule, or of black Africans having control of their own nations.

THE CHALLENGE OF FRONTLINE COVERAGE

The U.S. networks and their principal sources, the television news agencies VisNews and WTN, argue that coverage of the Frontline countries is difficult due to problems of expense and logistics, but these companies all too often take the easiest and cheapest approach to coverage. Even when news agency stringers and other producers in Southern Africa offer important stories about the Frontline countries, they are often rejected by U.S. and British television because of a perceived lack of interest, or more disturbingly, because they conflict with popular Western beliefs about the region.[9]

Only a small portion of U.S. network coverage of the Frontline countries is accomplished by sending in a correspondent and presenting a fairly comprehensive report several minutes in length (as comprehensive as the networks get). The same is generally true of European broadcasters. Instead, most news video comes from sources such as VisNews and WTN and is narrated by a reporter in a more accessible location, or by the news anchor.

When reports in the Frontline countries are narrated by a correspondent on the scene, the correspondent has, in most cases, flown in from the network's bureau in Johannesburg. A good deal of Frontline coverage by network correspondents, especially in the early eighties, was also done by London-based reporters. An example of "in-depth" network Frontline coverage using this "parachute journalist" approach was a series of reports by NBC's John Cochran in early 1984. Reports by Cochran about Zimbabwe, Mozambique, and Angola were broadcast within days of each other, after a period of nearly a year of no NBC Frontline coverage. The reports were not done through any journalistic imperative—there was no hot story—but through the desire to provide some exposure for the region as cost effectively as possible. It appears that after joining a British press tour accompanying Prince Charles to Zimbabwe, Cochran did a Zimbabwe story and an Angola story in Harare, flew quickly to Mozambique for a story on that country, and then back to London. Viewers would likely have had the impression from Cochran's reports that he had been touring the

Frontline countries for weeks.[10] The U.S. networks have repeatedly demonstrated that this superficial form of reporting is as much of a commitment
as they are willing to make to Frontline coverage.

Third World countries have often charged that Western television does
not report the background to stories about their countries—the information
necessary for the viewer to make an informed judgment about a story.
Stories are presented without any context, causing more misunderstanding, it is argued, than if the story was not reported at all. Television news
seems only capable of presenting events, not information about the issues
that lead to the events. The pursuit of emotionally appealing or visually
exciting stories is also said to prevent television from explaining issues.

Independent Zimbabwean TV producer Simon Bright believes the
international news producers in Harare would gladly do a larger number
of the positive, process oriented stories which could explain a country's
development, but complains that "editorial control is maintained in Britain," adding that the nature of stories is dictated by what editors in Britain
think their clients—primarily U.S. and European broadcasters—will buy.
Another Harare-based producer, WTN's Tony Liddell, admitted the limitations of the news work he does: "You fly into town, you spend five
minutes on the ground, you shoot the shit out of everything that moves,
you cobble together a story that's a minute and a half long, and you get
out. You don't have the time to get into what is really happening, what is
really going on."[11]

Critics of Western media point to this practice as an irresponsible way
to report news from the Third World, for "fireman" journalists cannot
develop the understanding required to report stories accurately, or spend
the time to look for the underlying causes of a story. And to be fair to
resident producers such as Liddell, who know their region well, no amount
of expertise can overcome the limitations of the fireman approach. The
news agencies and networks are alert to the criticism, but for economic
reasons they have done little to end the practice.

Western television's inherent economic limitations are often cited by
African officials who have been trained to a socialist tradition. News
decisions, they argue, are made on the basis of what will make money for
the news company, not through any objective journalistic wisdom. John
McManus conducted a systematic study of this problem, applying a
cost/benefit analysis to the process of television news gathering. He
observed,

Because every content decision involves an allocation of resources and an
estimation of whether the . . . viewership will "buy" the story, each decision

implicitly contains some economic thinking. . . . The presentation of issues particularly conflicts with the economic logic of television. In a medium where consumers must watch the same story for a set time, dull but consequential issues are likely to cost a station the interest of apathetic viewers. Further, issues are inherently more difficult to illustrate than events. Issues deny television its technological advantage over print, or force stations to spend money illustrating ideas.[12]

James Larson and many other critics of network foreign coverage have concluded that the news simply has to be longer to present anything even resembling an accurate picture of the world. Unfortunately, U.S. network affiliates have consistently fought against more international news. Even within the time limitations of the newscast as they stand now, more care can be taken to present informed, insightful reports that describe more than just isolated events.

The problems confronting television journalists in Southern Africa are formidable though, and often beyond the control of networks and news agencies. David Kogan, the managing editor of VisNews, summed up the problems of television coverage in the Frontline states: "It is very, very expensive to cover African stories because of the distances you have to cover. You're talking about using planes a lot of the time. . . . [Y]ou're talking about very poor communications in terms of satellite delivery, all of which means that there is a general orientation away from covering that particular region unless there is a major world grabbing story."[13] The cost of sending videotaped stories to London via the local satellite uplink is one of the expenses limiting coverage, especially given the poor quality of local facilities and personnel. One Harare news stringer tells a common story, saying that he has occasionally fed his footage to London through the Zambian satellite uplink, only to hear from London that they are receiving a Zambian football match. With the high cost of satellite time, such mistakes by local engineers have cost news companies thousands of dollars, and contributed to considerable mistrust of local facilities and a tendency to avoid stories that would otherwise be covered.

It is widely agreed that the least reported, yet most important Frontline story is the horrifying war and related refugee crisis in Mozambique. The major difficulty in covering Mozambique, according to Western reporters, is the lack of access to important events. While television's demand for immediacy is already at odds with Africa's more casual concept of time, the disarray in Mozambique makes rapid news coverage virtually impossible. Mozambique Director of Information Arlindo Lopes acknowledges that it is a problem, but not one he can do much about, noting that "it is a frustration both for Mozambican media and foreign media."[14]

A far broader question regarding expense is why only one American network, CNN, has a permanent presence in black Africa with its Nairobi bureau. The standard argument used by the networks when asked why they do not have more bureaus is the high cost of maintaining them. In 1982 James Larson was told by an ABC executive that the cost of maintaining even a shoestring bureau overseas was more than $1 million a year. That figure is astonishingly high because even more recently CNN has put the cost of their Nairobi bureau, which effectively provides coverage of the entire continent, at $250,000 a year.[15] With the networks spending more than $1 million each year on their Johannesburg bureaus (because these are much more than shoestring bureaus) they could obviously provide more even and thorough coverage of Africa with several smaller bureaus like CNN's scattered around the continent. The counterargument, of course, is that the major African story is in South Africa; in fact, the story is in South Africa largely because the networks have chosen to make their investment there.

The greatest problems for foreign news people in the Frontline countries are the restrictions placed on them by local governments. Zimbabwe began introducing restrictions on the foreign press within months of becoming an independent nation by reintroducing the old Rhodesian practice of issuing foreign correspondents temporary employment permits, enabling the government to authorize the work of journalists on a monthly basis. The measure was an attempt to "control undesirable and irresponsible reports in the overseas press." In 1982 the restrictions on foreign journalists were tightened and large sections of Zimbabwe were declared off limits to reporters.[16] New emergency powers also gave police the authority to confiscate cameras and film. Reporting about dissident activity in Matabeleland Province and tribunals for terrorist suspects were also forbidden, which effectively prevented the exposure of many human rights violations.[17] Several Western reporters fled during this tense period after being threatened by officials.[18]

A number of veteran correspondents in Harare told me that Zimbabwe's Matabeleland crisis in the mid-eighties demonstrated one instance when television did perform an important service and do its job well. Without the international pressure, specifically American pressure, that resulted from the television coverage, the genocide in Zimbabwe could have gone on much longer. But they add, President Robert Mugabe had, by 1985, wiped out a large portion of Zimbabwe's ethnic minority, the Ndebele, including virtually all of the political opposition.

The greatest international exposure of the Matabeleland crisis came after the BBC produced a documentary about it for their "Panorama" public affairs series. The documentary was later aired in the United States as a PBS "Frontline" program. The Panorama crew tried to find evidence of mass graves in Matabeleland without any success, but shortly afterward WTN was able to photograph a mass grave being uncovered. Panorama did videotape local people standing by what appeared to be grave sites, describing mass killings by Robert Mugabe's troops. The Panorama program began with just such a scene, immediately following a clip from a press conference, showing a furious Mugabe denying that any military excesses had occurred. That juxtaposition "went down like a lead brick" with the government, said WTN's Tony Liddell.[19]

The international pressure on Zimbabwe intensified when the CBS News program "60 Minutes" decided to do a story on the Matabeleland crisis. As is the tradition among the American networks, if a news story seems to have a substantial public impact on British television, as with the Panorama story, American producers scramble to duplicate the story for their own networks. The CBS report was produced in the classic "60 Minutes" manner, described by one media critic as "style over substance . . . the hunt, the chase, the triumph of good over evil."[20] The "60 Minutes" report featured an aggressive, accusatory interview by correspondent Diane Sawyer with President Mugabe. Mugabe is said to have been so deeply offended that he has not granted an interview to a Western correspondent since.[21]

The rash of negative reports about Zimbabwe's Matabeleland conflict has left an imprint on that country's information policy. Officials most often view the foreign press as hostile, as interested only in negative stories, even after a half decade of widely varied, and frequently upbeat, reporting. The Permanent Secretary for Information in Zimbabwe, Sarah Kachingwe, told me that Zimbabwe is consistently reported in terms of violence, comparing it to the situation of Britain being reported only in terms of the conflict in Northern Ireland.[22]

Although many of Zimbabwe's restrictive regulations still exist, Zimbabwe's Foreign Minister Nathan Shamuyarira indicated to me in a 1990 interview that he thought a general opening toward the press could begin to take place, and that much of the suspicion and hostility within the Ministry of Information is no longer useful. Unfortunately, Shamuyarira, now seen as one of the two most influential figures in Zimbabwe, relinquished control of Information in 1987, and the ministry has continued to echo the same sort of hostility to the Western press that was common in the early 1980s.[23]

After years of internal and external pressure to do so, Zimbabwe did lift its state of emergency in the middle of 1990. Zambia had been expected to follow suit, but repeated coup attempts are likely to keep restrictive emergency regulations in force.[24] With the return of the exiled African National Congress from Lusaka to South Africa in 1990, Zambia may have seen its last Western TV crew. All the Harare-based television news agency stringers said that they would be unlikely to cover a story in Zambia other than the ANC for fear of offending the government and not being allowed back.

For all the restrictions in Zambia and Zimbabwe, they are still generally the easiest Frontline countries for foreign television crews to operate in, with the exception of Botswana, which has done little to restrain foreign journalists. Malawi has permitted very few visits by Western television crews, and of the few that have been allowed, the story has usually been about Malawi's successes in coping with Mozambican refugees. Only a handful of Western TV crews have been permitted to work in Angola, and those that have tell of agonizing delays and a lack of cooperation and assistance from officials.[25] Former ABC producer Danny Schechter, probably the most influential American television producer to have worked in Angola, noted, "In contrast, Savimbi's UNITA, with its heavily financed Washington public relations firm, Black, Manafort, and Stone, well connected to the administration, has run smooth, well-orchestrated press tours [inside Angola]."[26] It was UNITA and the U.S. administration public relations campaigns, in 1981 and 1986, that resulted in heightened coverage of Angola, not any new openness on the part of the Angolan government.

Even in Zimbabwe, where Western reporters now operate with considerable freedom, a substantial degree of control is maintained through intimidation and the denial of access to sources. The Harare stringers for WTN, VisNews, and the British network ITN, who together provide most of the Western TV coverage of the Frontline countries, have good reason to be intimidated and practice self-censorship. In 1985 VisNews stringer Gavin Johnstone-Robinson was detained and beaten by Zimbabwean central intelligence agents. He dropped the story he had unearthed—and to this day will not reveal what it was—and has since taken much more care in what he reports.[27] The WTN and ITN stringers spent time in prison for making the mistake of anticipating a South African raid on Zambia, with one of them flying there before the attack took place. It took several weeks to convince Zimbabwean authorities that the correspondents were not in cahoots with the South African Defense Force.[28] And no TV correspondent in Africa can forget Anthony Joyce, an Australian TV reporter who was killed in 1979 while in Zambian police custody, after photographing the site of a Rhodesian attack.

Fortunately such severe repression is rare. Threats or expulsion are routine. Still, Zimbabwe's Nathan Shamuyarira disavows any knowledge of systematic interference with the foreign press, telling me: "They have had freedom so far—I do not think they have had their freedom curtailed. At the time I was in Information, there were about twenty-one foreign correspondents here—I only deported one." Despite the minister's assurances to the contrary, my study revealed that at least twenty journalists have been forced either through legal means or through intimidation to leave Zimbabwe during the 1980s. At least thirty-four journalists have been detained or jailed, including some who have been physically attacked by authorities as well.[29] Of course, Zimbabwe is not alone in its intimidation and repression of the press, but as the news center of the Frontline states, its actions have the most influence on Western reporting of the Frontline.

A more subtle form of control in the Frontline countries is the practice of restricting access by journalists to official sources of information. One brave Zimbabwean journalist, Jonathan Maphenduka of the government-managed Bulawayo *Chronicle*, put the problem this way: "Short of a break-in, a risky business indeed, there is no way one can get at the official source of the information without being made to feel like one is trying to leak state secrets to the enemy."[30]

THE SOUTH AFRICAN SLANT

As noted earlier, the Frontline countries have often been angered by their portrayal only as a minor aspect of the South African story. The South African orientation of U.S. network stories clearly demonstrates the extent of the problem. As independent producer Simon Bright noted, "Images of South African power reinforce South African power." Speaking of the dominance of South Africa in stories coming from Southern Africa, David Kogan of VisNews said the issue did concern him, but he believed coverage of South Africa is not disproportionate to its actual importance. He explained: "South Africa exercises an influence over the economies and over the infrastructure of all those Frontline states, be it good or be it bad (but) there's no doubt that the ease of communications in South Africa and the fact that you can satellite feed out of Johannesburg without any problem, and the fact that it is a nicer place to live, affects the international media's view of how to cover the story."[31] The "fact" that South Africa is a nicer place to live is echoed by many Western news people, suggesting that their raison d'etre often takes second place to their comfort.

Foreign Minister Nathan Shamuyarira told me that South African based journalists are viewed with suspicion because "they looked at us through South African eyes. . . . [T]hey were coming in with very biased views." Information Director Arlindo Lopes of Mozambique believes that South African disinformation dominated coverage of the death of the Mozambican president in a 1986 plane crash in South Africa. The South African press indicted the Soviet pilots, suggesting they were drunk and incompetent, and that version of the story was picked up by the international media. Mozambique attempted to convince the Western press that no proper investigation of the crash was ever conducted due to South African interference, and that there was strong evidence of South African military involvement in the crash. Only one U.S. network did a story on the allegations of South African involvement.

In 1983 the Frontline countries issued a declaration designed to correct what they perceived as distorted coverage in foreign media by banning Western correspondents based in South Africa. Foreign Minister Shamuyarira, who engineered the Kadoma Declaration, told me the declaration was an effort to "implement the New World Information Order [NWIO] in Southern Africa." As a practical application of the NWIO, it is unique in the Third World, but it was not surprising that Kadoma outraged most Western media outlets. In November 1983, the International Press Institute protested that the declaration "seriously constrained the free circulation of information and was contrary to the principles of freedom of the press as well as the United Nations Declaration of Human Rights and Freedom of Information."[32]

Only Zimbabwe has regularly, although inconsistently, enforced the declaration. Mozambican Director of Information Lopes explained, "There was an informal agreement amongst the Frontline states that we could not stick by this Kadoma Declaration strictly—it should be more flexible, considering that most Western media organizations have their correspondents based in South Africa and considering the costs of flying in journalists from Washington, from Paris, from London, we had to be more flexible and allow journalists based in South Africa."[33] Although no other Frontline information officials interviewed for this chapter admitted to such an agreement, Botswana disassociated itself from the agreement early on, saying that their man in Kadoma did not have authorization to sign it.[34] Angola and Zambia have frequently reiterated their intention to abide by Kadoma, even though both countries regularly admit South Africa–based, and in Zambia's case, South African, journalists.

THE AMERICAN SLANT

In his 1988 study of television's relationship to foreign policy, James Larson wrote, "Perhaps the most striking overall pattern in network television's coverage of international news is its congruence with the foreign policy priorities of the U.S. government. . . . Television, like other major media, gives heavy coverage to a small number of nations that somehow directly involve American interests."[35] ABC reporter Bill Blakemore agreed: "We most often follow what Washington and, in particular, the President and the State Department say is important. . . . We rarely have an adversarial or even critical relationship with Washington."[36] As expressed by Zambia's Director of Information Daniel Kapaya, "Developing countries look at the Western press as biased because they follow the policies of their state in which they operate."[37] The major example of U.S. orientation in Frontline coverage revealed by content analysis is the reporting of the Angolan war purely from the perspective of the U.S.-backed resistance army, UNITA. More subtle, but still obvious, are the stories on Zimbabwe and Mozambique that clearly reflect the U.S. government relationship to those countries at the time of the report. To provide one example, a U.S. State Department official told me in 1989 that the United States had begun to point to Zimbabwe as a model for South Africa to aspire to. With that change in U.S. policy have come a series of upbeat network profiles of Zimbabwe. Given the antisocialist network rhetoric of the early and mid-eighties, it is clear that the networks have not dared to present a positive picture of Zimbabwe until officially sanctioned by the U.S. government.

Cold War rhetoric has also been common in reports on Mozambique. Correspondent Mike Boetcher of NBC began his February 4, 1988, report from Mozambique by saying, "People are dying as a result of a Marxist-Leninist government, a drought, and a civil war," setting the tone for the rest of the report. South African involvement in Mozambique was never mentioned.[38] Changes in official U.S. policy toward Mozambique in 1988 and 1989 are responsible for an influx of American reporters and a shift away from Cold War themes. A CBS report from Mozambique in April of 1989 was facilitated by the U.S. relief organization CARE; it contained few political overtones, focusing instead on famine relief. But when CBS returned later in 1989 they relied on the United States Information Service in Maputo for local assistance. The resulting story again concentrated on Mozambique "abandoning Marxism."[39] In so doing, CBS demonstrated its unwillingness to stray too far from the U.S. government line.

The content analysis and the studies of famine coverage described

earlier offer considerable evidence of the tendency of Western television
to rely on American and European, usually white, sources for interviews,
regardless of their degree of knowledge, instead of using interviews with
Africans. This tendency, regardless of the views expressed by the white,
Western, interview subjects, does demonstrate an Anglo-American bias—
a bias against delivering information to the Western public from African
sources. It is a bias maintained at the editorial level—in New York or
London, not in the field. Television producers living in Africa get the bulk
of their information from African sources—it would be impossible for
them to do otherwise. Because news managers in the West deem Western
sources more palatable to their audience, field producers are forced to
distort and even misreport their stories to include those friendly faces. As
is also suggested by the famine studies and others, this choice of interview
subject reinforces comfortable stereotypes—that of the beneficent American or European helping the miserable African, that of a Western world
that is stable and filled with knowledge and a Third World in chaos, that
of a world where white is superior to black. These factors, in concert with
the presentation of news from an Anglo-American and South African
perspective, do indicate that some degree of racism is inherent in the
process of Western television reporting.

AN AFRICAN PICTURE OF AFRICA

Curiously, African broadcasters have never succeeded in establishing
their own exchange of television news as other regions of the Third World
have, a prospect which would alleviate the shortage of video images from
the region and show Africa to the world as Africa wishes to be seen. In a
study of the relatively successful Asian television news exchange system,
Dan Flournoy concluded that "Asians are getting their news about Asians
from Asians and they are getting it sooner than they would from the West."
He quoted a comment about the Third World by Johan Galtung, who
"observed how much more interested they would be, given a chance, in
news about their own countries and their own regions, and how much less
they would be 'mesmerized by the powers and superpowers.' "[40] That was
Unesco's hope in facilitating the creation of television news exchanges,
and they have generally been successful.

One long time observer of the media of Southern Africa told me that
the news exchange failure stems primarily from the political nature of
news—African governments are simply unwilling to cooperate on so
sensitive an issue. A number of countries also argue that an African news
exchange has become unnecessary because they receive TV news pictures

from so many other sources already, including the U.S. network CNN and the U.S. government. It is, however, news of the developed, not the developing world.

CONCLUSION

A picture of distrust and suspicion between reporter and reported is evident in television coverage from the Frontline states. Optimistic assessments see this hostility gradually yielding to mutual appreciation and cooperation. The research conducted for this chapter found both formidable obstacles to adequate television coverage of the Frontline countries and a surprising willingness by Western media and African governments to resolve many of the problems. At this juncture there is no Frontline government that needs to be so insecure, so ashamed of past or present misdeeds, that it must deny freedom and cooperation to the news media, be they local or foreign. Keeping the channels of communication closed, through the various means mentioned in this chapter, only delays, and perhaps prevents, the integration of the region into an increasingly interdependent global economy. A new openness is sweeping across Africa, and governments are demonstrating an increasing appreciation of the usefulness of Western media and the value of press freedom.

As new sources of television news emerge and political and technological change makes access to stories easier, the major news companies must also realize that a slightly greater commitment to African coverage, such as technical assistance to local facilities and the creation of more African bureaus, is in their best interest if they are to remain competitive and honor their commitment to thorough coverage of the world. In the longer term, the major news agencies should cooperate with African broadcasters to build a television news exchange system in Africa, to visually connect African countries with each other and with the world. VisNews has considered such an effort.[41]

Even if they do continue to report on the world from a purely national perspective, the U.S. networks must do a better job of informing the public about the foreign policy they sponsor—such as proxy war in Southern Africa, cooperation with South Africa, or politically motivated humanitarian aid. A continuation of the trend toward media sophistication and openness among Frontline governments and a slightly more balanced, responsible, and inventive approach to coverage of Southern Africa by Western media will do much to improve the quality and quantity of television coverage of the Frontline countries.

NOTES

1. Roper Organization, 1980, for the Television Information Office, cited in W. Phillip Davison, James Boylan, and Frederick T. C. Yu, *Mass Media: Systems & Effects*, 2d ed. (New York: CBS College Publishing, 1982).

2. Anne Messerly Cooper, "Third World News on Network Television: An Inclusion/Exclusion Study of Violence" (Ph.D. diss., University of North Carolina at Chapel Hill, 1984).

3. James F. Larson, *Television's Window on the World: International Affairs Coverage on the U.S. Networks* (Norwood, NJ: Ablex, 1984).

4. J. B. Weaver and Evens Porter, "Patterns of Foreign Coverage in U.S. Network TV: A Ten-Year Analysis," *Journalism Quarterly* 61, no. 2 (1984): 356–63. Weaver's 1984 study of network coverage of foreign affairs revealed that 6.7 percent of all network foreign news was about Africa. A PBS "Frontline" series television program entitled "Assignment Africa," about TV news photographers in Africa, included a token content analysis of network coverage of all of black Africa for the first six months of 1986. That analysis showed the coverage to be less than 1 percent of the network newscasts. Since 1986 was a year of heavier than normal coverage of the Frontline countries, the "Assignment Africa" study would have probably produced an even lower figure at any other time (Public Broadcasting Service, David Royal, producer, 1986).

5. Jean-Marie Higiro, "U.S. Television Network News Coverage of the 1984–1985 Famine in Sub-Saharan Africa" (Ph.D. diss., University of Texas, Austin, 1988); Livi Chibuike Ajuonuma, "U.S. Television News Coverage of Crisis in the Third World: The Case of the Sub-Saharan Hunger Crisis" (Ph.D. diss., University of Minnesota, 1987); Joanmarie Kalter, "The Untold Stories of Africa: Why TV is Missing Some Big Ones," *TV Guide* (May 24, 1986): 2–12.

6. *The Image of Africa*, final report of the International Exchange on Communication and Development between Africa and Europe (Rome, 1988).

7. For details, see Chris Paterson, "Western Television News and the Frontline States: A Case Study of Third World Coverage" (Master's thesis, College of Communications, Boston University, 1990). The content analysis was compiled using the *Vanderbilt University Index and Abstracts to U.S. Network News*.

8. Larson, *Television's Window*, and others.

9. One example was the refusal by the BBC of exclusive footage of a major South African military defeat inside Angola in 1988, a time when South Africa was claiming to have no troops in that country. According to the Zimbabwean producer responsible, Simon Bright, the footage was eventually accepted by other networks.

10. *TV Guide* (August 18, 1984).

11. Tony Liddell, Worldwide Television News, Harare Bureau, interview (1990).

12. John McManus, "An Economic Theory of News Selection" (paper presented to the Association for Education in Journalism and Mass Communications meeting in Portland, Oregon, 1988).

13. David Kogan, managing editor (Europe, Africa, and the Middle East) VisNews, interview (1989).

14. Arlindo Lopes, National Director of Information, People's Republic of Mozambique, interview (1990).

15. James F. Larson, "Global Television and Foreign Policy" (paper for the Foreign Policy Association) and "Assignment Africa" television program, 1988.

16. *Index on Censorship* 10, no. 2 (April 1981) and *Herald* (Harare, Zimbabwe, May 11, 1983).

17. *Index on Censorship* 13, no. 1 (January 1984); 13, no. 2 (March 1984).

18. According to several correspondents in Zimbabwe.

19. Tony Liddell, WTN, and "Crisis in Zimbabwe" (*Frontline* transcript, April 25, 1983, WGBH, Boston).

20. Jude Wanniski, ed., *The 1987 MediaGuide: A Critical Review of the News Media's Recent Coverage of the World Political Economy* (New York: Harper & Row, 1987).

21. According to journalists and other sources in Harare, and CBS News, "60 Minutes: Zimbabwe: Five Years After" (CBS News Public Affairs transcript of a television program with Diane Sawyer, correspondent, and Barry Lando, producer, on April 28, 1985).

22. Sarah Kachingwe, Zimbabwe Ministry of Information, Posts, and Telecommunication, interview (1990).

23. *Africa Confidential* 31 (February 2, 1990): 1, 5.

24. In the view of Zambian communications scholar Francis Kasoma, author of *The Press in Zambia*, and Western diplomats in Lusaka, all interviewed in February 1990.

25. Gavin Johnstone-Robertson, VisNews, Harare Bureau, interview (1990); Liddell; and London VisNews and WTN managers. Also: Danny Schechter, "How We Cover Southern Africa," *Africa Report* (March–April 1987): 8.

26. Schechter, "How We Cover."

27. According to Johnstone-Robinson, and verified by other Harare correspondents (1990).

28. Interviews with Leach, Liddell, WTN in London, and other reporters (1990).

29. *The Index on Censorship* and interviews with correspondents in Zimbabwe provided most of the information for the chronology of attacks on the press compiled for this study. See note 7.

30. Reprinted in John Edlin, "Perils of a Journalist's Profession," *Africa Report* (March–April 1987): 27–29.

31. Kogan interview (1989).

32. *Index on Censorship* 13, no. 2 (1984).

33. Lopes interview (1990).

34. *MOTO* (January 1984).

35. Larson, "Global Television."

36. Kalter, "Untold Stories."

37. Daniel Kapaya, Director, Zambia Information Services, interview (1990).

38. Danny Schechter, "South Africa: Where Did the Story Go?" *Africa Report* (March–April 1988): 31.

39. USIS sources in Mozambique, and David Neff, Director for Mozambique, CARE, interview (1990). Also, the *Vanderbilt Index and Abstracts*.

40. Dan Flournoy, "Satellite News Exchanges in the Third World," ERIC Document Reproduction Service #295598.

41. David Kogan (1989) and Gavin Johnstone-Robinson (1990) of VisNews.

15

Savimbi's Image in the U.S. Media: A Case Study in Propaganda

Elaine Windrich

The U.S. media played an important role in promoting the image of Jonas Savimbi, leader of the National Union for the Total Independence of Angola (UNITA), as a "freedom fighter" worthy of American support. However, this image did not originate with the media, which would have had little knowledge of or concern about an issue as remote to U.S. interests as a war in a former Portuguese colony in Africa. Instead, Savimbi was an essential element of South Africa's propaganda war to win American acceptance of its policy of destabilizing the black-ruled states on its borders, particularly those led by left-wing movements such as the Popular Movement for the Liberation of Angola (MPLA). This had been the Pretoria regime's strategy since its abortive invasion of Angola on the eve of that country's independence in 1975, providing military support for UNITA as well as another rebel group, the National Front for the Liberation of Angola (FNLA), then favored by the United States. Although South Africa had obtained American approval for the invasion, this support was withdrawn when it became evident that the South African–led forces would not be able to overcome the combined resistance of the MPLA and the Cuban troops brought to Angola to assist in the defense of the country. Also contributing to the American defection was the response on the home front, where opposition to a secret war in collaboration with an apartheid regime culminated in the enactment of the Clark Amendment prohibiting any future military intervention in Angola.

WAITING FOR REAGAN

Although Savimbi and his decimated UNITA forces survived the defeat inflicted on their South African patrons, retreating to a camp supplied and protected by the South African Defense Force (SADF) across the Namibian border, little was heard of his cause in the United States until the election of Ronald Reagan in 1980. During the intervening years that cause was kept alive by South African propaganda and by the publicity of various conservative organizations in the United States, such as the Heritage Foundation, the American Enterprise Institute, the American Security Council, and the American African Affairs Association. Although their promotional efforts had been generally limited to right-wing publications, their own and others such as *Human Events* and the *National Review*, in 1979 they attempted to extend their influence by inviting Savimbi to the United States. To ensure maximum publicity for the event, they arranged for the invitation to be personally delivered to Savimbi by *Newsweek*'s Arnaud de Borchgrave (a future editor of the pro–South African *Washington Times*),[1] who interviewed the UNITA leader and accompanied him to the United States.[2] However, because the Carter administration refused to receive Savimbi, and his meetings were mainly with the fringe groups that invited him, the media took little notice of the occasion. Nevertheless, the visit did result in the establishment and the renewal of contacts with the organizations that were to play such an important role in selling Savimbi to the media in the 1980s. Since these organizations had also been promoting a Reagan presidency, and many of their members were to obtain senior positions in the Reagan administration, Savimbi was assured of the official support that would enable him to attract media attention. This outcome was already evident in the 1980 election campaign, when Reagan as candidate promised American military assistance to Savimbi and his "freedom fighters" in Angola,[3] a pledge that was renewed by Reagan as president two months after taking office.[4]

With the adoption of Savimbi as part of the Reagan administration's strategy of destabilizing Third World governments that were supported by the Soviet Union, the media began to take an interest in this recruit to the international camp of "freedom fighters." As one critic pointed out, the tendency of the media to follow the agenda set by the government, whether on domestic or foreign policy matters, was nowhere more evident than during the years of the Reagan presidency.[5] Savimbi's cause certainly illustrated this tendency, since there was virtually no popular interest in the subject that would have generated media coverage. However, during

Reagan's first term (when aid to UNITA was prohibited by the Clark Amendment), there was an air of unreality about much of the media reporting on Savimbi. While articles about his anticommunist commitments and his prowess as a "freedom fighter" continued to appear in the mainstream press as well as in right-wing newspapers like *The Washington Times*, news of his clandestine contacts with CIA and other national security officials to obtain U.S. military aid went largely unreported.[6] Despite the availability of evidence to this effect in overseas media such as *The Observer* and *The Sunday Telegraph* in Britain, little notice was taken of it, although a *Newsweek* story on CIA intervention in the Third World in October 1983 did include UNITA among the right-wing rebels being armed and trained by the agency.[7] Nevertheless, the story was not pursued further, and even when the Iran-Contragate investigations later uncovered evidence that UNITA had been illegally supplied with arms,[8] these revelations also made little impact on the media.[9]

NEWS FROM NOWHERE

As a result of the new respectability conferred on Savimbi by the Reagan administration, American journalists began to make their way to the UNITA camp known as Jamba. While not all of those who made the visit were sympathetic, many of them were invited for that very reason, and many others had little knowledge or understanding of Africa in general or Savimbi in particular. Nevertheless, as a result of the authenticity associated with on-the-spot reporting, these dispatches were accorded more attention, and also more credence, by news editors than they merited. What these reporters rarely mentioned, however, was that their presence in Jamba was made possible by the SADF and that reports filed from South Africa (where many of them were based) were subject to draconian censorship regulations. Also limiting the credibility of these reports was the fact that few journalists could speak Portuguese (or Spanish), leaving them dependent on UNITA interpreters for such show pieces as interviews with MPLA or Cuban prisoners or kidnapped peasants held in a military camp.

In addition to these obstacles to credible reporting, visiting journalists were supplied with information that they were either unable or unwilling to confirm but unhesitatingly included in their dispatches. Many of the claims were repeated so often by journalists, sometimes quoting each other as sources, that they became part of the accepted wisdom of the trade. One example was the endless repetition of UNITA's claim to control one-third (or more) of the country. Few ever questioned this claim or asked what "control" meant in a very sparsely populated region said to contain less than 5 percent of the total population.[10] Other claims relayed by visiting correspondents related to UNITA's alleged military successes. These usually consisted of inflated body counts applied to alleged MPLA or Cuban casualties when in fact the civilian population accounted for many of the victims and the SADF for many of the kills. Maps were even provided to show UNITA's battlefield achievements and these often accompanied the dispatches. One of these maps, however, appeared in *The Los Angeles Times* with the label "the situation in Angola according to Jonas Savimbi."[11]

Most of the American correspondents visiting Jamba also tended to view Savimbi's cause in a Cold War context or in terms of South Africa's "total onslaught" propaganda. UNITA was invariably described as Western-backed, when in fact its only Western backer was the United States. Savimbi's Chinese support was rarely recalled, because it would complicate the simplicity of the anticommunist message, and recalling Savimbi's military collaboration with the Portuguese colonialists against the MPLA would detract from his image as a freedom fighter.[12] Since UNITA was to be seen as Western-backed, the MPLA could only be seen as Soviet-backed. As one critic of these ideological blinkers observed, the Angolan government's efforts to defend its country against continual South African aggression were "made to seem part of Soviet power play." Even those journalists who were able to get to Luanda and visit the countryside, to see for themselves the effects of UNITA's devastating attacks on civilian communities, displayed a remarkable reluctance to accept what they saw because it was pointed out to them by a "Marxist regime."[13] While such evidence was dismissed as part of the Angolan government's "continuing propaganda war," the disinformation put out by UNITA and its South African ally rarely aroused similar skepticism.[14]

Two examples of such reporting, nearly a decade apart, illustrate the pattern followed by many American journalists during this period. The first was by *The Washington Post* managing editor, Richard Harwood, who reported from Jamba in July 1981 in the company of British journalist Fred Bridgland, biographer of Savimbi and "a great admirer of the man."[15] Since Harwood admitted that he was "not an expert on Africa or Savimbi" and had "no definite knowledge about the rights and wrongs of the war," it was not likely that he would be able to recognize UNITA propaganda, whether it came from Bridgland or Savimbi himself. This was evident from his unstinted praise for UNITA troops("these lads knew what they were doing") and his dismissal of the charge that their military successes were the work of the SADF as racist. He was also convinced that South Africa was not providing UNITA with weapons or joint military operations, because Savimbi had denied it and the Cuban prisoners interviewed through a UNITA interpreter claimed that they had never seen a South African in Angola. On the basis of these observations, Harwood was determined "to carry his [Savimbi's] message and the reality [*sic*] of his situation to America to persuade opinion-makers and the new administration that UNITA is a strong and viable option to the Marxism in Luanda, that he is not a puppet of the South Africans."[16] However, despite his commitment to UNITA's cause, he was later to admonish an American correspondent in Mozambique for being "an advocate rather than a journalist" because he had expressed sympathy for the Front for the Liberation of Mozambique (FRELIMO) government.[17]

Nearly a decade later, visiting correspondents were still remarking about the "disciplined network of fighters" commanded by Savimbi (despite widespread allegations of human rights abuses) and relaying the claim that UNITA controlled one-third or more of the country. This was the message of the reports from Jamba by *New York Times* correspondent Christopher Wren, which also included denials of well-documented charges against UNITA. For example, while it was generally acknowledged that UNITA land mines were responsible for the fifty thousand or so amputees treated at government medical centers, this correspondent devoted an entire article to UNITA's care for the limbless and the maimed, alleging that the MPLA used land mines against the civilian population "because they are cheap." Some of the patients he interviewed through a UNITA interpreter claimed to be victims of toxic gas bombs dropped by Cuban pilots,[18] a widely publicized UNITA propaganda ploy that had been dismissed by scientific experts as "totally worthless" or "a real joke."[19] Another example was the matter of the missing elephants. Although world wildlife conservation groups had charged UNITA with slaughtering over a hundred thousand elephants[20] and Savimbi had often boasted of selling ivory to the South Africans to pay for his war, the explanation relayed by this correspondent was that UNITA's contraband trade in ivory was limited to "the tusks of elephants who died of natural causes."[21]

MEDIA EXTRAVAGANZAS

In addition to the reports from Jamba, Savimbi derived a considerable amount of media coverage from his visits to the United States. Although the 1981 visit was a relatively low-key affair resulting in the official recognition of UNITA as "a legitimate political force in Angola," Savimbi's appearance in 1986, when he was welcomed by President

Reagan, was a media extravaganza staged with great skill and precision.[22] Most of the credit for this achievement was due to the public relations firm of Black, Manafort, Stone and Kelly, hired by Savimbi at the rate of $600,000 a year to promote his image in the United States. Since the principals of this agency—Charles Black, Paul Manafort, Roger Stone, Lee Atwater, and Christopher Lehman—had managed the Reagan-Bush election campaigns and/or served in the Reagan administration, their access to the White House and its congressional supporters ensured that Savimbi would get a sympathetic hearing.[23] They also had their allies in the media, who could be relied on to arrange an address to the National Press Club, interviews with newspapers, op-ed articles, and letters to the press. In the run-up to Savimbi's visit, while the issue of U.S. military aid to UNITA was being debated, a series of articles by Jeane Kirkpatrick and Rowland Evans and Robert Novak appeared in the op-ed page of *The Washington Post* warning of a Soviet-Cuban threat to Southern Africa and calling for "something more than humanitarian assistance" to UNITA, namely Stinger and TOW missiles.[24] During the visit, *Commentary* editor Norman Podhoretz appeared twice in the op-ed page of *The Washington Post*, first to extol Savimbi's great "promise" and then to condemn "the hostile attitude that its directed toward any and all people—not just UNITA guerrillas—who are willing to risk their lives challenging communist rule."[25] The lobbyists' influence also extended to arranging appearances on prime-time television. Exposure on such programs as CBS's "60 Minutes," ABC's "Nightline," and the "MacNeil/Lehrer News Hour" gave Savimbi yet another opportunity to publicize his image as a freedom fighter, in this case to audiences reckoned in the millions.[26]

While much of the mainstream media was impressed by the packaging of Savimbi by his public relations advisers—CBS described him as "charismatic" and *The New York Times* characterized him as "magnetic"— an analysis of editorial opinion in newspapers across the country showed that most were in fact against aiding the UNITA leader.[27] This was certainly the case with leading newspapers—such as *The Washington Post*, *The New York Times*, *The Christian Science Monitor*, and *The Los Angeles Times*—with the latter pointing out that none of America's European allies shared President Reagan's vision of Savimbi as a freedom fighter. Other newspapers, for example *The Philadelphia Inquirer*, *The Burlington Free Press*, and *Newsday*, were most concerned that committing American prestige to the cause of an ally of South Africa would lessen the chances of achieving a negotiated settlement on Namibian independence and the withdrawal of Cuban troops from Angola. One of the most outspoken critics was *The Cleveland Plain Dealer*, which urged that

Savimbi be sent home without a penny of American assistance. Putting the case in its proper historical context, it recalled that the U.S. government, by failing to support a coalition government following the Portuguese departure from Angola, had helped create an opportunity for South Africa—a mistake that the Reagan administration and Congress were close to repeating by considering Savimbi's appeal.[28]

Opposition to Savimbi's cause also appeared in the op-ed pages of the mainstream press, where, in the name of balance, a hearing was given to "the other side." Among the columnists taking this stand were Anthony Lewis in *The New York Times*,[29] Joseph Harsch in *The Christian Science Monitor*,[30] and Mary McGrory, Richard Cohen, and Edwin Yoder in *The Washington Post*.[31] Other critics, the outside contributors, included TransAfrica's Randall Robinson,[32] Congressman Stephen Solarz[33] ("balancing" Congressman Jack Kemp),[34] and former diplomats Richard Moose,[35] David Newsom,[36] and Wayne Smith. As the latter described the lobbying efforts for Savimbi, "the American right wants to join Pretoria in exerting pressure against Luanda, the victim of South African aggression."[37] Both Cohen and Yoder were most concerned with the anticommunist hysteria surrounding the Savimbi issue. For Cohen, "Savimbi's groupies" were conservatives who found "virtue approaching sainthood" in anyone willing to fight Russia or Cuba: "Beatified as freedom fighters, they were compared to nothing less than the Founding Fathers."[38] And for Yoder, "Savimbi fever" represented "a recurring tendency to fawn, in a most undignified fashion, over any opportunist who pleads anticommunist credentials."[39]

SIGNS OF FADING ARDOR

After the 1986 visit, media interest in Savimbi declined considerably, since the debate over whether he should receive U.S. military aid, which most of the mainstream media had opposed, was abruptly ended by the Reagan administration's decision to provide covert aid which could not be debated or voted on by Congress as a whole. Also detracting from Savimbi's news value was the fact that what little media interest there was in Africa had been diverted to the U.S.-brokered peace negotiations involving South Africa, Angola, and Cuba. These were intensively pursued by the diplomats and closely followed by the media throughout most of 1988. Since Savimbi had been excluded from those negotiations, his American supporters turned their attention to ensuring a role for UNITA in the peace settlement. Expressions of alarm that he might be sold out in the interests of a diplomatic victory in Southern Africa before the Reagan presidency came to an end were frequently heard in the columns of such advocates as *Human Events* and the *National Review*, and even made their way into the op-ed pages of the mainstream press by way of Jeane Kirkpatrick and Lally Weynouth.[40] *Human Events*, for example, was continually asking, "Will the administration cave in to an Angolan sell-out?" or "What's happening to the Reagan agenda" in Southern Africa? As a leading purveyor of this alarm, Constantine Menges, a former National Security Council official, questioned whether the peace negoti-ations would produce a "communist victory" (in Namibia as well as in Angola), calling on President Reagan, while there was still time, to prevent "yet another incompetent deal in Southern Africa."[41] Also appealing to the president, Jeane Kirkpatrick urged him not to abandon the goals he had served for a lifetime. "Jonas Savimbi, the Mujaheddin, and American defense are what Ronald Reagan is all about," she wrote, and such friends and such principles should not be sacrificed to "deal-making, Soviet style."[42]

Also accounting for the change of emphasis from Savimbi the guerrilla warrior to Savimbi the symbol of "peace and national reconciliation" was the decisive defeat inflicted on UNITA and its South African ally by MPLA-Cuban forces in the battle for the key town of Cuito Cuanavale in southeastern Angola early in 1988. Although the humiliating military setback largely accounted for the Pretoria regime's acceptance of the provisions of the U.S. peace plan—to withdraw its troops from Angola and cease military support for UNITA—the connection between its defeat and its agreement to terms it had rejected for over a decade was rarely observed in the U.S. media. In fact, the MPLA-Cuban military victory made scarcely any impact at all, except on Savimbi's American supporters, who feared that once the South African "shield" had been removed "Savimbi's lightly [*sic*] armed fighters" would be confronted with "Castro's fresh force of elite Cuban combat troops."[43] As in the coverage of earlier battles of the war, correspondents tended to rely on briefings by the SADF or interviews with Savimbi and other UNITA spokesmen. Consequently, South Africa's invasion of Angola to save UNITA from defeat (as so often in the past) was reported as a hot pursuit raid on the Namibian South-West Africa People's Organization (SWAPO) guerrillas based in Angola, as the SADF initially claimed. Reporting the battle on the basis of news conferences at Jamba or UNITA press briefings in Washington also provided a distorted picture of reality on the ground. For example, while UNITA's chief representative in the United States told *The Washington Post* that Cuito Cuanavale was "half in control" of UNITA and would be "fully occupied in a matter of days,"[44] Savimbi told a news conference at Jamba two days later that "nobody was there," a claim he repeated to the Baltimore *Sun* correspondent several months later, when the battle was already lost.[45]

In promoting Savimbi's image as a peacemaker, his supporters also had to ensure that he would receive additional U.S. military aid to compensate for the alleged loss of some $80 million a year from South Africa. While they were in the midst of this campaign, *The New York Times* came out with a front page story, based on the testimony of Fred Bridgland and several UNITA dissidents, alleging that over the years Savimbi had committed gross violations of human rights. The essence of the charges, which were made on London Independent Television and in the London *Sunday Telegraph* the same weekend that they appeared in *The New York Times* (March 11–12), was that Savimbi had personally been responsible for the elimination of his party rivals by such means as detention, torture, assassination, and witchcraft trials. In support of the charges, the newspaper cited Amnesty International, which had evidence going back to the early 1980s to confirm many of them, including the cases of women and children being burned in bonfires at public rallies.[46] Also confirming the allegations was Africa Watch, an offshoot of the U.S.-based Human Rights Watch. But its report received little media attention because when it appeared a month later (April 1989), the concern aroused by *The New York Times* revelations had largely died down.[47] Although the PBS television program "The Jonathan Kwitny Report" attempted to stir the conscience of its viewers by showing a segment exposing the "murderous activities" of Savimbi (and also the responsibility of former Secretary of State Henry Kissinger for embroiling the United States in the war), this effort was allegedly aborted by the subsequent withdrawal of the program from the air.[48] In fact, media interest in the subject was remarkably short-lived and no public debate of any magnitude was generated by the charges that a recipient of American military aid had been abusing the human rights of its followers as well as other civilians among the country's population. Nor did the allegations have the slightest effect on the U.S. government; the additional military aid to UNITA requested by President George Bush was approved by Congress three months after *The New York Times* story.[49]

However, the long-term effect of the revelations was that less was heard of Savimbi as a freedom fighter, at least in the mainstream press; even those newspapers supporting military aid to UNITA (including the newly converted *Washington Post*) did not attempt to justify it on those grounds.[50] Another indication that the human rights issue had made some impact came from a completely unexpected source, the right-wing press. In a unique article in the *National Review*, roving correspondent Radek

Sikorski condemned Savimbi's human rights record, and also his megalomania, in far more compelling terms than anything that had appeared in the mainstream, or even the alternative press. By far his most damaging charge was that the publicity campaign carried out by Savimbi's lobbyists was largely based on fabrications, because UNITA's leaders were not only "compulsive liars" but also "briefed on how to lie most plausibly"—a charge that also reflected on the U.S. media which reproduced the fabrications.[51]

Another sign of the media's growing disenchantment was Savimbi's largely unheralded visit to the United States in October 1989. Although the UNITA leader's image had been temporarily rehabilitated by his acceptance of a peace plan initiated by African presidents at a meeting in Gbadolite, Zaire, on June 22, his reneging on the terms of the accord, including the cease-fire and his commitment to temporary retirement from the scene, soon dissipated the goodwill engendered by his highly publicized handshake with Angolan President Eduardo dos Santos.[52] As *Southscan*'s Washington correspondent observed, Savimbi's 1989 visit was not the "seamless media extravaganza" that his previous visits had been. This time his expensive public relations firm had been unable to prevent headlines suggesting that President Bush had chastised his UNITA client for undermining the African peace initiative or "to mitigate the sour press with the usual set pieces about 'Savimbi-the-soldier/democrat.' "[53] *Newsweek* had also arrived at a similar conclusion (a long road from de Borchgrave's portrayal of the "freedom fighter" in 1979), attributing the "signs of fading ardor" to Savimbi's human rights abuses, his obstruction of the African peace initiative and his loss of relevance in a transformed geopolitical scene. Nevertheless, Savimbi was still receiving the U.S. military aid that enabled him to continue a war that had become "a bloody stalemate serving no one's interest."[54]

Whether or not this advice was heeded, the war was finally brought to an end by U.S.-Soviet intervention in the peace talks begun under Portuguese mediation in April 1990. Following a summit meeting in Washington at the end of that year, negotiations were continued in Portugal until an agreement providing for a cease-fire and internationally supervised elections was concluded on May 31. Although the media generally welcomed the agreement as a victory for the Angolan people after thirty years of war or as "proof that the world is a better place for the end of the Cold War," Savimbi's supporters claimed it as a victory for their side and "a vindication of the Reagan Doctrine." But even *The Wall Street Journal* had to admit that the UNITA leader was not "a model Western democrat."[55] As his critics in the media warned, if Savimbi (bolstered by U.S.

and South African covert assistance) were to win the forthcoming elections, there would be little hope for the emergence of democracy in Angola.[56]

NOTES

1. See "Moon Shines on Apartheid," Washington Office on Africa, *Notes On Africa* (Summer 1982), pp. 1–3.

2. "Savimbi Asks for Help," *Newsweek* (November 12, 1979): 68.

3. Interview, *Wall Street Journal* (May 6, 1980).

4. Interview, *Washington Post* (March 29, 1981).

5. See Mark Hertsgaard, *On Bended Knee: The Press and the Reagan Presidency* (New York: Farrar, Straus, and Giroux, 1988).

6. See Edward Giradet, "Report from Angola," U.S. News & World Report (June 13, 1983): 30; and Fred Reed, "African Bush War," *Washington Times* (November 29–December 3, 1982).

7. *Newsweek* (October 10, 1983): 41.

8. House of Representatives, Sub-Committee on Africa, *Possible Violation or Circumvention of the Clark Amendment: Hearing before the Sub-Committee on Africa*, 100th Congress, 1st Session, July 1, 1987.

9. Notable exceptions were Steve Mufson, *Los Angeles Times* (July 26, 1987); and Sanford Ungar and Arnold Kohen, *New York Times* (January 20, 1987).

10. Tony Hodges, *Angola to the 1990s* (London: Economist Intelligence Unit, January 1987), p. 16.

11. *Los Angeles Times* (April 9, 1984).

12. William Minter, *Operation Timber: Pages from the Savimbi Dossier* (Trenton, NJ: Africa World Press, 1988).

13. Marga Holness, "Reporting Angola," *Africa Events* (June 1987): 9.

14. William Claiborne, "Angola's Twilight Zone," *Washington Post* (October 4, 1987).

15. See *Jonas Savimbi: A Key to Africa* (Edinburgh: Mainstream Publishing Company, 1986).

16. "Angola: A Distant War," *Washington Post* (July 19–25, 1981).

17. Harvey Tyson, ed., *Conflict and the Press* (*The Star* Centennial Conference on the Role of the Press in a Divided Society; Johannesburg: Argus Publications, 1987), p. 235.

18. "Angolan Rebels Try to Aid the Maimed," *New York Times* (October 21, 1988).

19. See David Aronson and Patricia Brett, "Chemical Warfare in Angola," *Facts and Reports* (Netherlands, December 1, 1989): 15.

20. *Time* (February 20, 1989): 76.

21. "Angolan Rebels Look to Life after the South Africans," *New York Times* (October 30, 1988).

22. *Department of State Bulletin* 82 (March 1982): 34.

23. Christopher Ladd, "Black, Manafort's Sweet Savimbi Connection," *Legal Times* (May 18, 1987): 1.

24. *Washington Post* (September 30; October 4, 25, 27; and December 23, 1985).

25. *Washington Post* (January 29 and February 6, 1986).

26. R. W. Apple, "Red Carpet Treatment for a Rebel," *New York Times* (February 7, 1986).

27. "Who Was That Man?" *The Guardian* (New York: February 19, 1986): 18.

28. Quoted in *Editorials on File* 17 (January 16–31, 1986): 98–100.

29. *New York Times* (January 27, 1986).

30. *Christian Science Monitor* (January 30, 1986).

31. *Washington Post* (February 4 and 6, 1986).

32. *Washington Post* (November 3, 1985).

33. *Los Angeles Times* (October 29, 1985).

34. *New York Times* (December 3 and 21, 1985).

35. *New York Times* (January 30, 1986).

36. *Christian Science Monitor* (November 7, 1985).

37. *Los Angeles Times* (January 19, 1986).

38. *Washington Post* (December 13, 1985).

39. *Washington Post* (February 6, 1986).

40. *Washington Post* (November 20, 1988).

41. *Human Events* (August 13, 1988): 3, and (August 27, 1988): 12; *National Review* (October 28, 1988): 26–27.

42. *Los Angeles Times* (October 30, 1988).

43. Senator Gordon Humphrey, *Human Events* (October 8, 1988): 1.

44. *Washington Post* (January 27, 1988).

45. Peter Honey, "Angola: The Bush War," *The Sun* (Baltimore, April 24 and 25, 1988).

46. *Amnesty International Report, 1988.*

47. *Angola: Violations of the Laws of War by Both Sides* (Africa Watch, 1989).

48. "Jonathan Kwitny Show Censored," *Propaganda Review* 6 (Winter 1990).

49. Elaine Windrich, "Savimbi in the U.S. Media: The Case of Human Rights," *TransAfrica Forum* 7 (Spring 1990): 3–15.

50. Editorial, *Washington Post* (November 23, 1988).

51. "The Mystique of Savimbi," *National Review* (August 18, 1989): 36–37.

52. Andrew Meldrum, "Angola: A Golden Handshake," *Africa Report* (July–August 1989): 34–35.

53. "Turn-Around Signalled in U.S. Media Battles on UNITA Issue," *Southscan* (October 13, 1989): 295.

54. *Newsweek* (October 16, 1989): 54.

55. "Reagan Doctrine Dividends," *Wall Street Journal*, editorial (May 9, 1991).

56. For views on the peace agreement, see *Editorials on File* 22 (May 1–15, 1991): 554–57.

16

The South African Story: A Correspondent's View

David Zucchino

Six days before I left South Africa for good, my children finally saw Soweto. I took them there to see a celebration. Something good had graced the life of a woman they loved. She was a black woman from Soweto, a place a few miles from our home in Johannesburg, but so impenetrable and distant that my children regarded it as something exotic, like a city in a fable.

The woman was Johanna Sebelebele, our housekeeper. She had come to me one day in April, her face alight, to tell me that her brother was coming out of prison, where he was serving a six-year sentence for terrorism. He was a trained guerrilla of the African National Congress. He had been caught smuggling rifles and grenades across the border. Now his older sister wanted a ride to Soweto to greet him and celebrate.

My two daughters, aged seven and four, begged to go along. They had heard Johanna Sebelebele speak of Soweto. They had heard their black friends from school say they lived there. But they had never been there. Apartheid had deteriorated enough to allow black girls to attend their private school, but it still ensured that blacks and whites did not live together. White children lived in the white suburbs. Black children lived far away in places with mysterious names like Soweto, the Southwestern Townships.

So off we went, a white man, a black woman and two little white girls on their way to the township. It took an hour, for Soweto was designed to be remote. The men who implemented apartheid did not want the township located too close to white Johannesburg. Nor did they want blacks getting the idea that Soweto would ever become anything more than a temporary "native location," a transient labor reserve. Decent homes and roads and street lights were signs of permanence, so these things never evolved in Soweto.

On this raw evening in April of 1990, Soweto looked more forbidding than usual. An autumn wind was scattering garbage from heaps that had been growing for days. The smoke from coal fires turned the sky black and stung the eyes. Shadowy figures brushed against the car windows as thousands of workers trudged home.

My older daughter studied this dark scene. It was like nothing she had ever seen in Johannesburg. "This is like Sodom and Gomorrah," she said finally. She had been studying the Bible at Catholic school. She imagined a great fire consuming the city. "Why are these people being punished?"

She was only seven but she knew: This was the other side.

She had always suspected Africans were somehow different. There were none in her neighborhood, save the servants who worked for whites. There were blacks at her school, sweet little girls with names like Motshabi and Mapabello. But they arrived by bus from a place called Soweto and disappeared back on the bus every afternoon, except for those wealthy few whose mothers collected them in a BMW or a Mercedes. So now my daughter had seen Soweto. And so, she thought, this was where they kept them all.

A few weeks before, the sad plight of Africans had been described to me by no greater an authority than F. W. de Klerk, the man whose political gambles led to, among other things, clemency for Johanna Sebelebele's brother. De Klerk was leaning against a wall of a reception room, a cigarette in one hand and a cocktail in the other. He was in Tuynhuis, South Africa's version of the White House, where he was receiving foreign correspondents.

I was in a small knot of reporters listening to de Klerk. I heard myself blurt out, "Why are you doing it?" I meant his overtures to blacks. To my surprise, de Klerk answered me. It was an informal, off-the-record reception, and so the man spoke in a passionate way I had never heard him speak in public.

He said it pained him to see blacks in the townships, to see their cramped houses and feel the overwhelming futility of their lives. He said he saw injustice in what his people, the Afrikaners, had done to Africans. He was determined to break from the past. The old ways were wrong, he said. He said he was going to change things—not because he was being forced to, not for political opportunism, but because it was the right thing to do.

That is how it was for me in South Africa. If apartheid could create two worlds, black and white, then it created for me a whole fractured universe. One day I could play the white South African, at home in comfort with a blue pool and manicured lawn and meat grilling on the *braai*. The next day I could be swept away by the crowd at the township funeral, feeling the earth tremble under the pounding of feet in the *toyi-toyi* dance of liberation. And the next day a Boer president would be speaking to me of atonement for his tribe's sins.

When I arrived in South Africa in 1986, the townships were in flames; there was no hope for an end to the nation's pain. Nelson Mandela was in prison and P. W. Botha was defying the world. When I left in the spring of 1990, Botha was a broken old man, Mandela was negotiating with his former jailers, and F. W. de Klerk was promising a "new South Africa" free of racial discrimination. During the intervening four years, I traveled to many troubled worlds inside one nation.

I sat *ukududuza*, in mourning, with a Soweto mother named Alvina Kheswa as she parted with her eleven-year-old boy, Bongani, who was shot dead by unknown white men as he celebrated Guy Fawkes Day. I saw the grief of two white widows named Mare and Clucas as they buried their husbands, who had been blown apart by an ANC bomb at a whites-only rugby match. I saw the horror on Gladys Mazibuko's face after the police killed her activist son, then hijacked his coffin and buried it to prevent an illegal—that is, political—funeral.

I had tea in a blue-collar Johannesburg suburb with a racist named Alan McCabe, who held a baseball bat as he described to me how he had chased away a "coolie"—an Indian—who had dared move into his all-white suburb. I watched Bannican Loate weep as he described the ritual murder of his activist sister, Masabata Loate, who was stabbed to death and her head hacked off by fellow blacks because she had denounced their necklace murders. I heard Father Smangaliso Mkhatshwa, a black priest who leads the Southern Africa Bishops Conference, recount his torture by the security police, who applied electrodes to his genitals. "No one is sacred anymore," Father Mkhatshwa told me one day in 1987. "The government truly believes it is God Almighty."

I saw black cops whip black protesters and white soldiers shoot black kids. I saw a black mob stone a black woman for sleeping with a black cop. I saw a black community called Oukasie disappear—uprooted and trucked away from growing too close to a white suburb. I saw a nearby Afrikaner farmer named Tom Weichelt removed to make way for a black homeland, then get paid $2.8 million by the government for his played-out farm. I saw the wreck of my local shopping center, blown up by a bomb. I saw the bodies of seven black children burned alive in Natal because their parents backed the wrong faction. I saw a squatter camp burned to the ground by vigilantes.

I asked Dr. No—Andries Treurnicht of the pro-apartheid Conservative Party—if he would ever let a black man in his home. No, he said, except perhaps a homeland minister, if he were well dressed and well spoken. I asked Archbishop Desmond Tutu why the whites hated him so, why they called him "that cheeky kaffir." He sat in lovely old Bishopscourt, the only black man in an exclusive white suburb, and replied with a cackle, "Because they don't like a black man getting too big."

I heard big, overbearing P. W. Botha tell a black American reporter that he, P. W., was more African because he spoke several African languages and the American spoke none. I sat in Nelson Mandela's tiny back yard in Soweto and heard him say that he did not hate whites; that they had a place in South Africa; that he understood why they were so afraid.

I saw small acts of kindness. A squatter family offered me their only meat for the week. A black father of three pulled over in the middle of the Natal wars to help tow my rental car out of the mud. A black marshall took my hand at a rally and led me away from a hostile crowd. Even the most frightened and hate-filled Afrikaners took me into their homes, set great meals before me and spoke earnestly of "us" and "them," the civilized West and heathen Africa.

And everywhere, I saw people weary of conflict. I saw black people in their matchbox township homes who wanted little more than to walk the streets without fear of being robbed or killed by gangs, or shot or detained by the security police. They wanted a say in their country's affairs and to be treated with dignity, of course. But they also longed for decent homes, paying jobs, and good schools for their children. They did not necessarily want to live with whites, but like whites. Some wanted absolute black rule. Some wanted to share power with whites. All wanted their rightful share of South Africa.

I saw whites who strapped on guns to defend their unique culture and their lives of dominance and privilege. I saw whites who said apartheid worked, who want to go back to pure apartheid or forward to their own *boerestaat*, their partitioned white homeland. These whites wanted change, but change away from de Klerk's "new South Africa" and back to *baaskap*, to the rule of the white boss.

I saw whites who genuinely wanted to share their country's wealth with blacks, but feared being swallowed up. I saw whites afraid to go to the grocery store for fear of being blown up by a limpet mine. I saw them hiding their homes behind security walls and razor wire and infra-red alarms. I saw them grab their children out of the path of black men at the shopping mall. I heard some of them say they would accept anything, even black majority rule, to live like normal people.

Most of all, I saw people ready for change. Two men gave them hope for something better, for something resembling peace. Nelson Mandela and F. W. de Klerk could inspire hatred and fear, but also hope. Together, they were killing off the old South Africa. They could not say what would emerge in its place. Like all of us, they knew only that a new and different South Africa was coming, and nothing could ever be the same again.

Sello Motanng, brother to Johanna Sebelebele, got out of a taxi in front of his mother's house. Sebelebele and the rest of Motanng's relatives rushed from the little Soweto matchbox to press kisses on his cheeks. There was a great roar from the street, where young black men danced and sang praises to the return of an ANC hero. One of them came over and kissed my daughters, who were relieved that festive parties and happy people could emerge from a place so forbidding.

All that night, there was singing and dancing in the little brick house. The next Saturday, relatives poured in from townships across the Witwatersrand. A goat was slaughtered and cooked in a pit. Tributes were paid to Sello Motanng, who, at 30, had given his youth to the African National Congress.

One day in 1982, Motanng had walked out the door of his mother's house and, without telling a soul, hitched a ride to Swaziland. He was off to join the ANC. His older brother had already fled the country and joined up. For that reason, the Special Branch of the South African Police was hounding Motanng. Sooner or later, he knew, he would be detained if he did not flee the country.

Both Motanng and his brother, Thabo Motanng, came of age on June 16, 1976. That was the day police opened fire on Soweto blacks protesting the teaching of the hated Afrikaans language in segregated black schools. Thabo and Sello saw their friends lying wounded in the streets.

"That was the day I realized the Boers would never stop killing us. We had to rise up and overthrow the system," Sello Motanng told me the day he got out of prison. Thousands of other young blacks drew the same conclusions, and they all shipped out to join the ANC in exile. They returned with guns and limpet mines.

Thabo Motanng was among the first to flee, stealing from home one night in 1976 without even telling his mother. He took military training at a secret ANC base in Swaziland and slipped back into South Africa, where he and his ANC comrades opened fire on several Soweto police stations with AK–47 assault rifles, killing four policemen. He was caught in 1982 and sentenced to hang.

One day in 1983, Sello picked up a copy of *Sechaba*, the magazine of the ANC's armed wing, *Umkhonto we Sizwe*, Spear of the Nation. Inside was a story about an Umkhonto we Sizwe soldier who had been hanged by the Boers in Pretoria. It was his brother Thabo.

That same year, Sello was sent on a mission to South Africa. He and two comrades were to slip over the border at night and deliver AK–47s and grenades to Umkhonto we Sizwe cadres in Soweto. They made it to a hotel inside South Africa, in the homeland of Bophuthatswana, where one of Sello's comrades betrayed them. The man turned out to be a police spy. The Special Branch crashed into the hotel room, and Sello was beaten and hauled away.

For three months, the Special Branch showed him photos of black "terrorists" and ordered Sello to identify them. They slapped him and punched him each time he said he did not know them, although he did recognize some as Umkhonto we Sizwe men.

"The Boers were slapping me and shouting 'ANC!' and 'terrorist!' " Sello told me. "I was saying, 'Jesus, help me!' And they were saying, 'There is no Jesus in the ANC.' "

Sello was describing all this to me in my kitchen. He had come to the white suburbs the day I was packing to leave. I think he wanted to see a white man's house. He seemed fascinated that a white man from America was interested in his circumstances. The black men from the moving company were fascinated, too. They strained to overhear Sello's talk of Umkhonto and limpet mines and savage Boer cops.

I asked Sello what he thought of de Klerk. "Well," he said, "de Klerk is not a stubborn old Boer, like P. W. Botha," the Afrikaner who ran South Africa when Sello went off to prison. He thought de Klerk was sincere. He thought he was trying. He thought he wanted to cut a deal.

De Klerk had certainly affected Sello's own fortunes. He had commuted the sentences of many blacks jailed, like Sello, for politically motivated crimes. Nelson Mandela had persuaded de Klerk that the government and the ANC could not begin formal negotiations with Umkhonto soldiers still in prison. De Klerk had released Mandela and other senior ANC men. The ANC wanted him to also free the ANC's "prisoners of war," as Mandela called them. De Klerk responded by commuting some cadres' sentences, and now Sello Motanng was in my kitchen.

I wondered how it felt to be suddenly legitimized. Almost overnight, the ANC had stopped trying to blow up its own country. It was no longer trying to "render South Africa ungovernable," the ANC battle cry of the

1980s. The ANC didn't have to sneak men like Sello Motanng into the country anymore. Their men could walk the streets openly. The ANC now had a modern, spacious suite of offices in the heart of white Johannesburg.

Sello, in fact, had just come from there. He had gone seeking work. He thought he was due some consideration for all he had suffered for the ANC, for his brother's martyrdom and his mother's pain. And the men at the ANC did indeed thank him. They were setting up a ceremony to honor the Umkhonto cadres coming off Robben Island. But there was no job. The ANC men told Sello they were still setting up. He should check back in a few weeks.

Sello was crushed; somehow he had expected an immediate reward. He couldn't wait for the ANC. He needed money now. He had a son to raise. He spoke to me of an idea he had. Perhaps he could get a job using the new skills he had acquired. I didn't know what he meant. Who would hire a man trained to plant limpet mines?

No, Sello said, he meant the skills he had learned on Robben Island. In prison, they had taught him to be a carpenter.

Prison was something black people seemed to know all too well in South Africa. They would say, "When I was in prison . . ." the way Americans of my generation would say, "When I was in college. . . ." The week I arrived in South Africa, I kept running into prisoners—people coming out of detention, people going into detention, people hiding from detention, people about to be detained.

It was early July 1986. P. W. Botha had just imposed a state of emergency. His cops were raiding the townships, dragging activists from bed, hauling them off to jail without charge or trial. The number eventually reached 30,000. People were afraid to go home. I spent one evening in Soweto with two distraught black activists named Sophie and Patience, who were hiding out on a friend's living room floor. The women couldn't go home because the police were waiting for them, camped out in their parents' living rooms.

People were going to jail for possessing ANC literature. The ANC and anything associated with it was banned. It was illegal to wear the ANC colors of gold, green, and black. People hid their copies of Mandela's banned biography; I made my first flight into Jan Smuts airport with the book buried deep inside my luggage. A black man named Matthews Ntshyiwa was sentenced to three years in jail for engraving the initials ANC on his coffee cup at work. The sentence was later reduced, but Ntshyiwa's boss fired him anyway.

Now, four years later, everybody wears ANC T-shirts. Mandela's face is on neckties and umbrellas. White cops clear traffic for ANC protest marches. The number of detainees is less than one hundred. Some political prisoners and ANC cadres are coming out of prison. Political executions have been halted. Former ANC exiles—the men the government was calling terrorists a year ago—are posing for pictures with de Klerk. A state-run assassination squad has been exposed. Most of the emergency decree has been lifted.

What happened? Some people say it was sanctions, or the pain of international isolation and the cutting of foreign bank loans, or the wrecked South African economy, or the sheer weight of black resistance, or the open defiance by millions of South Africans, black and white, of apartheid and repression. It was probably all of these things. What really mattered was that F. W. de Klerk decided he could no longer defend the indefensible.

The president's men had dropped hints for more than a year, but few people noticed at the time. As early as 1988, I heard a young government deputy minister named Roelf Meyer, 42, make a telling remark outside parliament one day. "Look, we didn't invent apartheid," he said, speaking for the generation of Afrikaners who were children when the National Party came to power in 1948 and institutionalized apartheid.

In July 1989, the month before de Klerk forced Botha from the presidency, his law and order minister made a startling comment. Adriaan Vlok, the man who put 30,000 people behind bars without a single warrant, was suddenly calling apartheid "an albatross around our necks." He said it would "crucify us if we don't get rid of it."

De Klerk was eleven years old when Afrikaners began passing apartheid laws. So now he and his suddenly progressive followers seemed to be saying: Don't blame apartheid on us. We didn't impose it, but we will end it. It can't be justified. It's wrong. We want to do the right thing.

It was difficult to believe that this was the same man who, as Botha's minister of education, wanted to withdraw government money from liberal colleges whose students were involved in antiapartheid protests. As recently as 1986, de Klerk said: "The National Party stands by its policy of separate residential areas, schools and institutions for different race groups." Now he was abandoning the very system that had nurtured him.

I saw state repression in country after country of black Africa long before Pretoria ever gave me permission to report inside South Africa. I expected South Africa to be far more oppressive. It wasn't. It was just different. Materially, South African blacks live better than blacks in the rest of Africa. Government ministers would often cite this fact to Western reporters, as if it somehow proved white South Africans to be morally superior to other African rulers.

But because South Africa has so much more wealth to share, the low status of blacks seems even less excusable. South Africa claims to abide by Western norms; the whites there beg to be included in the family of Western nations. Few black-ruled nations make any pretense of democracy, so it is only logical that the West holds Pretoria to higher standards. Much of South Africa even looks like America, with skyscrapers and shopping malls and Pizza Huts. That makes the indignities suffered by blacks all the more reprehensible.

The West rightly refuses to allow South Africa both acceptance and apartheid. That is why South Africa is punished with sanctions and disinvestment. That is why American congressmen who tour South Africa demand an end to South Africa's state of emergency, but tolerate much longer states of emergency in Kenya and Zimbabwe, as well as the killing and torturing of blacks in Angola, Burundi, Somalia, Mozambique, Ethiopia, Sudan, and elsewhere.

Yes, South Africa is different. Apartheid makes it so.

When I visited African countries, the government would send a "minder," an official from the Information Ministry, to shadow my every move. His job was to make sure I interviewed only approved citizens and saw only what the government wanted me to see. African governments are not satisfied with state control over their own news media. They want to control the foreign media as well.

I expected a minder in South Africa, too, but there never was one. There was only a man from the Bureau for Information, who summoned me to Pretoria during my first week for an elegant lunch. There, he warned me that I had better report "both sides of the story." I already knew one side. The other side, the information man told me, was the terrorist ANC, with its bombings and intimidation of moderate blacks, and its master plan to make South Africa a black-ruled, one-party, Marxist state.

Pretoria, as it turned out, didn't need minders. My phone was tapped. My mail was opened. From time to time at funerals or rallies, a police video crew would videotape me and my fellow foreign journalists. And Pretoria could always refuse to renew our work permits, a threat that was subtly but firmly held over our heads. Even so, most foreign correspondents wrote openly about things nominally prohibited under South Africa's emergency press restrictions—police torture, police actions, descriptions of unrest, protest marches, banned funerals, detentions, draft resisters, riots and removals. And almost without fail, a new work permit would be approved every three months.

South Africa deported a few journalists, of course, but they were almost always TV people or still photographers. The authorities despised cameras; they showed truths that could not be denied. They did not concern themselves as much with the written word. They could always say a newspaper article was biased or slanted or misinformed. So they let us bend the media restrictions rather than kick us out and draw undue attention to our work.

South African newspapers defied the restrictions, too, and they antagonized the authorities at every opportunity. On my first day in South Africa, I read an editorial in the liberal *Star* newspaper calling P. W. Botha a fool and a tyrant. I expected the paper to be shut down the next day. In all my travels through black Africa, I had never read the slightest criticism of a government or head of state. Most newspapers in black-ruled nations are state-run, and the few independent papers are thoroughly cowed by dictators or military leaders. So I was surprised to see the head of state ridiculed in South Africa, where I had assumed such insolence was forbidden. I was even more surprised by the authorities' reaction. They ignored it. I soon discovered that South African newspapers, even during the worst days of Botha's censorship, routinely called the white authorities criminals, racists, rogues, and demagogues—and got away with it.

There was an essential difference between South African censorship and that imposed by, say, Daniel Arap Moi. In Kenya, President Moi actually gave speeches, printed verbatim by a fawning press, warning Kenyans not to speak to foreigners, particularly foreign journalists. The message got through. I couldn't do interviews; Kenyans recoiled when they saw my notebook. I once tried to get a Kenyan government functionary to tell me Kenya's annual rainfall. He refused. He said it was a state secret.

In South Africa, blacks welcomed me into their homes. They poured out tales of cruelty and deprivation, then wrote their names down in my notebook and begged me to print their stories. Again and again, they would say: "Tell them in America what is happening to us." They knew the white authorities would be angered by what they said, but they were not afraid. Most of them already had been harassed, detained, shot at, and beaten. What else could happen? And they knew that millions of fellow blacks were also rising up and speaking out. They believed their cause was just, and that gave them courage.

This sort of quiet and relentless defiance was like a waterfall beating down on solid rock. It wore away the old iron-fisted Boer rule even under Botha's authoritative presidency. By the time de Klerk maneuvered Botha from power, the cumulative tide of resistance forced his hand.

Blacks were flying the ANC flag and reading ANC pamphlets long before de Klerk legalized the ANC. They flooded white hospitals before de Klerk declared them open to all races. They infiltrated white beaches, white train coaches, and white buses before de Klerk opened them up. They lived in nominally white city centers more than a decade before de Klerk proposed turning urban cores into "open areas." They held peaceful rallies, often in the face of police guns and whips, long before de Klerk authorized peaceful protest. They defied their restrictions before de Klerk ordered an end to restrictions.

When I first arrived in South Africa, I saw signs reading, "Slegs Blankes"—whites only—on the toilets in Johannesburg's city hall. On the men's room door at the Johannesburg Zoo, a sign said, "European Males Only." Tiny white stick figures were painted on some toilet doors in the parks and black ones on others. Then one day they disappeared.There was no announcement, no celebration. Nobody really noticed. Blacks had been ignoring the signs for years.

But for every barrier that is falling, others still stand. Though the Group Areas Act is widely flouted, the law still dictates where South Africans can legally live. Though blacks may now own their homes—in black townships only, of course—the Land Act still reserves just 13 percent of South Africa's land for blacks on a trial basis. Though the pass laws were scrapped in 1986, the Population Registration Act still classifies South Africans by race at birth. (As of early 1992, the Group Areas Act, the Land Act, and the Population Registration Act had been repealed.) Though de Klerk proposes letting certain neighborhoods open schools to all races, public schools are still segregated, and black schools are woefully inferior.

All of these prescribed inequities are negotiable, de Klerk says. Drawing on his cigarette during his informal bull session at Tuynhuis, he assured us that he could convince whites that they no longer need apartheid laws to protect their interests. The next day, de Klerk's Afrikaner minister of constitutional affairs said publicly that the National Party will probably negotiate itself out of power within ten years.

Even as apartheid laws are softening, the hatred between some black factions is hardening. Afrikaners like to say that blacks are not a majority in South Africa, but a minority of a dozen separate tribes. That is a convenient exaggeration, but it is true that more blacks are killed by fellow blacks than by the white-led security forces.

One of the first stories I covered in South Africa was the fighting in Natal Province between blacks who support the ANC and those loyal to the Zulu tribal movement called Inkatha. Four years later, I was still covering the Natal wars. Nothing had changed except the death toll.

One day in early 1990 I interviewed an Inkatha widow whose husband and sons had been murdered by a pro-ANC mob. The next day I interviewed a pro-ANC woman whose son had been murdered by Inkatha gunmen and whose house was under 24-hour guard by ANC comrades to prevent Inkatha from burning it to the ground. Both women seemed surprised when I told them that there was another black mother sharing the same grief and fear on the other side of the war zone.

Sometimes South Africans literally don't speak the same language. One Christmas, my white neighbors went on vacation and left their home and pool in the care of their black maid. The woman's children came down from the rural Transvaal to enjoy white living for a while. Though the maid's eighteen-year-old son could not swim, he dove into the pool one morning while his mother was away. Soon he was face down at the bottom. His younger brothers and sisters ran to fetch the gardener, screaming in their Northern Sotho tongue. But Edward the gardener was a Coloured from the Cape, and he spoke only English and Afrikaans. By the time Edward realized what the black children were saying, dragged the young man from the water and ran next door to ask me to phone the black ambulance service, the maid's son was dead.

For all the misery I encountered, I shared small victories with South Africans who resisted the system in a million small ways. In 1986, I sat with Albertina Sisulu, a prominent antiapartheid leader, alone and cold in her Soweto house after the authorities cut off the electricity during a rent strike to protest township conditions. Four years later, I watched her smother her husband with kisses the day Walter Sisulu came home after twenty-seven years in prison. The electricity was back on, and the authorities announced they would negotiate with activists—and not with the toothless black councillors imposed by Pretoria—to end the rent strike.

In 1988, I visited Henry Klotz, the white mayor of Durban. Klotz had just been suspended from Botha's National Party for daring to suggest that Durban's beaches be opened to all races. He struck me as a visionary too far ahead of his time. In March 1990, shortly after de Klerk had ordered the nation's beaches integrated, I visited Klotz again. He reminded me that he had told me that change would come one day. "I just never thought it would come so soon," he said.

By February of 1990, I knew the old days were gone for good when I went to visit the head of Broederbond, the secret Afrikaner society that invented and implemented apartheid. For more than half a century, the Broederbond has ruled South Africa; every head of state since 1948 has been a Broeder, including de Klerk. The society is dedicated to Afrikaner supremacy, with apartheid as its tool.

The Broederbond president is J. P. de Lange, a mild little Afrikaner professor. I asked him point-blank if apartheid had been a mistake. De Lange stared at his hands for a long while. Then he looked up, and I thought he was going to launch into the old self-serving Afrikaner justification of racial separation I had heard a hundred times before. Instead, he took a breath and said: "Yes."

But even with apartheid dying, old attitudes persist. On a personal level, South African blacks and whites know little of one another. The only regular contact is still between *baas* and servant, supervisor and employee, customer and cashier. In Johannesburg, virtually every checkout clerk in the grocery store is black. Virtually every supervisor is white.

Most whites cannot imagine a black supervisor, much less a black member of Parliament or, God forbid, a black president. I know. I lived among them. Living in the white suburbs was like taking a never-ending safari ride through an African game reserve. You would ride along, safe in your Land Rover, never seeing the dangerous beasts lurking in the veld. A few brave whites would step off into the wild unknown, but the rest would roll the windows up tight and shut out Africa.

Even the most liberal whites could be unintentionally demeaning toward the blacks they were committed to help. At the multiracial Catholic school my daughter attended, my wife noticed one day that a sign over a type of candy sold in the school snack shop read: "Nigger Balls." When she explained to the nuns what the term meant in American, they were horrified and the sign quickly came down.

Over four years, I never saw a white man perform menial labor. Every janitor and maid, every street sweeper, coal miner, motorcycle messenger, and gas station attendant is black. Virtually every foreman, office manager, and personnel director is white. I went to white homes where the madam would complain about her maid in front of her, as if the poor woman weren't there. Again and again in the townships, blacks used the same word to describe to me how they felt in white South Africa: invisible.

If some blacks were invisible, some whites were blind. Most had never been to a township. Until early 1990, few among them had ever heard an ANC member speak or seen an ANC flag. Few had watched a black protest march or seen police whip mourners at a political funeral. Until de Klerk legalized the ANC in February 1990, such things were almost never shown on government-run TV. Whites even had their own TV channels, where they could forget Africa and tune in to "Dallas" and "Thirtysomething."

They had an invasion complex. They all lived in compounds surrounded by high walls with sharpened stakes imbedded along the top. They had infrared alarms and panic buttons that summoned security guards with guns strapped to their hips. I had these things, too. They came with the territory.

I also had them in Kenya, as did my black and Indian neighbors. One night in Nairobi, a machete gang battered down our barricaded doors with a tree trunk before security guards answered the panic button and chased them off. It was a common occurrence, and everyone in Nairobi had their own tales of true crime. But the Kenyans were afraid of criminals. The South Africans were afraid of blacks.

Like all foreigners in South Africa (even Asians, who are known as "honorary whites"), I lived among the ruling class. But I would leave the white cocoon to prowl the townships and the homelands, to see the funerals and the marches, to tell the tales of the dispossessed. I lived in the white suburbs. I worked in Africa.

I once spent weeks in a township called Tembisa with rebellious young blacks who called themselves comrades. They told me how black collaborators in Tembisa were necklaced. They claimed they only watched as others carried out those executions by fire, but the joy they took in describing them made me think they did more than just watch. One day the comrades dropped by my house to borrow some money. They saw that their white friend lived far more comfortably than they did. One of them laughed and told me: "Comrade, we are going to have to nationalize this house of yours."

In the suburbs, white acquaintances would learn that I was a foreign reporter and they would always ask: Have you been to the townships? It was like asking: Have you been to Mars? They assumed I had some oracular insight into their own country. What were the blacks thinking? What was de Klerk really up to? Was Mandela as frightening a man as they had been led to believe?

Africa scared them. Sometimes it scared me. The day Mandela was released, I was trapped in a volatile crowd of 40,000 blacks awaiting his arrival in downtown Cape Town. As each hour passed without Mandela, young men in the crowd grew more surly. Archbishop Tutu and the Rev. Allan Boesak begged them to stay calm. They cursed the clergymen, who gave up and got out of the way. Soon there was wild shoving and charging. People were crushed against walls. Some of them fell down and were trampled. Thousands of us were lifted off our feet by the crush of people and carried on a wave for half a block, our feet never touching the ground. People's bones were broken. Skin was scraped from faces and arms.

Then Mandela arrived and from the throng rose the richest and most plaintive sound I had ever heard from a gathering of human beings.

Mandela raised his arms and people fell to their knees, weeping. Again we were all lifted and carried on a wave, but a gentle wave of rejoicing.

Three days later, I sat in Mandela's yard and heard him speak of controlling black rage and addressing white fears. His voice was soft and soothing. He was like an old sage, and I felt blessed. I wanted every white in South Africa to watch this man on their TV sets inside their houses hidden behind stone walls. That night, I drove home from Soweto to the white suburbs with a sense that the trip was shorter than ever before.

IV

Changing African Coverage

17

Dateline Africa:
Journalists Assess Africa Coverage

Tami Hultman

On March 21, 1990, scores of world leaders gathered in a soccer stadium for a dramatic midnight ceremony. After a long war against South African rule, the last colony in sub-Saharan Africa became an independent nation. The independence of Namibia marked the end of an era that began when the European powers divided Africa among themselves at the Berlin Conference of 1884–85. It was also, many hoped, a sign of things to come in Africa. The constitution that came into effect that night is one of the world's most democratic.

The historic event made the ABC "World News Tonight" as a concise tag at the end of another item: "Meanwhile, at midnight, the flag of South Africa was replaced by a flag of Namibia, marking the independence of the last South African colony. A black government took over power of the country, which has a 7 percent white minority." NBC also devoted two sentences to the item; CBS doubled the coverage with four sentences. Only CNN reported the independence of Namibia as more than a backdrop for talks between U.S. Secretary of State James Baker and Soviet Foreign Minister Eduard Shevardnadze, who attended the ceremonies. Although the cost of transporting reporters and camera crews long distances is cited by network executives as a major reason for infrequent African coverage, Namibia was a reminder that the most important reasons may lie elsewhere. All four commercial networks had crews on the spot.

"I think we might have done better on Namibia," says Bill Wheatley, who for five years—including the period when Namibia gained independence—was executive producer of the NBC "Nightly News." "[Namibia] certainly is an important place with ramifications for Americans, given the American involvement over the years, and also because of the South African connection. So I think that deserved more time than it got."

David Gergen, communications director in the Reagan White House and now editor-at-large for *U.S. News and World Report*, says the Namibia reporting was part of a pattern. "The history of American media," he says, "has been one of general inattention to Africa, except when there's been major famine or conflict." Gergen says parachute journalism—a quick in-and-out during crisis situations—has been the most common response to African events.

Africa "has to be undercovered," says John Leonard, media critic for CBS's "Sunday Morning," "because I read all the time—I read hundreds of magazines, I get five newspapers a day—and I don't know what's going on."

Washington Post associate editor Jim Hoagland, who won a Pulitzer Prize for his reporting on South Africa, says the African continent has gotten short shrift in the media for a long time. "I was foreign editor and assistant managing editor [at the *Post*] for about eight years," Hoagland says. "And I would have to be honest in saying that Africa weighed relatively lightly on the scales of newsworthiness. As a former correspondent in Africa, I regret that."

ABC's Ted Koppel agrees that Africa gets insufficient media attention. The "Nightline" host says that "a certain fundamental racism in this country" means that half a million Ethiopians dying doesn't provoke the same response as would the deaths of half a million Italians.

It is the complacency of many television producers that irritates Ed Turner, executive vice-president in charge of news gathering at Cable News Network (CNN). The first step toward improved reporting, Turner believes, is acknowledging the problem. "I'm here to tell you that we are *not* doing a good job," he says emphatically, "but at least we know it! So much more needs to be done, and we'll do more, and even that won't be enough." The feeling that Africa is somehow escaping its fair share of media scrutiny seems to be gaining ground among media gatekeepers—the people who make the decisions about what gets into the newspapers or onto radio and television broadcasts across the nation.

But does a sense that Africa may merit more space and airtime mean that it will get more? What do journalists themselves see as the factors limiting Africa coverage? To explore those questions, Africa News Service interviewed several dozen editors, producers, and reporters from major print and broadcast media in the United States. Unless otherwise cited, all the quotes in this chapter are from those conversations.

THE AFRICAN ADVENTURE STORY

The future is built on the foundations of the past. Before looking at the prospects for more complete coverage of Africa, it is important to trace the roots of images that still shape today's reporting.

From the earliest days of the republic, Americans have viewed Africa as a continent of savages and wild beasts. The reading public was alternately fascinated and repelled by accounts like those of reporter Henry Morton Stanley. Sent by *The New York Herald* in 1866 to find the British missionary and explorer David Livingstone, Stanley regaled audiences with front page accounts of his journeys. His later books about his African travels—including *Through the Dark Continent* in 1897 and *In Darkest Africa* in 1890—shaped opinions in Europe and North America. In his book *Dark Continent: Africa as Seen by Americans*, Michael McCarthy says explorers' images of Africa were widely accepted by blacks as well as whites.[1] "During the late nineteenth and early twentieth centuries, especially," McCarthy writes, "a majority of black Americans subscribed either consciously or unconsciously to the dangerous and fallacious idea of African inferiority."[2]

Yet the observations of the popular writers were often ill-informed and misleading. African societies appeared to Europeans to be stateless. Africans seemed to have no religions. Even their fields looked uncultivated. Scholars now know that whatever the flaws in African societies, many African cultures built powerful empires, African theologies were complex and intricate, and crop rows that looked jumbled or untended were often scientifically sound examples of productive intercropping or of shifting cultivation that let marginal tropical soils recover by lying fallow.

But the explorers' reports were used to explain and justify the subordination of people of African descent. "The case against black people in America," says McCarthy, "was advanced by showing that their African ancestors had failed to develop a fully civilized way of life. If Africans could not do it in their homeland, then how could their progeny possibly do any better in America?"[3] In 1889 the second issue of *National Geographic* magazine featured an article by the geographic society's founder, Gardiner Hubbard, asserting that Africans had developed a degree of civilization only after coming into contact with Western culture. When that contact was cut, Hubbard wrote, Africans "deteriorated into barbarism."[4]

According to McCarthy, the most important source of reporting on Africa in the nineteenth and early twentieth centuries was an African-American paper called *The Freeman*, published in Indiana. Articles by explorers and other African travelers were supplemented by cartoon caricatures depicting Africans with bones through their noses and necklaces of teeth. The comic savages spoke in crude dialects, often about their next human meal. School textbooks, travel writings and children's literature reinforced the media images. But it wasn't always that way.

Pictorial art was the mass media of fourteenth- and fifteenth-century Europe. A study of the period by the Menil Foundation's *Image of the Black in Western Art* project has unearthed and catalogued thousands of images from artworks and has published several large volumes of its on-going research.[5] In the stunning reproductions, blacks appear as royalty, saints, and sages as well as servants, pages, and musicians. Imperial Europe gave Africans a large place in its veneration of saints, its heraldry and its art. The institution of slavery changed all that.

Large-scale contacts between Europeans and Africans coincided with the development of the slave trade in the sixteenth century. Explorers found that, despite its fabled wealth, Africa did not readily yield its riches to European entrepreneurs. "From an economic point of view," says Volume 2 of the Menil study, "Africa had only one thing to offer: manpower."[6] The establishment of colonies in the Americas, built on labor-intensive crops such as cotton, intensified the demand for chattel slavery—and the need to justify it. Christian doctrine, which taught that all people were part of the human family and equal before God, was transformed into the dogma of polygenesis, which held that races had been created as distinct and unequal. Twelfth-century enamels of apostles addressing a white man and a black man, symbolizing the variety and unity of humanity, were made obsolete by the evolving theory that Africans had been divinely fitted for servitude.

Even the abolitionist art of the eighteenth and nineteenth centuries helped erase the diverse, often positive, earlier perceptions of blacks, says art historian Hugh Honour in the latest of the Menil volumes. So potent were the images of blacks as victims, he says, "that they reduced the possibilities of representing blacks in the former roles of saint or devil, proud Magus, regal personification of Africa, or even richly dressed and petted page boy."[7]

Like the abolitionist's crusade that solidified an image of blacks as victims rather than actors, the fly-encrusted, stick-thin children portrayed in late-twentieth-century antihunger campaigns have had an unintended result. What is being called compassion fatigue has fused with a contemporary view of Africans as either brutal and corrupt or passive and exploited. The dark continent has come to be seen as the lost continent. Rather than being sensationalized, it is most often simply ignored.

UNDERREPORTING AFRICA

We have not come as far from Stanley's conception of Africans as we like to think. During a 1978 uprising against the government of Mobutu Sese Seko in Zaire, the Associated Press called the rebels' campaign "a rampage of murder and rape," while United Press International dubbed it "a frenzy of killing and looting"—characterizations based on government press releases and later proved incorrect.[8] During another uprising fourteen years earlier, when Zaire was still known by its Belgian colonial name of the Congo, *Time* magazine said that the "rebels were, after all, only a rabble of dazed, ignorant savages."[9]

One young American reporter who arrived in central Africa during that chaotic period, which came to be known as the Congo crisis, was Joseph Lelyveld, now managing editor of *The New York Times*. Like Jim Hoagland, Lelyveld later won a Pulitzer for a book based on his South Africa reporting. And like Hoagland, Lelyveld has sometimes questioned the way news decisions are made. He recalls his stint in the Congo as marked by the tyranny of pack journalism—still a constant complaint of reporters covering Africa. The world's media, he says, congregated in the Congo capital, practicing journalism by press release. His own stories made the front page regularly. "At a time when a place is recognized as being hot," he says, "almost any reasonable development can be front-page news or make the network news simply because there's a concentration of journalists there. That creates a media momentum, unrelated to what's really important. Sometimes very fundamental and important coverage gets lost at moments like that as the herd tramples around."

Lelyveld says he began to feel "a little fraudulent that I was writing authoritatively about a subject I knew very little about. I knew the capital—and this was a vast country. The rest I was doing mostly on hearsay." So, "almost with a sinking feeling," he left the pack, venturing into the countryside and filing stories quite unlike those of other reporters. Although his dispatches ran in the paper, they were buried deep on the inside pages. And when *The New York Times* downplayed the story, other papers followed suit. Years later, Lelyveld said he still felt a bit guilty that "in a sense, I had taken the Congo off the front page."

Codi Simon, the foreign editor at National Public Radio, acknowledges that what's being reported in other media influences coverage at NPR. "It's a combination of factors," she says, "like what's in the papers, what's on the wires."

"Africa hasn't been a priority of ours," Simon says, "not because we're not interested and not because we don't care—but because so much else is happening in the world. It's very hard to find the air time to fit in an important but frankly secondary story from anywhere else."

One of the reasons Africa can be perceived as a secondary story, Jim Hoagland says, is that it "is becoming increasingly irrelevant economically to the rest of the world." Economics is always a difficult topic for mass media to tackle, but the economic restructuring of Eastern Europe and the social costs of austerity programs there and in Latin America have received far more extensive coverage than similar stories in Africa. In fact, the debt burden, which is proportionately heavier for Africa's economies than for countries anywhere else in the world, is reported in the U.S. press as though it were almost exclusively a Latin American problem.

Roger Wilkins, who teaches at George Mason University and has served on the editorial boards of both *The Washington Post* and *The New York Times*, doesn't buy the argument that Africa's weak economies account for the lack of press attention. "I think Africa is undercovered," he says, "and I don't believe that decisions are made on the basis of its economic importance." Like others who have questioned editors and producers about the lack of Africa coverage, Wilkins has heard, time and again, that there is no constituency for news about Africa in the United States. "Let me tell you something," he says. "A very substantial proportion of the people in the United States are of African descent. And it's only the ignorance and the racism of people who make news decisions that keep those stories—real stories, powerful stories, interesting stories—from reaching our television screens and our newspapers."

Wilkins's assessment gets strong reactions from media decision makers. "That is something which I categorically reject," says NPR's Simon. "I do not think it's a question of racism. That's something I completely disagree with. It is not because these are black people who are starving. There are starving people everywhere who are not covered."

If you don't think racial factors play a role, Wilkins counters, look at who's making the choices. "What is news and what is newsworthy," he says, "is basically decided by middle-class, middle-aged, white American males—people who have a very narrow slice of human experience but who overvalue the ability of their limited experience to give them a broad worldview. Most of these are people who have never had a close African-American friend, let alone an African acquaintance."

Probing Wilkins's charges is no easy task. News organizations whose daily business is asking tough questions of others are remarkably reluctant to give straight answers about their own institutions. Katherine McQuay, media relations manager for the NBC "Nightly News," says that asking about the ethnic composition of the show's editors and producers is "unfair." Neither ABC, *The Washington Post, The New York Times, The Christian Science Monitor*, nor *The Wall Street Journal* would provide any information about the racial make up of their editorial staffs. Round-about inquiries, though, suggest that there is not a single African-American making decisions about foreign news at the television networks or at any major national newspaper. (There is more diversity at some of the strong regional papers, such as *The Detroit Free Press*, where a black foreign editor reports to a black managing editor for news.)

Bill Kovach, curator of Harvard's Nieman Foundation for Journalism, agrees that the backgrounds of decision makers help define what is news and what isn't. "All major news organizations are run," he says, by people who are "white, generally Anglo-Saxon, predominantly male. And they see the world through that prism." Kovach, who was Washington bureau chief of *The New York Times* and for two years edited *The Atlanta Journal and Constitution*, uses himself as an example. "I'm Albanian-American," he says, "and things that happen in the Balkans are inherently important to me. No matter how good an editor I am, I'm not going to follow African news in the same way."

Howard French, Caribbean bureau chief for *The New York Times*, has covered Africa for a variety of papers. He raises the same issue Kovach does, but from the perspective of a black reporter. "Africa," French says, "is about as remote as you could get from the things editors think about on a daily basis." He says editors tend to be captives of "the axis-of-world-history school of thought"—what happens in Africa is not considered important to the future of humanity. Like Wilkins, French sees race as a factor in that perception. "Africa is populated by a bunch of black people," he says. "If it were populated by a bunch of Albanians, Africa would suddenly be more interesting." Those dynamics won't change, Kovach says, "until newsrooms have more blacks who consider their African heritage important."

There is, apparently, a long way to go before that happens. Joseph Foote of Southern Illinois University conducts an annual visibility survey that identifies the network television correspondents who are seen most often on the major networks' evening newscasts. His latest survey received press attention for its finding that there are only six women among the fifty most visible reporters. But Foote says he found *no* black reporters in the group and only two in the top one hundred, ranked fifty-ninth and sixty-ninth. Not a single black woman made the list.

At the print newsroom level, though, there were significant, if limited, changes in the 1980s. What *Newsday* deputy editor Les Payne used to call the unwritten rule against assigning black reporters to cover Africa has been relaxed. Payne was among the journalists who complained that the same editors who would think it absurd to refuse to send a Jewish reporter to the Middle East would routinely bar black reporters from Africa, on grounds of potential bias. Now, *The Washington Post*, *The New York Times*, *The Baltimore Sun*, and *The Detroit Free Press* have all assigned black reporters to the Africa beat—and the experiment has been judged a success.

Jim Hoagland says that *The Washington Post*'s former Nairobi-based reporter, Neil Henry, has great storytelling abilities, and he "simply wrote a lot of stories into the paper that wouldn't have gotten there solely on the typical, and somewhat stereotypical, 'newsworthy' valuations that we place in drawing up the front page."

Roger Wilkins concedes that it is difficult to alter the prevailing pattern at the editorial level, even with the best of intentions. He uses *The New York Times*, where no major editing job has ever gone to a black, as an example. "Now that's the premier news organization in the United States," he says, "and it's run by people who would like to do better, I think, but the legacy of the past lives on." Too often, Wilkins says, black talent wasn't nurtured and black reporters weren't promoted. Many of the best left journalism for other fields. "So people who are in charge now," he says, "who would very much like to promote blacks into news decision-making jobs, can't do it."

There is general agreement among editors and producers—as well as reporters—that if African issues were regarded as important for U.S. policy considerations, they would cease to be seen by the news media as fringe concerns, outside the mainstream. But paradoxically, it is often media attention that sparks policy debates. "There's a circle that exists here," says David Gergen, "and it's not necessarily a virtuous circle. American foreign policy tends to reflect the geopolitical interests of the country." And Africa, Gergen says, has not been seen as geopolitically important.

Most of the journalists interviewed concede that even crisis situations and geopolitical concerns that would command attention elsewhere tend to be overlooked when they carry an African dateline. Before Nelson Mandela's release from a South African prison attracted notice to the fighting in that country's Natal province, for example, the killings there went largely unreported in the U.S. press. Yet from 1987 to 1989, according to several estimates, more people died in Natal than were killed in Lebanon and Northern Ireland combined.[10]

An informal survey of reporters interested in Africa, both black and white, reveals a deep frustration that seems to go beyond the normal dissatisfaction most journalists feel about not getting enough print or air time for their stories. But individual reporters feel too vulnerable to voice their critiques openly. Editors are defensive, they say, and respond poorly to charges of bad news judgment, especially if there is a suggestion of racial bias in the decisions. Over and over, though, reporters tell stories of major African developments being ignored by the media gatekeepers.

As the 1990s began, there was ample evidence that the pattern of limited Africa coverage was continuing. Across the continent, in Ethiopia, Sudan, Mozambique, and Angola, massive human suffering was largely unreported. The decade was ushered in by a Liberian war that raged for months before it was treated seriously in most of the press. Liberians, whose West African nation was founded by freed American slaves and hosts several strategic U.S. communications and intelligence facilities, persisted in thinking that the U.S. government would intervene to halt the bloodshed. But as the regime of Samuel Doe tottered, even a major massacre by government troops could claim only fleeting media attention. On July 30, public television's "MacNeil/Lehrer News Hour" bumped a scheduled report on the killing of over six hundred Liberian refugees in favor of a discussion about a continuing hostage crisis threatening the government of Trinidad and Tobago.

Two months earlier another massacre—of pro-democracy university students by soldiers in Zaire, a key U.S. ally—was all but ignored in the U.S. press. In Europe, by contrast, news reports of the incident touched off a furor that forced Belgium to suspend all new aid and loans to its former colony.

Several journalists tried to interest their editors in the democracy movement that began to sweep the African continent in 1990. By the end of 1991, at least twenty former autocratic governments had been forced to hold elections, share power, or leave office. The dramatic events were accompanied by powerful visual images. In Madagascar, for instance, the democracy campaign mobilized hundreds of thousands of demonstrators day after day. But Americans, whose media were focused on developments elsewhere, were denied a glimpse of the breathtaking pace of change in Africa.

"Nightline" would like to cover such issues, says Ted Koppel. The prime obstacle to doing so, he says, is the logistical requirements of television. The show needs a filmed segment, he says, to launch each topic. "We have roughly thirty-five people who work on 'Nightline,' " Koppel says, "and we have five programs a week. On average, that means you've got seven people per program." Taking a correspondent and crew out of the mix for two or three weeks to do an Africa piece can be done—and

"Nightline" did it to cover the Liberian fighting—but it's too difficult and expensive to be done frequently, Koppel says.

CNN's Ed Turner cites logistical problems, too, including the shortage of satellite uplink equipment in Africa. "But that's an explanation," he says, "not an excuse."

"There comes a time," Turner says, "when you say, 'Dammit, we have to do these stories on Africa. These are important things that people need to know about.'" CNN's immediate bid to improve international coverage was the creation of a program to air stories contributed by television agencies, many of them government-controlled, from countries around the world—a kind of global soapbox, Turner says. For the longer term, Turner is pinning his hopes on portable mini-broadcast stations now available that can take advanced transmission technology into the field.

Although he expects to encounter opposition from African authorities who would like to control news sent from their countries, Turner says such attitudes are not unique to Africa. "We have the same problems in countries as 'civilized'—that's in quotes," he says, "as the United Kingdom and across Europe. Africa is not alone in its desire—desire by the governments—to want to control what goes out of there."

OVERCOMING OBSTACLES TO COVERAGE

NPR's Codi Simon thinks the problem of access to official sources is severe enough in Africa to kill stories that would otherwise be aired. "What do you do as an American journalistic institution," she asks, "when you have got to have the other side, and the other side won't give it to you?"

Victoria Brittain, assistant foreign editor at *The Guardian* newspaper in London, hears similar complaints often, but she thinks they're unfair. The principal obstacle to access, she says, is the economic crisis in African countries. "The infrastructures of all these countries are very frequently on the verge of collapse," she says, "which means that their level of information is extremely poor, their [government] ministers are all too busy to brief journalists, it's extremely difficult to get around in their countries."

"It's the physical, economic and social crisis in Africa that makes it difficult to cover," she says. "It's not, in my view, something to do with Africans being particularly unwilling to cooperate with journalists."

But the worst problem for reporters covering Africa is not indigenous to the continent, says Brittain, who has reported for *The Times of London*, *The New Statesman*, and the BBC. "Dealing with all the Third World's issues is extremely difficult," she says. "But it's mainly difficult because

you have to bludgeon your editors to give you space to cover these issues."
As an editor now herself, she tries to be sensitive to the Africa stories that
may not be getting the exposure they merit.

Despite reporters' frustrations, African journalists are tempted to think
that foreign reporters are the problem—or at least part of it. It takes a great
deal of time and patience for a journalist to understand the complexities
of African societies, says NPR's former South Africa correspondent John
Matisonn, and most don't take the time. And that, he says, makes it harder
for those who do. In South Africa, Matisonn says, "you have millions and
millions of black South Africans who are very politically sophisticated—
often more sophisticated than the whites." Journalists who understand that
sophistication, he says, have a hard time conveying it persuasively to
editors who are accustomed to more superficial reporting.

South African newspaper editor Zwelakhe Sisulu, who served as press
spokesman for Nelson Mandela in the period following his release, shares
Matisonn's dismay about some of the incidents the two have witnessed.
Sisulu was disappointed with most of the U.S. reporters, especially television people, who flooded into South Africa after the Mandela release,
and he came to see their attitudes as symptomatic of an American approach
that leads to the superficial understanding and poor reporting. "[The
Americans] tended on the whole to be very arrogant," Sisulu says. "They
expected people to lie down and let themselves be trampled over" because
of the importance of the networks. Some of the U.S. crews, he says, hired
"bouncers" to clear the way for them in crowds. And sometimes the hired
muscle came into conflict with the security arranged for Mandela. "The
sheer competitiveness of it all was quite terrifying," Sisulu says. "I'd
always thought of TV people as journalists. I've now changed my mind.
I think they are a breed of their own."

Among the most frequently cited reasons for the dearth of Africa
reporting is a low level of public interest. Some editors say that even if
Roger Wilkins is right that the black community is as important a constituency for Africa as, for example, the Polish community is for news of
Eastern Europe, the pressure for greater coverage isn't felt in the nation's
newsrooms. That's important, Bill Kovach says, because as print and
broadcast media have been bought by larger corporations, commercial
considerations have become increasingly important components of news
decisions. In 1982, fifty corporations controlled most of the business in
all major media. By 1987, the number of such companies had shrunk to
twenty-nine.[11]

In the wake of that concentration of ownership, editors and producers
have felt a growing pressure to cut costs. In 1989, the "Today" show

planned a week-long series of live broadcasts from Africa with host Bryant Gumbel. The planned ten hours of programming would have been the largest exposure Africa had ever had on commercial television. Five reporter/producer teams were assigned to develop story ideas. But before filming could begin, the project was suspended. Executives at General Electric, which owns NBC, had balked at spending the money for Africa, according to network sources.

As for print media, Kovach says, newspapers are giving more attention to "issues that concern the consuming public, which inordinately is white, middle-class/upper-class, suburban." Editors are under pressure, Kovach says, to increase circulation among that kind of constituency. "I've worked for news organizations," he says, "where we've done African stories that gained a wide following among the black readers of the community. But the advertising department and the business side of the newspaper were not interested in those stories because the advertisers weren't interested."

Jonathan Kwitny, a former *Wall Street Journal* reporter and public television producer, says that the quest to attract desirable readers with soft news—such as stories about celebrities—means something else has to be eliminated. "And Africa," he says, "would be near the top of most editors' lists."

News executives agree that if a broader interest in Africa were demonstrated, all the obstacles to better African reporting would be overcome. "I don't think there's any doubt," says NBC's Bill Wheatley, "that if editors and producers feel there's substantial public interest that they'll find a way to do coverage."

Whether the media gatekeepers are good judges of public interest is a topic of debate. Many editors and producers assumed a widespread fascination with the dramatic changes in Eastern Europe, and intensive media coverage in 1990 reflected that assumption. But surveys by the Times Mirror Center for the People and the Press—established by the company that owns *The Los Angeles Times*—suggests that the assumption was wrong. The American public watched closely the fall of the Berlin Wall, Center Director Donald Kellerman says, but "a few days later, a few weeks later, they told us repeatedly in one way and another that they are confused by the events, the cast of characters change, they do not have a sense that this is something with which they can empathize." The center's surveys suggest that the same factors that cloud public understanding of Africa also apply to areas of the world that get far more sustained press attention.

So how can Africa get a better deal? David Gergen thinks that what the continent needs is an organized constituency to argue its case. The Middle East, he says, gets coverage that is "disproportionate to the number of people who live there and, if you're a sub-Saharan African, I think you'd probably argue it's disproportionate to the importance of the Middle East."

"We've got to develop a stronger citizen interest in Africa," says Roger Wilkins. "African interest organizations have to become more acutely aware of these issues and begin to act as intelligent and critical consumers of the news product. News executives respond to pressure just like other executives, and they are not getting the pressures." The potential power of an Africa lobby has been demonstrated in the case of South Africa. Organizations such as TransAfrica, with its daily demonstrations outside the South African embassy in Washington, forced media attention to the issue. In the wake of the publicity, Congress passed economic sanctions against South Africa.

Charlayne Hunter-Gault of the "MacNeil/Lehrer News Hour" says there is no shortage of African stories that can interest and move Americans. "It's the human side of the story," she says, "that tends to tap into the interest of people. Every story that I have ever done, every issue that I have ever approached—when I have done it in terms of how people are affected, the reaction has been incredible. I think that's what's missing in a lot of the Africa coverage."

Educating Americans to the fact that they live in an interdependent world is one place to start, says Ed Turner. "Why is it smart to invest in schooling?" he asks. "Why is it clever to understand your neighbor?" Because if we don't know more about the nations of Africa, he answers, "we are absolutely guaranteeing ourselves more and more difficulties and troubles ahead. Without the understanding of each other, you're bound to be in conflict with each other." David Gergen agrees that out of both morality and self-interest, Americans should be giving Africa more attention. But he's not sure how or when that will happen. "I think, to be realistic," he says, "we ought to see that there are some big mountains to cross to get from here to where we ought to be, and I think those mountains are going to be higher in the next couple of years, not lower."

But some journalists find signs of hope. Jon Kwitny says that while the easing of tensions in Europe may have focused attention away from Africa, it may also make Africa coverage less distorted. Despite the tragedy of the Liberian conflict, he says, it was refreshing to "finally read about an African conflict without one side being identified as 'communists' and the other as 'freedom fighters.' " If that Cold War perspective is gone, Kwitny says, "that's one thing to be thankful for."

John Leonard of "Sunday Morning" says that what gets in the papers and on television "are those things that the people who run news organizations or work for news organizations care about. Individual energies, biases, passions—that's how things change." So a few people in the right places who care about Africa, Leonard believes, can begin to change the journalistic agenda.

"It's a real chicken-and-egg situation," says Charlayne Hunter-Gault. "People look at it and say, 'There's no interest in Africa.' Well, there's no coverage of Africa. If there was coverage of Africa, there would be interest in Africa. It's as simple as that, I think."

NOTES

1. Michael McCarthy, *The Dark Continent: Africa as Seen by Americans* (Westport, CT: Greenwood Press, 1983), pp. 35, 41.

2. Ibid., p. 146.

3. Ibid., p. 28.

4. Gardiner Hubbard, "Africa, Its Past and Future," *National Geographic* (April 1889): 99–124.

5. Ladislas Bugner, ed., *The Image of the Black in Western Art*, Vols. 1 (1976), 2 (1979), and 4 (1989) (Cambridge, MA: Harvard University Press).

6. Ibid., Vol. 2, part 2, p. 242.

7. Ibid., Vol. 4, part 4, p. 18.

8. See "The Media: Massacring Zaire," *Africa News* (June 5, 1978), pp. 2+, and "Dog Bites Man Isn't News," *Africa News* (June 18, 1990), p. 14. Post-mortems of the coverage that examine why early reports had been so exaggerated include: Dierdre Carmody, "Despite Black Toll, Zaire Killings Are Viewed as a White Bloodbath," *New York Times* (May 27, 1978), p. 4. David Ottaway, "Figures Got a Political Twist," *Washington Post* (May 28, 1978), p. 1.

9. "Congo Massacre," *Time* (December 4, 1964): 28–32.

10. "Legacy of Apartheid Challenges ANC," *Africa News* (April 9, 1990), pp. 1–2+.

11. Ben H. Bagdikian, *The Media Monopoly* (Boston: Beacon Press, 1987), p. ix.

18

Changing Policy: An Editorial Agenda

Thomas Winship and Paul Hemp

The starting point in any discussion of Africa coverage is that American newspaper readers—and most American editors—don't know much about Africa and don't care to know very much more about Africa. On a typical day, editors faced with limited news space and competing local and national news tend to rank most foreign news in general and African news in particular as a "maybe." The standard response to this attitude is that editors shouldn't respond only to readership surveys but should also help raise the public's consciousness about important issues.

At the moment, Africa has less strategic or economic importance to the United States than do other parts of the world. But the difficulties facing the continent—political instability, foreign debt, drought—have world-wide implications. Simmering tensions in Africa could erupt into conflict that would have an even more direct impact. And for humanitarian reasons alone, the U.S. public should be informed about the problems and successes of a continent that is home to one-tenth of the world's people.

First, we outline some basic elements of the African story making it a particularly difficult challenge for the American media and, in turn, particularly vulnerable to charges of bias and imbalance. Some of the most prominent of these elements follow.

Enormous Continent-wide Problems. The experts, unfortunately, agree that economic and living standards in Africa have been steadily declining since the 1970s. Political instability is rampant. Natural disasters are locked in a deadly cycle with resource exploitation. The news is generally not too good, causing a preponderance of negative reporting, as the critics say.

General Public Lack of Interest. As hard as it is to admit, the African story does not elicit a great deal of day-to-day interest in the United States. Part of this has to do with the comparative lack of a strong African constituency in America. Immigrant ties to Europe are a main reason why European news still sells pretty well in the United States. But, by and large, American blacks—cut off from their culture during the slavery years— have not yet come to identify strongly with Africa. Cultural differences, the gulf between industrial and rural societies, depressing news events, and lingering racial prejudice undoubtedly help contribute to this indifference.

Difficulties of Access. Africa is also a pretty hard place to cover because of vast distances, transportation and communication obstacles, and political barriers. One result is the inordinate expense of covering Africa. It costs an average of $200,000 a year just to keep one correspondent going in Africa. A small press corps, spread thinly, focuses its limited resources on the hit-and-run big story (often trouble) or an overly generalized and simplistic overview. Visa problems and government bureaucracy compound the access problems, while suspicion and resentment between official and journalist feed on one another.

Anti-American Feelings. Widespread opposition to U.S. foreign policy in Africa, particularly on the issues of South Africa and our preoccupation with East-West relations, makes the American correspondent's job tougher and fuels criticism of the U.S. media's role in Africa. Suspicions of conspiracy, monopoly, and outright journalistic dishonesty abound in many African opinions of the U.S. media.

Differing Perceptions of the Media's Role. Another element in the hostility to the American press is the difference in philosophies between an adversarial and a supportive press. In many African countries, the press is viewed as a tool of national development, and this is not the case in the United States. In most African cases, the media is to some degree controlled by governments, which require a supportive press. While journalists the world over yearn for free expression, many leading African journalists sincerely believe that their role is to further the cause of nationhood and development. For this reason, the American press system is often regarded as counterproductive.

Declining Resources. A 1986 survey by *PressTime* magazine indicated U.S. newspapers had nine full time correspondents covering black Africa, and about twice that many working for U.S. news agencies. That number has since declined with reductions by the networks and UPI, to an estimated 15 full-time U.S. correspondents in sub-Saharan Africa.

American Insensitivity and Ignorance. One cannot address the subject of press coverage without mentioning this sad fact. The number of

Americans who speak Hausa or Swahili is minuscule. Americans generally do not understand the problems of trying to achieve self-sufficiency and stability in a post-colonial atmosphere. They do not understand or empathize with the fundamental challenges of survival that face much of Africa. And they also do not understand the impact news can have in a volatile political atmosphere.

There are reasons for optimism. The American press, by and large, is not an ideological institution. It goes where the news is, generally without regard for self-interest and colonial baggage. It tries to do a good job of telling its audience what happened. Without American journalism, the world—and this includes Africa—would be a far more ignorant place. The American press is quite aware of its shortcomings; so much so, as a matter of fact, that it is often accused of excessive masochism. At every editors' convention, there's a rip-roaring debate about credibility and responsibility. This kind of introspection is good for the profession. (Incidentally, shortcomings there may be, but monopoly, conspiracy, and outright dishonesty are not usually among them.) Vowing to pay more attention to Africa doesn't solve the problems of African news coverage.

The tougher question is: What news do we print about Africa? Most American newspapers don't really have much choice. They are limited to using reports from major syndicated press services. The tremendous expense of maintaining an overseas bureau is something only a handful of U.S. papers can afford. And with increased interest in Eastern Asia and Eastern Europe, more resources of even these papers are being directed to those areas. Press services traditionally report breaking news. And following the traditional American definition, breaking news usually is something extraordinary, often something bad—the standard fare of coups and famine that Africans say gives an inaccurately negative portrayal of the continent. Another staple of African reporting are stories on government corruption and abuse of power, furthering the bad news coming from the continent.

When a newspaper does send its own correspondent to Africa to look beyond breaking news, the reporter not surprisingly often writes about things that are striking to a Westerner. That frequently is the offbeat, the bizarre, the colorful—a traditional practice such as voodoo, for example— resulting in what might be called the *National Geographic* coverage syndrome. The unusual subject that catches the attention of the reporter also catches the attention of editors and readers back home, so the story gets prominent display. It may be one of only a few stories on Africa that a U.S. reader will look at in a year, furthering stereotypes about Africa and leaving the reader ignorant of developments in important areas such as agriculture.

What can the U.S. media do to improve coverage of Africa? To begin, there needs to be increased reporting of trends, not just newsbreaking events. Instead of reporting the blips on the screen—the coups and famine—we need to show the underlying trends that cause them. An occasional overview is a more effective use of limited space than scatter-shot reporting on breaking news that isn't place in context. In 1989 *The Boston Globe* ran a major three-part "whither Africa" series. They deployed three reporters and a photographer for one month to find out where Africa is today and where it is heading. The series was a valuable, compact primer on the continent for the typical reader whose knowledge is limited. Such reporting of contextual information is rare and should be expanded.

The American press also should try to put "color" stories in context, using them to illustrate—by example or contrast—broad social or political trends. Michael Hiltzik of *The Los Angeles Times* did a piece in 1989 about the Liberian defense minister's arrest for allegedly using witchcraft to further his political aims. The politician was charged with killing a policeman so that a sorcerer, or "heart man," could use the blood and organs to increase the defense minister's powers against President Samuel Doe. The article, focusing on the stereotypically bizarre rather than on the constructively mundane, was just the sort of story that Africans criticize the American press for highlighting. It ran on the front page of *The Los Angeles Times*, unusually prominent play for a story on Africa. And yet who could deny its grisly fascination? What set it apart was its careful and fair analysis of the origins of this kind of witchcraft and its place in Liberian society. Although the news was sensational, it was used to elucidate broader themes.

Similarly, market women—petty traders in colorful dress, with uncouth manners and bags bulging with goods for sale—are a colorful subject for a story. But a piece about them and their work can serve as a platform to discuss the problem of widespread unreported trade between West African countries and the important role women play in commerce there.

The U.S. media—which usually see their role as a watchdog—also should make a special effort to find the occasional positive story about progress in Africa. Most good African journalists see their role as two-fold: They aid their societies not only by uncovering wrongdoing but also by highlighting successful development efforts. They refuse to accept a role of blindly supporting government policies; but they also see a special responsibility for promoting development. U.S. journalists may look askance at such a dual role. But reporting the successes—albeit with the caveat that they may be the exception rather than the rule—is important if Africa is to progress. Incidentally, what U.S. newspaper has not at one time shamelessly served as a cheerleader for a sports stadium or some other local development project? A story about a UNICEF program in Sierra Leone that has succeeded in vaccinating 90 percent of babies against childhood disease can help development in Africa, if only by lessening cynicism that all development projects have little to show for the funds devoted to them.

Perhaps the most effective way the American media can help improve African coverage does not involve their own reporting, but rather the training of African journalists. U.S. journalists, no matter how objective and professional they may be, are inevitably going to view Africa through an American lens. They bring to a story their preconceptions and major gaps in their understanding of Africa. One way to broaden the understanding of Africa in the international marketplace of ideas is to add the reporting of skilled African journalists. There have been efforts to do this, including the formation of indigenous news services such as the Pan African News Agency (PANA). Unfortunately, PANA has not become a credible source of news to Western readers and editors, in part, because the participating national news agencies often serve as government propaganda mouthpieces. But the problem of credibility arises more from African journalists' lack of training, in the basic skills of objectivity and fairness. U.S. journalists can help through programs designed to share professional skills with their African colleagues. In the long term, the training of African journalists will do more than anything to shape our impression of Africa.

We should not despair. Africa's image in the U.S. press can—and will—improve over the next decade, if only because the universe is shrinking so fast.

19

South Africa Now: The Challenge of the South African Story

Danny Schechter

In the summer of 1986, while covering Jesse Jackson's visit to Southern Africa's Frontline states, on assignment for a well-known prime-time TV network news magazine program, I spoke with Zimbabwe's President Robert Mugabe outside his office in Harare, the capital city. I asked about the destabilization campaign that South Africa's neighbors said was costing them billions of dollars and millions of lives.

I asked Mugabe if he would welcome American military help as a way to protect his region from South African attack. His reply was immediate. First, he told me that I was the first American reporter to ask him that question. Second, he immediately took up the idea, explaining that a U.S. arms flow would enable Zimbabwe to divert its scarce resources from military expenditures into badly needed educational and agricultural development efforts. Such a U.S. commitment, he said would serve as a powerful signal to Pretoria. In a crisp response—what we TV people call a good sound bite—he appealed for Washington's help.

After confirming that this was indeed the first time such a statement had been made—and because such scoops are often the adrenaline of news organizations—I called our foreign news desk in New York to find out how I should ship the tape for consideration by our nightly news show. I explained the circumstances, why his statement was newsworthy, and that it had won Jackson's immediate endorsement. The response from New York startled me. The news editor on the other side of the line had only one reaction, a question: "Where is Harare?"

It was clear that not only would I have no sale, but the story, and by extension noncrisis news from Africa, was hardly a blip on the network radar screen. I might as well have been calling from the moon.

"WHEN IT'S NOT ON TV, IT DOESN'T EXIST"

It has become axiomatic that when an issue is not on television in the United States, it does not exist for most Americans who rely on TV news for most of their understanding of world issues. And for the most part, on an ongoing, regular basis, news and developments about Africa in general and Southern Africa in particular are not frequently covered. The exceptions are usually moments of high drama or when the video is particularly evocative as in the case of the bloated bellies of Ethiopia's famine victims, an ongoing coup or civil war, violence in South Africa's townships, or when a well-known personality—say a famous celebrity such as Nelson Mandela—is released from prison.

TV news for the most part is what the people who run TV programs say is news, although they are influenced by what is in the papers or on the wires. Few media critics—or area specialists—are happy with network news offerings overall, so it is not surprising that so many Africans, and journalists or scholars who follow Africa, are particularly distressed by the quality and quantity of African coverage.

In the case of South Africa, network news coverage has played an important role in bringing the apartheid issue to world attention. There is no doubt that graphic reports of police violence and township responses helped galvanize world opinion against apartheid, and fueled antiapartheid movements and their demands for sanctions. To stop such images from getting out, the South African government imposed media restrictions between 1985 and 1986 that sought to, and did, limit what the cameras could see and transmit. Their rules were designed to intimidate and to encourage self-censorship. They worked.

A year later, the Canadian government commissioned a quantitative study of the effects of those restrictions and concluded that Pretoria had been "successful in driving images of violence, human rights violations and poverty in South Africa off the television screens of the Western world." The report documented a sharp drop in coverage, even though as those TV images decreased, the rate of detentions and human rights abuses inside South Africa increased. Just why the networks, so passive for so long, were so cooperative with those restrictions has become a matter of debate.

MEDIA APPEASEMENT

The argument started when a former senior-level CBS producer penned a *New York Times* op-ed piece calling on the networks, his among them, to unilaterally withdraw from South Africa if they were unable to do their job. "They've kept us from covering the story because of the fear that by breaking the rules, we'll get thrown out," wrote Richard Cohen. He charged "media appeasement" with apartheid. A congressional committee that deals with African issues took this issue so seriously that it convened hearings, inviting network officials to testify about their news coverage problems. The committee was startled when not one broadcaster agreed to testify. The hearing itself was not even considered newsworthy and no news crews except C-SPAN's were even assigned to cover it. Citing First Amendment freedom of press concerns, the networks would not even cooperate with an official inquiry intended to call attention to South Africa's effort to suppress the flow of news.

In their defense—when any defense has ever been offered—news managers claimed that they must agree to obey the laws in the countries in which they operate or they would not be able to operate at all. In any case, the argument continued, they had to protect their people, and guard against their expulsion. A few went further, explaining the decrease of coverage by claiming that the story in South Africa had changed, and was no longer as vivid. By that they meant that the street fighting—and the pictures it produced—had in TV parlance "gone away." One network foreign news editor told me he thought competitive pressures also dictated a cautious response. Everyone wanted to make sure they were there when a "big one," a story such as Mandela's release, broke. So for nearly two years, TV stories from South Africa were few and far between. And that is not simply because there were no stories to shoot, or that material could not be shot or acquired from many free-lance crews. In this period, many reports were shot, only to be put "on the shelf" rather than on the air in New York.

While it is true that major events were happening elsewhere in the world at this time—in Eastern Europe and in the Soviet Union for example—and that the traditional twenty-two-minute newscast can't cover everything, it is also true, to quote a MacNeil/Lehrer report, that the networks were "tip-toeing around." They did not challenge a system of state-imposed media censorship of the type which would later be taken up by governments in Israel and China. Not one American TV correspondent was expelled from South Africa in this period.

Was racism a factor? Some critics thought so, charging that most

American news coverage remains Eurocentric and that overwhelmingly white news organizations were not, at bottom, committed to covering a black freedom struggle. Kenneth Walker, former "Nightline" correspondent, one of the few black reporters ever assigned to that show, and to report from South Africa, told a TV interviewer that the reason for diminished coverage was that "news decisions in this country are made by about ten white guys who live within a 25-mile radius of Manhattan." Walker called the lack of coverage a "failure of nerve and a failure of will," even claiming that "Nightline" only went to South Africa for its first series of week-long programs in response to pressure from black staffers at the network.

Other media critics have contended that poor coverage of blacks in South Africa is not surprising in light of the benign neglect of black community issues in America. There is no question that America's newsrooms tend to be racially homogeneous with few blacks in decision-making positions. Some who are, such as Les Payne, the managing editor of *Newsday*, have committed their newspapers to enhanced coverage of South Africa. TV anchor Charlayne Hunter-Gault has done the same at PBS's "MacNeil/Lehrer News Hour." Many individual journalists—black and white—are committed to the story. There seem to be far fewer broadcast institutions that are.

CONSTRUCTIVE ENGAGEMENT

Another factor which may be more central is political, rather than racial. Network news tends to march in lockstep with U.S. government policy, often sharing its worldview and Cold War biases. The Reagan administration considered South Africa an ally, and practiced a policy of constructive engagement. Network news programs never dissented sharply from that view, for example, by looking at our South Africa policy as skeptically as they came to see America's Vietnam policy in the last years of the war.

The opposition movements there, especially the African National Congress (ANC), were not taken terribly seriously in those years either. They were frequently tainted in our media the same way they were tainted in South Africa's pro-government white press as communists, frequently labeled "Moscow-backed" without much background offered about their histories or political goals. Liberation movements in other parts of the Third World received similar treatment although dissident movements in Eastern Europe and the Soviet bloc were usually treated much more sympathetically. Perhaps that is because network news programs, like the

U.S. government, have always been more focused on East-West issues than North-South concerns.

Overall, most TV news editors cannot be accused of having too much intimate knowledge or interest in African liberation movements. When a story is perceived as of only limited interest by those at the top of a news organization, it is given only limited coverage by the rank and file.

It is possible that network news managements would disagree with my assertions. They would probably point with pride to their coverage of Nelson Mandela's release from prison. And it is true that the three networks and CNN sent a small media army to South Africa to chronicle that event. Yet the monthly *Tyndall Report*, a trade publication that surveys TV news coverage, noted in the aftermath of that coverage in March 1990: "South Africa received 176 minutes of coverage in one month. The total for the previous 30 months (August 1987–January 1990) was 412 minutes. Thus this month's coverage was higher than the *annual* coverage of South Africa (165 minutes) over the last two and a half years." In the period before Mandela's release, South Africa ranked twenty-seventh—next to last—on the Tyndall list of major news stories being covered on television.

The undeniable bottom line is that South African coverage levels are episodic and inadequate—and even when they are not, on such stories as the Mandela release—the levels of analysis and background contextual reporting is usually very weak. There have been some exceptions—and exceptional programs—including some hosted by Ted Koppel who cannot be accused of just parachuting over, in the manner of so many network superstars. What Koppel had going for him was more extensive air time and a virtually unlimited budget.

ENTER "SOUTH AFRICA NOW"

It is against this background, in April 1988, that former CBS producer Rory O'Connor and myself started the weekly television news magazine called "South Africa Now." We believed from our own experience that the networks respond more to competition than to criticism. We wanted to demonstrate that the story of upheavals in the region, and the aspirations of the people who live there could be told weekly on American television, despite the censorship there and indifference here.

We recognized early on that we would only have a running chance of defeating the censors by working with black journalists and video teams who were already in place in South Africa and looking for TV outlets overseas. Collaboration became our watchword—and training South African blacks in TV journalism part of our mission. Our staff now is multiracial, multicultural, and multinational, a mix of seasoned broadcast journalists and novices. We believe that the people who are closest to the news on the ground are in the best position to explain what is going on. Since Southern Africans are most committed to getting their news out, we have been seeking to equip them with the tools and skills to tell their own story. "South Africa Now" is a TV vehicle for Africans to report an African story, and for Americans to see and hear African voices.

MULTIPLIER EFFECT

We hoped that "South Africa Now" 's existence—and what publicity we could attract to promote it—would have a multiplier effect, keeping the issue of the suppression of news from the region in the public eye. We want to prod the networks to improve and increase their coverage by example. We were and are very aggressive in this respect and have been accused of being "guerrilla journalists" and advocates as a result.

We were able to start "South Africa Now" with a small grant from the United Nations. Most charitable foundations or corporate sponsors would not touch us initially, arguing that if the networks with their vast budgets— $1 billion per annum—could not provide coverage, why did we think that our small company, Globalvision, could? They were skeptical and not without good reason.

So we had to get on the air first, to prove that it could be done. Then, we could refine our product as we went along. Globalvision has, as its credo, the view that regular on-going programs—weekly series, not occasional documentaries—are what's needed to reach and build an audience for the information that Americans are not getting elsewhere. We started transmitting the show on one satellite network, and soon found our way onto leading PBS stations. We had hoped that once we proved we could produce a quality program, other funding could be found. Fortunately that is what happened. Unfortunately, the funding has been at a subsistence level.

WHERE "SOUTH AFRICA NOW" IS SEEN

As of September 1990, "South Africa Now" had been on the air for two and a half years, adding new stations in the United States and overseas during each thirteen-week season. At this writing the show is seen on leading public television stations nationwide, in the Caribbean, Japan, and Southern Africa. Having the program seen in the region we cover has been very important in the sense that the people who are making the news we are covering can now see and react to our work. We also contribute weekly segments to CNN's "World Report" sent by satellite to eighty-two countries.

Our budget went from $200 a week to a $15,000 cash outlay with many in-kind services provided by friendly PBS stations. To put this in perspective, our *annual* budget for fifty-two shows approximates the amount spent each week for network news magazines such as "60 Minutes," "Prime Time Live," and "20/20." We were forced to rely on foundation grants to pay for the show, which we produce on a non-profit basis, in association with the Africa Fund. Unhappily, we could find no corporations to sponsor or underwrite the show. One programmer at a PBS station in Dallas was quoted as saying that "South Africa Now" is considered "not corporate friendly." The lack of corporate interest in the show is no doubt linked to the fact that so many corporations have been on the firing line for their business dealings in South Africa.

FORM AND CONTENT

We were as concerned with what we would put on the air as with winning air time. We started with a determination to provide stories that were not being covered. We also wanted to forge a style of presentation that might make the program more accessible to ordinary viewers. We wanted the program to be unique in both its form and content.

In form, we opted for a high energy presentation with many quick stories, flashy graphics, and grabby features. We decided on a magazine format with a diverse mix of elements rather than a talk show loaded down with experts. The idea was always to reach out to a large mass audience and not just talk to the small circle of the initiated. We did not want to become the TV show of the African Studies Association!

Our program mix was consciously designed to include news, background reports, and cultural segments. Because culture often leads politics in Southern Africa and is certainly an arena for the expression of ideas, values, and aspirations, we gave it a priority. Unlike traditional news shows that deal with culture as a second thought—in cutesy "kicker" stories at the end of the newscast or with "What's Hot" type segments—we devoted a third of the program to substantive reports on music, film, theater, and the arts. Many of these reports are lively and entertainingly produced to please the ordinary viewer.

We had serious internal debates over how to cover the news. That has been a major challenge. We wanted our news section to focus on the news of the black majority, not the white minority. So when the networks featured reports on the white elections, we focused on the black voter boycott and explained their unrepresentative character. When some reporters feted President de Klerk as the "Gorbachev of South Africa," we looked analytically at his record and at the limited nature of his reform vision. We emphasized the role that the mass democratic movements and their defiance campaigns played in pushing the government onto that road of reform. Unlike the network cameramen that tend to shoot from behind police lines, we wanted our images to come from within the movements of change, looking the other way.

On one occasion we were able to compete head on with network efforts. That occurred when we produced a prime-time special for PBS on Mandela's release that aired nationwide on February 11, 1990, the day of his walk to freedom. For that occasion, we had a professional budget and satellite access. So our show carried all the news the networks had but with a distinctly different frame. Our coverage of Mandela's release, for example, stressed two points conspicuously absent in most network coverage. First, that Mandela himself initiated the negotiations that resulted in his freedom, and second, that he did so from behind bars. Later we reported on how he ended up in prison in the first place—a rather important dimension of the story the networks ignored—we spotlighted the role played by the CIA in tipping off the South African police about his whereabouts.

In our reporting, we also try to be careful about our use of language. We avoid such phrases as *black-on-black violence*. The stories on this subject usually miss the political, as opposed to the racial or tribal character of local conflicts. Violence against black township officials or fighting between activists of the ANC/United Democratic Front and the Inkatha movement led by Chief Gatsha Buthelezi stem from ideological differences that must be explained. The role of the South African police and army in this conflict has been central, although you might not know it from most TV reporting.

GETTING THE STORY RIGHT

We have tried to get the story right rather than have it first. We want to explain how and why events occur, and to look at the forces behind the scenes. To do that, we have investigative reporters looking into many controversial stories including South Africa's nuclear weapons program, its chemical and biological research, military efforts, sanction busters, and the like. Weekly, we seek out analysis and background from leading experts, analysts, and activists. We have always tried to get the broadest range of viewpoints as well, including that of the South African government. But its officials have refused to cooperate, denying us interviews, comments, and even access to the country by turning down, without explanation, our requests for visas.

Perhaps they hoped that we would go away once we were spurned or that public television stations wouldn't carry the show because of an alleged lack of balance. Thanks to our association with CNN, as a contributor to a program to which South African Broadcasting also contributes, we are able to use their material and so ensure that government viewpoints are represented on "South Africa Now."

THE SINCEREST FORM OF FLATTERY

The South African government has done more than show us its displeasure. They actually attempted to compete with us by covertly subsidizing their own show, cloned after ours but riddled with government propaganda. Called "Inside South Africa," it too was formatted as a half-hour news magazine with a black host. The show drew on a wide range of reports from government-controlled television and was produced by a company called Global News, which is headed up by a former SABC executive.

Despite the similarity of the names of the two producing companies, Global News and Globalvision, the shows were completely different. For one thing, "Inside South Africa" had a big budget for post-production, special effects, and satellite transmission. When "South Africa Now" exposed this look-alike competitor, and tipped off a South African newspaper which confirmed that it was being covertly subsidized with government funds, it soon became less visible. Perhaps it was unable to find a broadcast outlet in the United States. I guess we should be pleased about this attempt: imitation is still the sincerest form of flattery.

"South Africa Now" has constantly sought to explain the character of apartheid itself since it is not well understood by the American press and American TV viewers. Our reports tend to explain apartheid as more than a system of legalized racial domination; we view it as a framework for economic exploitation and ethnic division and manipulation. We believe that apartheid needs to be reported as a labor system as well as a tool for preserving racial privilege. Issues of class need to be covered as thoroughly as questions of race. We believe that the economic impact of apartheid—vast disparities between white wealth and black poverty—is as cruel as its racially discriminatory effects. "South Africa Now" seeks to give its viewers an insider's view of the struggle for majority rule and economic transformation, not just for civil rights under the current system. Our reporting reflects that understanding. "South Africa Now" carries a "Labor Watch" segment because trade unions are often at the center of the fight for economic justice. It is important to cover their demands and the highly concentrated economic institutions they are up against. That means also covering the international dimensions of the issue—the role transnational corporations play in propping up apartheid and the impact of sanctions. In an increasingly global economy, you cannot cover South Africa without also covering the countries that trade with South Africa. Thus, we have run many stories about how Pretoria has worked to evade sanctions, and the support they have received from Israeli arms dealers, Arab oil suppliers, and the country's own monopoly corporations such as Anglo-American and DeBeers. You cannot cover apartheid without looking at its economic underpinnings.

From our first programs, we decided also that our focus would be regional because apartheid policies have impacted on all of South Africa's neighbors in such a devastating manner. As a result we frequently feature reports from and about the Frontline states. We have carried reports from Angola television and an excerpt from a Cuban film about the battle in Southern Angola at Cuito Carnivale that may have been a decisive factor in ending South African intervention and assuring Namibian independence.

At a time when no other regular reports were being aired on Namibia, we started a "Namibia Watch" segment hosted by Joseph Diescho, a black Namibian scholar; this segment ran every week from the implementation of UN Resolution 435 to that country's independence, which we covered on the spot. One of our Namibia stories aired charges of a massacre of SWAPO combatants by South African trained forces. It was given page one treatment in the South African press and led to a denunciation of the show by that country's defense minister in Parliament, a sign that we were being taken very seriously indeed. Diescho now hosts a weekly "Frontline Focus" segment reporting on events in Angola, Mozambique, and Zimbabwe as well as Namibia. In 1990, we established a Zimbabwe bureau.

Finally, we also critique news coverage itself through a regular "Covering the Coverage" segment. Since filling the void in coverage is our goal, we often cover gaps, omissions, distortions, and disinformation in other media as a regular part of our program. This type of reporting is also unique on television where there is very little direct media criticism by one program of another.

EVALUATING OUR IMPACT

How can we evaluate our work? What have we achieved, and what do we hope to achieve? For starters, we have won recognition in our industry. An Emmy Award. A Gold Medal from a New York video festival. And a citation of "Excellence in Television" from *Channels* magazine. We have been proud of the kind endorsements we have received from journalists we respect in South Africa and overseas, from Allister Sparks to Bill Moyers, Gwen Lister to Anthony Lewis, Les Payne to Peter Magubane.

We have been called "indispensable" by *The Village Voice*, praised for "filling the void" by *Time*, called "hip and stunning television" by *Vanity Fair*, endorsed by Oprah Winfrey and featured on MTV and the "Today Show." Television writers around the country have sung our praises, too, from *The Detroit Free Press* ("puts the networks to shame") to *The Los Angeles Times* ("remarkable") to publications in Europe and Africa.

The point of citing this favorable attention is not just to pat ourselves on the back; it shows that TV programs about Africa do not have to be marginalized or ignored. They can become popular and respected. For years PBS stations have run expensively produced "Nature" shows about Africa and specials on African animals. They have been big ratings boosters. Can we do the same for the African people?

We are very mindful of our limits, problems, and shortcomings. Our staff is young and largely inexperienced. (Our salaries are probably the lowest in television, and not by choice!) Our reports can be rhetorical or rely on too much file footage. Our lack of access to satellites makes electronic news gathering slower than it could be, making it hard to always be as timely as we want to be. It is sometimes tough also to transcend charges of bias, a frequent contention of the South African government which would prefer that we not exist. Organizational rivalries also impact on us. For example, PAC members say we are too ANC-oriented, and ANC people hate it when we cover the PAC.

Perhaps the most public controversy around our work followed the program's cancellation by the Los Angeles public television station in October 1990 on the grounds that we lacked balance. *The Los Angeles Times* revealed that for some time, without our knowledge, "South Africa Now" had become the target of a campaign to drive it off the airwaves by a conservative media advocacy group, the Committee on Media Integrity. The group's chairman, writer David Horowitz, publicly claimed the station's decision as his own victory. *The Los Angeles Times* explained that he had "met with station executives a half dozen times and conducted a year-long letter writing campaign." His charge: "South Africa Now" represents "hard-line Marxist propaganda posing as news."

Many of the program's viewers rejected this characterization. While the station denied that it had been pressured, more than a thousand viewers flooded the station with calls and letters. Organizations threatened to picket the TV station and launch a boycott. City council members and congressional representatives spoke out on the program's behalf, so did two Pulitzer Prize–winning journalists. *Los Angeles Times* television critic, Howard Rosenberg, praised "South Africa Now" coverage, calling the cancellation decision "bone-head[ed]" and publicly wondering if it represented the "intellectual sterilization of PBS." Clarence Page of *The Chicago Tribune* called "South Africa Now" "one of the most enlightening programs on television" and called the cancellation part of an "ominous trend." "President de Klerk's happy and soothing diplomacy," he wrote, "may be accomplishing what his government's onerous State of Emergency failed to do: silence important news and criticism of the South African government while the battle to end apartheid continues to rage. As a loyal viewer of 'South Africa Now,' I think the bias excuse is bogus."

The Los Angeles station reconsidered after a barrage of pressure that the station's manager called a "firestorm." But more insidious than right-wing attacks or decisions by conservative programmers was a larger problem—a growing view among many PBS stations that the show was no longer needed because the situation in South Africa was changing and that news was more accessible. The Boston PBS station took that view, canceling the program because it had "outlived its usefulness." "Conventional media are covering the story in depth now," contended Broadcasting Director Dan Everett. Researchers from Fairness and Accuracy in Reporting responded with statistics to show that this conventional wisdom is way off base. Looking at the period between July 1 and October 15, 1990, they noted that the three network news programs devoted no more than thirteen minutes per network per week to South Africa. In the first two weeks of October 1990, when the station's decision to cancel "South Africa Now" was being made, NBC ran one three-minute report on white South Africans, ABC had a twenty-second anchor mention of a change of law, and CBS aired nothing.

The trend seemed clear: whatever beachhead "South Africa Now" had established for coverage of African news was being eroded. The news business, on commercial and public channels, was once again limiting coverage. The deeper reasons were discussed by some of the country's top journalists who met at Harvard in May 1990 under the auspices of the Nieman Foundation in Journalism to bemoan the paucity of news coverage about the continent. Anthony Lewis, the Pulitzer Prize–winning *New York Times* columnist who frequently writes about South Africa explained the problem this way: "We have a short attention span. This is the age of ten-minute fame and the nine-second sound bite. After a week or two, Mandela dropped down to small type and left the screen—and with him Africa went out of American consciousness. As it happens, South Africa is only at the beginning of a profoundly important story, what could be a transforming process."

Some corporate executives have complained about our reports on divestment campaigns and one accused us of not adequately covering Chief Buthelezi. (He finally helped us get an interview with the Inkatha leader after we assured him that we wanted his perspective on the air.) Like other news organizations, we have had our share of gaffes and inaccuracies. You certainly cannot please everyone, and as someone who has known the benefits of professional network production budgets, I am not pleased by the quality of some of our footage. I have had to lower my expectations along with the production budget.

CHANGING TELEVISION

"South Africa Now" has not achieved all of its goals, but it has gotten its message across. Although we know we have not changed television, we would like to think we have not left it the same either. Hopefully the show's approach, its fusion of information and culture, and some of our experience in low cost production will find its way into a democratic South Africa where the program's style, sensibility, and attitude could become one model for new television programs there.

The battle for more TV coverage of Africa here will be a long one despite the fact that millions of Americans turned out to welcome Nelson Mandela during his American tour, demonstrating their interest in the issue. If anything should have convinced the media gatekeepers that millions do care, that massive response in city after city should have done the trick. A survey by the Times Mirror Company at the time of Mandela's release indicated there was more interest in that story than the uprisings underway in Lithuania. Not all American news executives got that message, even after coverage of the Mandela events proved ratings blockbusters for local TV stations that went live to Mandela events.

A month after the trip, on August 8, 1990, *The Wall Street Journal* reported that the executive producer of "NBC Nightly News" had decided to ax a story filed by their South African correspondent on apartheid and its effect on the education of South African children, "insisting that viewers were becoming bored with the South African story." The segment, which was two minutes long and therefore considered practically documentary length, was screened for staffers who were reportedly enthusiastic about it and thought it should run. The executive producer said he would broadcast it only if they could "prove it was a piece that would interest a housewife in Queens."

Fortunately one of the staff members had a mother in Queens who was actually invited to screen the story without being told quite why. Incredibly, when Mrs. Sonia Perez of Astoria, Queens said she liked it, NBC ran it. This episode is one more sign that the audience is more open to watching news from South Africa than media guardians are willing to provide it.

WHAT IS TO BE DONE?

The challenge to American television is to respond to the interest that is there, and not to abdicate its responsibility to better inform Americans about the world we live in. The challenge to those who care deeply about Africa is to find ways of doing something to improve media coverage of Africa, especially on television, and to find ways to change the situation detailed in the many chapters of this book.

So what can be done? If you agree that the television media is too important to be left to its own devices, then there are efforts to be made by viewers and producers alike. For one thing, individuals and organizations can monitor TV news coverage to pinpoint inaccuracies or misinformation. Letters to the editor can be written and individual journalists can be approached with suggestions and criticisms. Organized efforts can be made to meet with network executives; letters can be sent to correspondents at African news bureaus. (None of the big three networks have African bureaus outside of Johannesburg!) Writing more about media issues—in the spirit of the essays in this book—can be useful in raising public awareness about media deficiencies.

And "if you don't like the news," to quote the legendary San Francisco radio broadcaster Scoop Nisker, "you can always go out and make some of your own." "South Africa Now" is doing just that.

POSTSCRIPT

In late April 1991, after three years of weekly broadcasts, "South Africa Now" won a special George Polk Award—considered one of the highest honors in American broadcast journalism—for its coverage of South Africa. A week later, the program went off the air, owing to a lack of sustaining funding and a desire to transfer the show to colleagues in South Africa. The final edition aired a pilot program produced entirely within South Africa, with segments contributed by a variety of local video units. "South Africa Now" 's New York–based anchors spoke of passing the baton from North to South, from New York to Johannesburg. "Like a phoenix," one said, " 'South Africa Now' may rise again."

The South African producers are struggling to find their own financing and secure a place in a South African broadcasting industry still controlled by the white minority. Six months after the program's demise in the United States, supportive letters from viewers worldwide are still arriving at the program's New York office. Globalvision is now attempting to use "South Africa Now" as a model for a new global television series on human rights. Copies of "South Africa Now" programs are available for personal and educational use from Globalvision, 215 Park Avenue South, New York, NY 10003.

Selected Bibliography

Adams, William C., ed. *Coverage of International News*. Norwood, NJ: Ablex, 1982.

Bagdikian, Ben H. *The Media Monopoly*. Boston, MA: Beacon Press, 1987.

Bodie, Charles A. "The Images of Africa in the Black American Press, 1890–1930." Ph.D. diss., Indiana University, 1975.

Bonnah-Koomson, Anthony. "News of Africa South of the Sahara in Six U.S. Newspapers, 1977–1988." Ph.D. diss., Ohio University, 1991.

Braley, Russ. *Bad News: The Foreign Policy of The New York Times*. Chicago: Regenery Gateway, 1984.

Buni, Andrew. *Robert L. Vann of the Pittsburgh Courier: Politics and Black Journalism*. Pittsburgh: University of Pittsburgh Press, 1974.

Cohen, Bernard C. *The Press and Foreign Policy*. Westport, CT: Greenwood, 1983.

Cooper, Anne Messerly. "Third World News on Network Television: An Inclusion/Exclusion Study of Violence." Ph.D. diss., University of North Carolina at Chapel Hill, 1984.

Davis, Angela. *Women, Race and Class*. New York: Random House, 1983.

Edelman, Murray. *Politics as Symbolic Action*. New York: Academic Press, 1971.

Frederikse, Julie. *The Unbreakable Thread: Non-racialism in South Africa*. Bloomington: Indiana University Press, 1990.

Fried, Morton. *The Notion of Tribe*. Menlo Park, CA: Cummings Publishing Company, 1975.

Gans, Herbert J. *Deciding What's News: A Study of CBS Evening News, NBC Nightly News, Newsweek and Time*. New York: Vintage Books, 1979.

Gates, Henry Louis, ed. *"Race," Writing and Difference*. Chicago: University of Chicago Press, 1986.

Giffard, C. Anthony. *UNESCO and the Media*. White Plains, NY: Longman, 1989.

Gitlin, Todd. *The Whole World Is Watching: Mass Media in the Making and Unmaking of the New Left*. Berkeley: University of California Press, 1980.

Gurevitch, Michael, Tony Bennett, James Curran, and Janet Woollacott, eds. *Culture, Society and the Media*. London: Routledge, 1988.

Hachten, William. *Muffled Drums: The News Media in Africa*. Ames: Iowa State University Press, 1971.

Hachten, William. *World News Prism*. 2nd ed. Ames: Iowa State University Press, 1987.

Hachten, William, and Anthony Giffard. *The Press and Apartheid*. Madison: University of Wisconsin Press, 1984.

Haile, Reesom. *Africa on Television: U.S. Network Coverage of African Affairs, 1977–1980*. Ph.D. diss., New York University, 1987.

Harriman, Ed. *Hack: Home Truths about Foreign News*. London: Zed Books, 1987.

Harris, Phil. *Reporting Southern Africa*. Ghent: Unesco, 1981.

Harrison, Paul, and Robin Palmer. *News Out of Africa: Biafra to Band Aid*. London: Hilary Shipman, 1986.

Hartley, John. *Understanding News*. London: Routledge, 1988.

Herman, Edward S., and Gerry O'Sullivan. *The "Terrorism" Industry: The Experts and Institutions that Shape Our View of Terror*. New York: Pantheon Books, 1989.

Hertsgaard, Mark. *On Bended Knee: The Press and the Reagan Presidency*. New York: Farrar, Straus and Giroux, 1988.

Hogan, Lawrence D. *A Black National News Service: The Associated Negro Press and Claude Barnett, 1919–1945*. Rutherford: Fairleigh Dickinson University Press, 1984.

Jackson, Henry F. *From the Congo to Soweto: U.S. Foreign Policy Toward Africa Since 1960*. New York: William Morrow and Company, 1982.

Kelly, Sean. *Access Denied: The Politics of Press Censorship*. Beverly Hills, CA: Sage Publications, 1978.

Larson, James L. *Television's Window on the World: International Affairs Coverage on the U.S. Networks*. Norwood, NJ: Ablex, 1984.

Lentz, Richard. *Symbols, The News Magazines, and Martin Luther King*. Baton Rouge: Louisiana State University Press, 1990.

Mankekar, Dinker Rao. *One-Way Flow: Neo-Colonialism via News Media*. New Delhi: Clarion Books, 1978.

Manoff, Robert K., and Michael Schudson, eds. *Reading the News*. New York: Pantheon Books, 1987.

Markham, James. *A Comparative Analysis of Foreign News in the Newspapers of the United States and South America*. State College: Penn State University Press, 1959.

McCarthy, Michael. *The Dark Continent: Africa as Seen by Americans*. Westport, CT: Greenwood Press, 1983.

Minter, William. *Operation Timber: Pages from the Savimbi Dossier*. Trenton, NJ: Africa World Press, 1988.

Mohammed, Umar. "Nigerian News in Four United States 'Elite Dailies': An Analysis of the Coverage of Civilian and Military Governments (1960–1966; 1966–1979." Ph.D. diss., The Florida State University, 1981.

Nwosu, Ikechukwu Enoch. "Crisis Reporting: A Comparative Analysis of Four Black African Cases (1967–1979)." Ph.D. diss., University of Minnesota, 1981.

Onwochei, Gil. *U.S. Television Coverage of Africa: Geopolitical, Economic, and Strategic Policy Implications*. Ph.D. diss., University of Oklahoma, 1987.

Righter, Rosemary. *Whose News? Politics, the Press and the Third World.* New York: Times Books, 1978.

Rodinson, Maxime. *Europe and the Mystique of Islam.* Roger Veinus, trans. Seattle: University of Washington Press, 1987.

Rosenblum, Mort. *Coups and Earthquakes: Reporting the World for America.* New York: Harper and Row, 1981.

Said, Edward W. *Covering Islam: How the Media and the Experts Determine How We See the Rest of the World.* New York: Pantheon, 1981.

Smith, Anthony. *The Geopolitics of Information.* New York: Oxford University Press, 1980.

Smith, Anthony C. H., Elizabeth Immirzi, and Trevor Blackwell. *Paper Voices: The Popular Press and Social Change.* Lanham, MD: Rowman and Littlefield, 1975.

Stokke, Olav, ed. *Reporting Africa.* New York: Africana Publishing Company, 1971.

Suggs, Henry Lewis. *P. B. Young, Newspaperman: Race, Politics and Journalism in the New South, 1910–1962.* Charlottesville: University of Virginia Press, 1988.

Tomaselli, Keyan. *Myth, Race and Power: South Africans Imaged on Film and TV.* Chicago: Lake View Press, 1986.

Tuchman, Gaye. *Making News: A Study in the Construction of Reality.* New York: Free Press, 1978.

Vail, Leroy, ed. *The Creation of Tribalism in Southern Africa.* London: James Curry, 1989.

Index

About the Contributors

CHARLES A. BODIE is a lecturer and writer with interests in African-American affairs and Virginia history. A teacher of history at Virginia Military Institute, 1982–86, his research experience concerns African-American press coverage of Africa in the interwar period.

KIRSTEN NAKJAVANI BOOKMILLER is a doctoral candidate in Foreign Affairs at the University of Virginia, with a research concentration in government and media studies, and the co-author with Robert Bookmiller of "Palestinian Radio and the Intifada," *Journal of Palestine Studies*, 1990.

ROBERT J. BOOKMILLER is a doctoral candidate in Foreign Affairs at the University of Virginia, specializing in Middle East Studies, and the author of "The Algerian War of Words: Broadcasting and Revolution, 1954–1962," *Maghreb Review*, 1989.

LISA BROCK is Assistant Professor of African History and Diaspora Studies in the Department of Liberal Arts of the School of the Art Institute of Chicago. She has done extensive research on the political economy of Mozambique. Her contribution to this volume emanates from her research interest in the symbolic uses of tribalism and primitivism in Western accounts of the African experience.

ANNE COOPER is Director of the Center for International Journalism and Associate Professor in the E. W. Scripps School of Journalism at Ohio University. Cooper worked in the mass media for more than ten years in the United States and overseas.

BOSAH EBO is Assistant Professor in the Department of Communications at Rider College in Lawrenceville, New Jersey, where he teaches international communication. His research concerns the cross-cultural transfer of media professionalism and the New World Information Order.

HASSAN M. EL ZEIN is Head of the Department of Journalism and Mass Communication at the Faculty of Arts of Omdurman Islamic University in Sudan.

JO ELLEN FAIR is Assistant Professor in the School of Journalism and Mass Communication at the University of Wisconsin, Madison. Her research interests include the role of the mass media in national development, media representations of Africa, and women, communication, and development.

JULIE FREDERIKSE served as Southern Africa correspondent for the U.S. National Public Radio from 1979 to 1985, and continues to report for NPR, the Canadian Broadcasting Corporation, and Africa News. She works for the Popular History Trust, a documentation center on South Africa located in Zimbabwe, and is the author of three books on Southern Africa, *The Unbreakable Thread: Non-racialism in South Africa* (1990), *South Africa: A Different Kind of War* (1987), and *None But Ourselves: Masses vs. Media in the Making of Zimbabwe* (1984).

RODGER M. GOVEA is Professor of Government at Cleveland State University, where he teaches methodology, international relations, and world politics. He is the author of various articles on the impact of the Cold War on media coverage.

WILLIAM HACHTEN is Professor Emeritus in the School of Journalism and Mass Communication at the University of Wisconsin–Madison and the author of various works on press censorship and African media, *Supreme Court on Freedom of the Press* (1968), *Muffled Drums: The News Media in Africa* (1971), *The Press and Apartheid: Repression and Propaganda in South Africa* with C. Anthony Giffard (1984), and *The World News Prism: Changing Media, Clashing Ideologies* (1987).

BEVERLY G. HAWK is Assistant Professor in the Department of Government at Colby College. Her research concerns the image of Africa in America, its sources, and its policy implications.

PAUL HEMP is a reporter for *The Boston Globe*. He previously conducted seminars for working journalists in West Africa on behalf of the Center for Foreign Journalists, an independent, non-profit organization based in Reston, Virginia.

TAMI HULTMAN, Executive Editor of Africa News Service, has twenty years experience covering African affairs. Her photographs and articles have appeared in numerous books and publications, including *The New York Times*, *The Washington Post*, and *The Los Angeles Times*. Her series on hunger in Africa won the Judges' Award for Radio at the World Hunger Media Awards, and her productions have been aired by the BBC, National Public Radio, and CNN, among others.

MINABERE IBELEMA is Associate Professor of Journalism at Eastern Illinois University. His research concerns the implications of news and entertainment programming for African and African-American communities.

WUNYABARI MALOBA is Assistant Professor of History at the University of Delaware. His research interests include colonialism and its impact in Africa, peasants and revolution in Africa, and social and cultural history. He is the author of *Mau Mau and Kenya* (forthcoming).

STANLEY MEISLER is the United Nations correspondent of *The Los Angeles Times*. He was a correspondent for the *Times* in Africa from 1967 to 1974. In his twenty-one years of overseas experience, he has also represented the *Times* in Mexico, Spain, Canada, and France. Before joining the *Times*, he was a Washington correspondent for the Associated Press and Deputy Director of the Office of Evaluation and Research of the Peace Corps.

CHRIS PATERSON is currently an independent producer in Boston. His research on Western television coverage of the Frontline states was funded by the Kaltenborn Foundation and Boston University. A former television news photographer and director with national credits, he has also worked as a reporter and photographer in Southern Africa.

DANNY SCHECHTER has been covering Southern African issues in print and broadcast since the early 1960s. He worked as a TV producer for CNN and ABC News for nearly a decade before co-founding Global-vision Inc. and becoming Executive Producer of "South Africa Now." A Nieman Fellow in Journalism at Harvard, he has won several Emmy Awards.

ELAINE WINDRICH is currently a visiting scholar at Stanford University. She has taught at several universities and has been an advisor to the Zimbabwe Mass Media Trust and the Commonwealth Group of the Parliamentary Labour Party. She has also written widely on Southern Africa, including *The Mass Media and the Struggle for Zimbabwe* (1981), *Britain and the Politics of Rhodesian Independence* (1978), *The Rhodesian Problem: A Documentary History* (1975), and various articles and reviews concerning South African censorship and propaganda.

THOMAS WINSHIP is currently President of the Center for Foreign Journalists. He began his career as a reporter for *The Washington Post* and served as editor of *The Boston Globe* from 1965 to 1985.

DAVID ZUCCHINO is a foreign correspondent for *The Philadelphia Inquirer* in Africa and winner of the 1989 Pulitzer Prize for Feature Reporting.